'A conflicted love letter to her European origins and the uncrushable spirit of her glamorous, at times difficult parents, this lyrical page-turner made me laugh and made me weep.'

MAGDA SZUBANSKI, author of *Reckoning*

'*Only* is a wild and deeply felt tale. With her unflinching gaze, Caroline Baum explores the inheritance of being an "only", contrasting an exotic cast of the glamorous and the famous with her unconventional, often solitary childhood.'

AILSA PIPER, author of *Sinning Across Spain*

Caroline Baum has had a distinguished career in arts journalism and broadcasting working for the BBC, ABC radio and television, *Vogue* magazine (in the UK and Australia), and as founding editor of *Good Reading* magazine. She is a regular contributor to national media and her writing has appeared in two anthologies: *My Mother, My Father* and *Rebellious Daughters*. In 2015 she was awarded the Hazel Rowley Fellowship and is currently working on a biography. She lives on the south coast of New South Wales.

www.carolinebaum.com.au

# Only

## A SINGULAR MEMOIR

# Caroline Baum

## ALLEN&UNWIN
### SYDNEY·MELBOURNE·AUCKLAND·LONDON

First published in 2017

Copyright © Caroline Baum 2017

Allen & Unwin
83 Alexander Street
Crows Nest NSW 2065
Australia
Phone: (61 2) 8425 0100
Email: info@allenandunwin.com
Web:  www.allenandunwin.com

Cataloguing-in-Publication details are available
from the National Library of Australia
www.trove.nla.gov.au

ISBN 978 1 76029 397 0

Set in 12.2/18.6 pt Goudy Old Style by Bookhouse, Sydney
Printed and bound in Australia by Griffin Press

10 9 8 7 6 5 4 3 2 1

*For Jacqueline and David*

# Contents

# PART TWO

# PROLOGUE

# Triangle

There are supposed to be two sides to every story but in my case there are three. His, hers, mine. Two parents, one child. Our personal geometry: triangulated. The shape of our family: a tricorn hat, as worn by gentlemen, pirates and highway robbers. Together, we form a wedge of cheese, a piece of cake, a segment of a pie chart.

There's something uncomfortable about a triangle: it's all elbows, suggesting awkward unease. Sharp edges. Not like the gentle symmetry of a square or the harmonious flow of a circle. Isoceles, equilateral, scalene: the words themselves sound pointy and acute. A triangle is easily distorted, pulled in one of several directions. Although its three sides are supposed to represent the most stable of forms, making it the preferred design for medieval fortresses, its shape rarely felt balanced to me: more often teetering, a warped and lopsided trivet that would not lie flat.

Countering the story of the three wise men and fairy tales granting three wishes, superstition suggests that bad things come in threes, from Macbeth's witches to plane crashes. Roadside danger signs are framed in a triangle. It is the outline of alarm. In the orchestra, it is the percussive voice of warning.

When I visualise a triangle, I see the jumbo-size Toblerone chocolate mountains my father would consume, nougat-studded, peak by peak, breaking off two or three from the whole sweet row of Swiss Alps they represent. Then these mountains melt, replaced by real whipped-cream snowy summits, like the ones we used to visit during annual winter ski holidays. Mostly my father is at the apex, dominant and domineering, looking down on us from a lofty altitude. Occasionally I imagine myself at the top with my parents at the base, each tugging me towards their corner of the valley, with more or less persuasion or force. That was our dynamic. My mother never challenged either of us for the highest spot: the air up there was too thin. She preferred to let us slug it out. 'You two are so alike,' she would say, with a Gallic shrug.

Three barely felt like a family. It felt like it did not count. Like we were unfinished. Incomplete. There was always a gap at the table, room to set places for others. But visitors were few and far between. Mostly, there was only me.

# PART ONE

PART ONE

# CHAPTER 1

# All the cherries

L et's start with happy. A colour photograph. A dimpled dumpling infant captured in a moment of pure, unambiguous singleton delight: enthroned in my high chair, I have a *gamine* chop of hair that looks as if it was done with kitchen scissors but almost certainly wasn't and am hogging a bowl of cherries. My ears are festooned with stems of plump glossy fruit. One dark cherry sits on my tongue like a giant bead, about to be swallowed. I am looking at the camera, or rather, at my mother behind it, clapping my hands in glee, more cherries within easy reach. The expression on my chubby cheeky face screams, 'All these are for me!' Sharing is as unknown to me as algebra.

Cherries have been uplifting ever since. Their appearance sudden, their season short, a fleeting treat to be seized at any opportunity, their rarity enhancing their appeal.

Twenty years after that photograph, I was lucky enough to be in the south of France with a friend, picking cherries from heavily laden boughs in a vast orchard. Despite the wicker basket on my arm, I mashed most of them straight into my mouth, drunk on their bloody juice and meaty flesh. Spheres of flavour both tart and sweet—impossible to tell which from their shiny eat-me exterior. There may be more messy sensuality to a ripe mango or the sun-warmed velvet of a peach, but cherries remain my favourites, perhaps because of their miniature size, which makes them as covetable as gems.

I keep that cherry snap of myself within my eye line at my desk, a frozen frame of what uncomplicated, unadulterated joy looks like. It's a good reminder that sometimes, all it takes is fresh fruit.

The photograph was taken in the flat in St John's Wood where my parents lived when I was born. Five years later we moved south of the Thames to Wimbledon—a deliberate ploy of my mother's. She was keen to put some distance between herself and my father's business partner's family, whom she considered nosy and intervening. Determined to carve out a life of her own, she chose exile to a part of town where she knew no one but could suit herself. With my father's business established and doing well, my parents bought a large two-storey brick home with a big garden and renovated extensively. Though I never liked the house, which had a gloomy atmosphere intensified by wood-panelled hallways and pelmetted curtains, it was undeniably comfortable and extravagantly spacious. A lot of shouting between floors went on to locate one another. My mother banged on the central heating radiators to summon us to dinner. It was only when I visited friends that I realised having two rooms plus their own bathroom was not usual for most children.

One of the best things about our street was its proximity to Wimbledon Common and all its wildlife. In summer my mother and I walked there to pick abundant blackberries. Woodpeckers, jays, robins and nuthatches visited our garden regularly, especially when my mother put up a bird feeder, as did hedgehogs, for which she left out saucers of milk. On snowy mornings, there was nothing lovelier than to see a fox slink across our lawn to scavenge in our bins, its russet brush tail like a flame against the frozen whiteness.

At Christmas, which was an entirely secular occasion celebrated only for my benefit, my parents exchanged gifts with the formality of court emissaries swapping ceremonial offerings—Hermès for him, Gucci for her, hardbacks for each. All the rest were for me. As soon as I woke up I would lean over the bannisters to survey the landing below piled high with parcels of all shapes and sizes. Sliding backwards down the carpeted stairs on my tummy, enjoying the friction of every tread, I landed in a sea of boxes and sat tearing away wrapping paper, surrounded by booty while my parents looked on with the satisfaction of benefactors. Everything I wished for materialised: large tins of Caran d'Ache colouring pencils, dolls in national costume to add to my extensive collection, new outfits for Cindy (I was never a Barbie fan), a subscription to my favourite nature magazine, snow-white ice skates, a tennis racquet, an orange space hopper, a pogo stick my father almost bent out of shape with the sheer force of his bouncing, and those ugly little Moomin trolls whose hair I liked to comb out.

There was no ambiguity as to the origins of this haul. I never put out a stocking for Father Christmas because my own father was more than able to satisfy my every desire, and keen for me to know that he and no one else was the provider of all bounty.

Birthdays were even more extravagant occasions of conspicuous consumption. Like a small buddha, I was adorned with jewellery before I could even walk. As I teethed, I sucked on gold medallions and charms for comfort. I have some of these still—a snowflake, a heart-shaped locket—indented with the marks of my milk teeth.

Each year was marked with fine gold pieces in small powder-blue boxes—the name TIFFANY printed on their lids meaningless to me until decades later. I remember a finely hinged bangle I accidentally bent out of shape and a stylised wishbone brooch (I loved pulling the real thing from my mother's roast chicken dinners) that I eventually downgraded, to her displeasure, using it as a safety pin.

Because my father had business connections with the top hotels in London, my parents hosted my early birthday parties at the best establishments in Mayfair. Magicians entertained me and my friends from kindergarten and then primary school. Films of Buster Keaton and Laurel and Hardy were screened in between boisterous rounds of pass the parcel and musical chairs. Best of all was the jewel-like fruit jelly served for tea, which shivered and shimmered in paper bowls with pleated edges and which I much preferred to the creamed gateau centrepiece that held the candles I blew out. It never occurred to me as odd that these celebrations were not held at home, any more than I thought it peculiar that annual prize-giving at my school was held at the Royal Albert Hall, where the 3000-strong student body filled the stalls, while the proud parents occupied the red velvet boxes. You just take it for granted as a kid that the world you live in is normal. My normal just happened to be privileged.

Although I had a large collection of dolls, they were mostly neglected. Instead of playing with them, I turned my own high-sided baby cot into a crib, preferring to tuck them in, sometimes side by side, sometimes more carelessly heaping them on top of one another, a mêlée of piglet-pink plastic articulated limbs sticking out at odd angles.

Some were almost as big as me, usually blonde with eyes that blinked thick black lashes over bright blue irises. My favourite was Chatty Cathy. She had a string in her back that I pulled to make her talk. In her high-pitched American accent she invited me to brush her hair, give her a bath and change her dress. Once her high-maintenance repertoire was exhausted, she'd say 'I'm tired' in a slightly whining tone and get put to bed with the others.

But none of these creatures held my attention or affection. What need did I have of dolls when somewhere, deep inside, I knew that I was the doll? My dresses were nicer than any of theirs, my wardrobe more extensive. I was loved, admired, cuddled, hugged, squeezed, kissed and groomed with far more care. To punish the dolls for the temerity of their pretensions, I twisted their heads back to front and arranged their arms and legs the wrong way round, distorting their perfect prettiness into freakish deformity. There was only room for one princess in our household, and I knew who she was.

Not all gifts were received with equal enthusiasm. The night before my seventh birthday I was in bed when I heard bumping along the hallway outside my bedroom. Something large was being manoeuvred into the playroom. As soon as the coast was clear, I got up, unable to wait until morning for the intended surprise. There was a hulk against the wall, covered in a chenille bedspread. Lifting a corner, I was dismayed to discover an upright piano. It was loathing at first sight.

The next morning, I was vocally ungrateful, protesting tearfully that I had never played a note, never expressed any musical aptitude or interest. But my father was adamant: it was a skill that well-brought-up young ladies, of which I was to be one, whether I liked it or not, simply had to possess. His old-fashioned Viennese notions of gentility and discipline were not to be argued with. I was lucky he did not summon a dancing master to teach me the waltz.

That wretched instrument became the bane of my life. I had no desire to learn and no enthusiasm when it came to practice, but an hour a day, under my mother's half-hearted supervision, was insisted upon. When no one was looking, I tormented the piano in every way I could: stuffing chewing gum into its innards and encouraging our dog Sasha to jump up and run along the keys. We never achieved any semblance of harmony, the piano and I. Ten years later, when I finally persuaded my parents to get rid of it, I could not resist giving it a spiteful little shove as it was manoeuvred down the stairs.

That was the first act of real defiance and self-assertion I can remember, the first time I refused to conform to an ideal and standard set by my father. Until the piano revolt, I was docile and compliant. My rebellion coincided with my going out more into the world and noticing that a piano was not a standard fixture in every home. Equally, that other children did not enjoy such palatial amounts of space to themselves, more commonly sharing a bedroom and all their toys. That they helped wash up after dinner or had a weekend job like cleaning the car or a paper round. That some mothers worked and did not have au pairs. I was formulating my own theory of relativity, beginning a lifelong habit of comparison, endlessly weighing up the pros and cons of every situation and circumstance, fuelled by my father's competitive insistence that everything we were and owned must be the best.

Convention dictates that only children are spoiled. What does that even mean? Spoiled like milk that has soured naturally past its use-by date? No. More like an overindulged brat, who as a result of too much attention, becomes selfish? Yes, that's it. This tired nostrum has gone unchallenged for centuries, recently boosted by stories of how China's generation of so-called Little Emperors has turned out: pampered, demanding, unfit for marriage. The world over, we are labelled as being socially maladjusted, needy, attention-seeking and incapable of forming meaningful relationships. Common wisdom says we lack generosity and basic interpersonal skills. We have a terrible reputation, an image problem that needs a serious makeover.

I had always understood that my mother, herself a singleton, could not have more children for medical reasons; only recently she told me otherwise: she made a deliberate decision not to have more in order to devote herself exclusively to her only child. In the purely material sense, it's true that I was indulged in all the ways the cliché suggests. At the epicentre of my parents' universe, I had few chores or duties for pocket money and was raised in an atmosphere of comfort, exclusivity, praise and reward. But I was also captive.

When I was an infant, it was common for toddlers to learn to walk wearing harnesses like small ponies. There was nothing sinister about it, the leather straps just kept them safe and within reach in case they stumbled. My mother disapproved of these reins. The invisible restraints came not from her but from my father, when I was steady on my feet: a raised voice at the least sign of insubordination or a look of disappointment when I failed to score top marks. I loved the element of performance that went with being admired in my newest smocked dresses with stiff petticoats and my straw boater. Despite a self-conscious shyness, I was enough of a show-off to strike a pose for my mother's camera. But there was an expectation that I should perform in the sense of always doing my best away from the camera too. The role I was expected to play began to seem constricting, as if that pretty dress had shrunk in the wash.

From infancy to puberty I was self-contained and entertained myself with solitary pursuits. Swaying on my painted dappled grey rocking horse, wearing a cowboy outfit complete with gun holster and red felt stetson purchased by my father on his annual business trip to the US. I had a slightly macabre fascination with dead insects for a while, collecting the corpses of bees from windowsills and saving them under my pillow. In season, I gathered up conkers as they fell from our vast horse-chestnut tree, fascinated by the natural gloss that made them look polished. Like cherries, their shiny quality fascinated me. I wanted some of that varnish for myself, perhaps guessing it was a protective coating that might shield me from knocks to come. But kept in my coat pocket, they wrinkled, dried and lost their sheen.

Although I could amuse myself well enough, I was lonely a lot of the time. Hours spread out endlessly before me like an edgeless glassy pool, especially during holidays. I spent a lot of time looking out of the window of my playroom on to the street below, sometimes waving at strangers if they happened to look up, or listening out for the rag-and-bone man who came past on his horsedrawn cart shouting 'Any old iron', or the Breton with the weatherbeaten face who sold ropes of garlic from the pannier on his bicycle, having come across on the Channel ferry. It became a habit to curl up next to the radiator in my room and listen to the water running through the pipes, pretending that its warm-blooded gurglings were the sounds of a friend talking to me. But the radiant heat was no substitute for human playmates.

Until I went to school I don't think it occurred to me that most other children had siblings. If they did, I had failed to notice them. But suddenly they were impossible to ignore; there were brothers and sisters everywhere. In most books I read growing up, same thing. Siblings to look up to, copy, play with and annoy. To teach you about teasing and sharing and all those other life skills you take for granted when you are one of many. Fitting in, group dynamics, tag teams, relay-style cooperation. Singularity suggested a handicap to be overcome.

When a Belgian aristocratic brood moved in next door with five children, the message was clear: a real family was bigger, louder, messier. They were pale and plain, big-boned and heavy. When they came over to play, it was like an invasion from a cloned Teutonic platoon. You could see their DNA replicated in each family member: the prominent nose, frowning brow and straight thick hair, the ungainly gait and thick ankles. Slightly diluted in each iteration but unmistakable nonetheless. Their consistent guttural accents were abrasive and ugly, as if they were permanently choking. The volume of their exchanges bewildered me: they seemed always to be shouting at each other. Their tribal tone was one of aggression. Two of them had spectacular tantrums, turning puce, as if they had been boiled, while they wailed at some perceived injustice. I was fascinated by their hair-pulling rough and tumble, but often could not wait for them to go home.

They only had to look at each other to know who they were. As a child, I could not identify with anyone or recognise myself anywhere—my own features too wobbly like unset custard to draw any obvious comparisons. Once the flesh had settled on my bones in my teens, friends and acquaintances commented on my resemblance to my mother—her olive skin, deep-set eyes, long neck and high brow. It took me much longer to see that I had also inherited my father's crooked smile along with invisible, less appealing traits.

I found the whole concept of games and play baffling or tedious. With no regular experience of catching a ball, I was splay-fingered, clumsy and uncoordinated. Board games were unfamiliar, meaning I usually lost, lacking the competitive edge of my rivals. I even threw the dice badly and found shuffling cards embarrassingly awkward: others knew how to keep the deck tightly held, while in my inexpert hands, the cards slipped and spilled. Marbles, which enjoyed huge popularity in the playground of my French school, seemed just an excuse to collect pretty shiny spheres. My mother encouraged me, prompted by her own nostalgia. I swapped the glassy beads for more precious agates, but had no interest in the rules of the game.

Shaky when it came to balance, I was slow to learn to ride a bicycle, preferring instead to wheel sedately along the leafy streets to Wimbledon Common on my tricycle. Long after other children had graduated to two wheels, I chose stability over speed. I was careful with myself, sensing the burden of being what the French call *un enfant unique*.

When I visited friends at home, I generally preferred to talk to their parents, developing a precocious appreciation for conversation.

Up close, the personal habits of other families were often shocking. They shared things I had never shared. At about the age of eleven I was finally allowed to go for a sleepover at my best friend Antonia's house. After dinner, she and her sister popped into the same bath and invited me to join them. I am not sure I had seen anyone naked before. Alarmed and disgusted at the murky soapy water, I politely asked if I could use the telephone. Unaware of social niceties, my message was crisp and to the point: 'Please come and get me, they're dirty.'

When I repeated the sleepover experiment in other homes, I was not used to sharing a bed and found the kicks and snufflings intolerable. My parents were so fastidious about bodily functions that I only learned what a fart was when we got a dog.

⌒

Since games, whether physical or mental, required partners, reading and crafts were the alternatives, and I grasped at them enthusiastically. I pressed leaves, cut out figures from felt, lost myself in the hypnotic symmetry of Spirograph drawing and the sensual feel of Play Doh and clay. The pleasing click of a Lego window fitting into the bricks I was assembling to build a house was sometimes the only sound in my playroom.

But I was agonisingly lacking in social confidence, so hesitant about inviting friends to play that I wrote out a script with a list of all the possible responses I might get to be prepared for all eventualities. If they said no, I quickly scanned my follow-up options (*What about tomorrow? Or can I come to you?*). I was totally unused to rejection.

Aware that I needed to keep myself active and amused, my parents installed an impressively professional gymnastic set of rings, trapeze, rope ladder and swing on a large steel frame in the garden. Professionally assembled and concreted into the lawn, it looked forbiddingly like the equipment at a penitential bootcamp rather than a place to play. After attending that year's Royal Tournament at Earl's Court, I was very taken with the military obstacle course and tried to recreate it single-handedly with my version of commando rolls. But the effect was not the same. A general needs troops.

One summer, when I was about six or seven, without warning or explanation, a French boy came to stay. Bruno was the son of my mother's friends. Five years older than me, he was of a somewhat sullen disposition and no doubt furious at having been sent away from *copains* (mates) his own age to a quiet English suburb. Totally unprepared for the presence of this instant brother, instead of welcoming his company, I saw him as a threat. It was the first time anyone had attempted to annexe my territory. I refused to share my toys. When Bruno helped himself, I retaliated with wild scenes until my exasperated mother had to separate us like warring nations with a quickly drawn-up frontier: me in the front garden, Bruno in the back. Grudgingly, we shared an inflatable pool. Surprisingly, in water, we were able to submerge our hostilities and our splashings were relatively cordial. Eventually, poor Bruno was introduced to the brainy boy next door, who took him off my hands. The experiment in sharing had been a dismal failure.

A few years later my father bought a ping-pong table. Little did I know that he had been something of a champion player at university. It was a natural outlet for his aggression and lightning reflexes. When we played, I spent most of my time dodging the ball as if it were an oncoming bullet, such was the velocity of his strokes.

The same was true when we had snowball fights. My father packed his projectiles so hard they were like cannon balls, knocking me backwards. Also keen at fencing as a student, he loved to lunge, parry and thrust with sabre-like icicles picked from the gutters of chalets when we holidayed in the Alps. Fortunately, the point of his frozen rapiers would snap on impact, preventing serious injury. But if my ski jacket had not been padded, I would have had bruises from his jabs and stabs. He was always dangerous, forgetting his own strength and unable to rein in his natural competitive aggression.

My chief pleasures were watching television and ice skating. In the afternoons after school I watched my favourite children's shows (*Animal Magic* with Johnny Morris, *Crackerjack* and *Blue Peter*), but on Sunday evenings I graduated to more adult fare. We lined up our armchairs like the three bears: Papa Bear in the large velour recliner where he would work his way through a box of chocolates without sharing them and smoke himself into a cloud of cigarettes until he was barely visible; Mama Bear in the wing chair with footrest, knitting elaborate Aran and Fair Isle patterns without any visible signs of counting stitches, never dropping one, her eyes on the screen; and Baby Bear in the small bucket seat, positioned halfway between them. Together we watched *Upstairs Downstairs*, *Rowan and Martin's Laugh In* (one of the few things that injected unanimous mirth into our otherwise serious household) and the BBC's latest literary adaptation—in my pre-teen years it was *The Forsyte Saga*, which fascinated me with its formal dialogue and heaving bosoms. To keep track of the plot twists, I wrote a synopsis of each episode in my diary:

*January 5: Soames finds out about Elderson, Victorine sits for Greer in the nude.*

*January 12: Fleur (my favourite character, played by Susan Hampshire) has a baby boy.*

*January 19: Irene and John come back. Soames resigns.*

On our weekly sports days I went to the Richmond ice rink. The journey on a specially hired coach was a treat because it was my only experience of travelling with friends. To my endless frustration and despite weekly pleading, I was not allowed to use public transport to get to school until my mid-teens, and even then, an au pair had to wait with me on the platform see me safely on. At the rink I enjoyed the ritual of tightening up the laces on my boots and slipping into my blue skating dress with its flared skirt and matching knickers. A pair of white gloves completed the outfit.

The rink offered a magical opportunity to slide with balletic grace, however fleetingly. I learned basic moves and spins from a patient ex-Olympian, Mr Nixie, duly noting weekly progress in my diary:

*February 12: did a twizzle*
*February 19: another twizzle*
*February 25: skating backwards and crossovers*

Graduating to the rudiments of ice dancing, beginning with the foxtrot, meant whirling round the rink at speed facing forwards, holding hands with a friend, feeling the wind in my hair. This exhilaration culminated in the interval, during which we adjourned to the cafeteria to buy egg mayonnaise sandwiches, possibly the most delicious thing I had ever eaten. No one anywhere has ever got the proportion of egg to mayonnaise as right as the caterer at the Richmond ice rink.

But mostly, I played in my head. I imagined myself as a spy or a secret agent, and kept my parents under close observation. I listened behind doors or stealthily picked up the phone in another room while they were talking. I riffled through the papers on my mother's spindly-legged bureau and my father's more solid home-office desk.

Or else I devised new ways to torment our good-humoured, gap-toothed Cockney housekeeper, Mrs Barns. My favourite tricks were to switch off the power point for the vacuum cleaner or floor polisher while she was rooms away or to creep up behind her and tie her apron strings to the door while she was ironing. Nothing rattled her: she chuckled at this mischief, though I was a proper pest.

Mrs Barns was far more than a housekeeper in our lives. She didn't just clean: she kept my mother company. Every weekday at eleven, they shared a coffee break (Nescafé was considered sophisticated in those days, especially when it switched from powder to granules), during which they dissected the day's headlines and any local gossip that Mrs Barns felt it necessary to impart. Her husband, Bob, who was considerably smaller than his hefty spouse, worked 'on the buses' so there was also much talk of public transport and its many vexations. Delays on the route to her favourite shopping destination in Clapham were a frequent topic: 'I could only take the 74 up the junction but then I had to wait for the 93 and it never come, Mrs *Bawm*, it never come,' her mournful repetition turning her account into an almost poetic lamentation of disappointment.

She also had the habit of repeating the last syllable of every single word my mother said, as if to demonstrate her attention, creating an echo chamber that could become so hypnotic my mother never spoke to her for too long, fearing the effect would put her in a trance.

Mrs Barns was also a champion malapropist, with my mother trying to keep a straight face before rushing off to a notebook hidden in the pocket of her corduroy gardening jacket to jot down her latest turns of phrase. The only one I can remember is when describing the process of getting a perm she said her head had been covered in swastikas. This sounded alarming until we worked out she meant Schwarzkopf hair products.

At Christmas she gave us hideous gifts we were obliged to display: multicoloured crocheted skirts attached to luridly pink naked plastic doll torsos, meant to hide loo rolls. Every summer she took a coach holiday with her family to the British seaside, from which she sent us a postcard of crowded beaches covered in large uncomfortable-looking stones and where the weather was almost unfailingly foul. My mother commented wistfully that the Barnses seemed to enjoy each other's company no matter where they were or how much it rained. Mrs Barns always returned with a stick of Brighton Rock for me. After she retired, my mother made several efforts to stay in touch, all of which were met with silence. It was puzzling and hurtful. Her big-hearted loyalty was missed and mourned.

Thinking that a pet might teach me responsibility and to care for something other than myself, my parents bought me a puppy, a pedigreed West Highland terrier that made up for his short-legged stature with a defiantly outsize personality. He had the hunting instinct of his genes and would regularly return from garden skirmishes involving hedgehogs with his handsome muzzle as stuck with spines as a pincushion. Sasha became immediately devoted to my mother, who was the only one to take regular care of him. He followed at her heels from room to room, sitting on her feet while she watched television, emitting a low rumbling growl if anyone came too close.

I was ambivalent about him: I loved grooming his long silky coat with a steel comb, but had no interest in the daily chores of walking or feeding him. Though undoubtedly a companion, he also stole some of my limelight with his antics: he chewed a neat fringe in every coat in the cloakroom, from my father's cashmere to my mother's camelhair, to indicate his displeasure at being left on his own.

My solution was to see him as a surrogate brother to tease and torment. (As with a brother, his was the first penis I ever saw. Unlike a brother's, I found the way it would pop out and retract like a glossy pink lipstick when he humped a visitor's leg fascinating.) I occupied his bed so he was forced to lie elsewhere and even ate his Good Boy choc drops when there was no other chocolate in the house. Best of all was his Pavlovian reaction to the word *shampoo*: to say it was to trigger an inexplicable but cartoonish, lunatic run through the house, with him bumping into furniture, knocking obstacles in his path flying, like a frenzied greyhound at the track. Poor creature: he hated water as much as a cat. We took him to the beach once, encouraging him to follow us into the sea. No sooner had he done so than we discovered he was the only canine that did not know how to dog paddle, as he promptly started to sink.

Not surprisingly, he viewed me with distrust. But if we were alone in the house for too long he would often seek me out. I was always touched when he pushed my door open, even if I was a companion of last resort.

Sasha lived for fifteen years. The day he died was the only time I ever saw my parents in the same bed together, sitting up like the effigies of couples on Etruscan coffins, his tartan collar between them on the covers. They had slept in separate rooms since I could remember, supposedly because of my father's snoring. I don't know what was more shocking: to realise I would never see Sasha again or to see them in this unprecedented intimacy.

# CHAPTER 2

# *Papa et Maman*

In her late twenties, my Parisian mother Jacqueline Legout was at the height of her striking and considerable beauty. In photographs taken then she looks like a cross between Frida Kahlo and Picasso's lover, Françoise Gilot. With sculptural cheekbones, strong arched brows framing liquid dark eyes, hair pulled back dramatically like a ballerina to accentuate her long neck, she had the severe look of a Spanish flamenco dancer, which she accentuated with flaring full skirts and necklines that showed off her handsome *décolleté*. Blessed with a naturally perfect set of teeth, she dazzled admirers with a smile of film-star wattage. From the moment he saw her, my father was, to use one of his favourite words, smitten.

Maman has always been coy about her romantic life and was never someone I felt I could confide in about crushes or advice on how to handle boys. I was an adult before she told me that before she'd met my father, she'd had a casual romance with a high-profile married man.

Roger Thérond was a film critic at the time who went on to become the flamboyant founding editor of *Paris Match*. Dark-haired, horse-faced, with a long misshapen nose, Thérond took Maman to jazz clubs to see Juliette Gréco. He showed her off at the Cannes Film Festival premiere of *Jeux Interdits*, a film that left her devastated. I would only understand why much later.

'I think his wife died while he was with me, but I was too amoral at the time to care,' my mother once admitted. I wondered about the choice of that word, 'amoral', particularly since my mother has always had an unerring and pretty inflexible moral compass. It would be many years before I would understand the reasons why she might describe herself that way.

When I looked Thérond up on Google I saw that he had subsequently remarried, to a model who had been a muse for both Christian Dior and Yves Saint Laurent. Photographs of her gave me a shock: she could have been my mother's identical twin.

Jacqueline had met Thérond through her best friend at the time, Arlette (later Agnès, when she began her career) Varda, a high-spirited tomboyish gadabout. Their friendship began at the Girl Guides during the Nazi occupation, when the organisation was banned. Disregarding its illegal status, guides met in secret locations, favouring mysterious places including rooftops and abandoned buildings. Petite, bossy and fearless, Arlette wore her coal-black hair in a long thick plait. Together with three sisters from her home town of Sète, she dreamed up rock-climbing adventures and organised camping trips in the forest of Fontainebleau, despite there being German snipers on the city's outskirts. Disregarding danger, the gang roamed every inch of Paris on foot, choosing a different suburb to explore for a day. A wild child given free rein, Arlette scandalised her parents in late adolescence by going off to Corsica to live with a community of fishermen before returning to France, changing her name, and becoming the only female member of cinema's *nouvelle vague* and one of the country's most celebrated film directors.

Her older brother Lucien fell in love with Jacqueline and they became engaged when she was nineteen. Having secured a place at l'Ecole Polytechnique, one of France's elite higher education institutions, Lucien stunned my mother by volunteering for active duty in Indochina, staying away for eighteen months. During his absence she bumped into Thérond, who asked her out.

As the wedding date drew closer, my mother felt increasingly uneasy. 'I liked the whole family very much and wanted to belong, but at the same time I could not handle their kindness, and thought they would swallow me up. I mistook Madame Varda's care for interference. I could not cope with anyone taking an interest in me,' she said, looking guilty, but without further elaboration.

Two weeks before the wedding, Jacqueline broke it off with Lucien. She gave no reason. Sensitivity was not her strong point in that moment. Like a cornered animal, she only knew she had to escape. She was deeply apprehensive about marrying someone who had fought in a war and who might have killed someone. 'When his mother showed me the trousseau of bed linen that had already been embroidered with our initials I knew I could not go through with it,' she told me.

Her instinct was sound. Years later in Paris I went to visit Agnès, still hard at work in her cutting room at the age of eighty-seven. She revealed that Lucien, to whom she was never close, had for a time become a violent man.

There may have been another unconscious reason for my mother's reticence. When I was in my twenties, my mother told me a secret she had shared with no one. Not with her best friend Arlette, not with Thérond, of whom she started to see more after her break with Lucien, and more revealingly, not even my father once they were married.

Nineteen and still a virgin, my mother went for her first proper job interview for a secretarial position, pretending in her application to be twenty-one. Her prospective employer, a ship's chandler, had asked her to come for an interview at the end of the day. A woman admitted her to the offices above the famed Lido nightclub on the Champs-Elysées, and then left. The man locked the door, raped and assaulted her, only stopping when my mother told him she was under-age. Although her face was swollen as a result of being hit, no one asked for an explanation and she told nobody the reason. When she trusted me with this confidence, abruptly and out of the blue, I felt like I had been assaulted. We were not in the habit of exchanging these kinds of confidences.

By the time she was twenty-eight, Jacqueline was desperate for a family of her own. She had left it quite late, and when she made her choice of partner, from the way she told me, I felt her motive was driven by a cool pragmatic urgency more than genuine passion.

What did my mother see in the young Harry Baum? Black-and-white photographs from the 1950s show evidence of a certain debonair confidence in his assured bearing: he held himself well. His straight-backed, military posture increased his stature and made him look like a leader, someone in charge. Never a dance-floor lothario, he must have made his conquests thanks to the force of his personality and a certain vitality that colleagues described as charisma.

Daughters are hardwired not to find their fathers attractive, but Harry Baum was not handsome by anyone's standards. Of average height with sloping shoulders, by the time I came along, his luxuriant light chestnut hair had thinned, emphasising his high forehead and moon face. Spectacles framed his small pale grey-green almost lashless eyes. His nose was broad, his mouth thin. When he was angry, his lips seemed to retract as they twisted into a grimace that suggested he'd just bitten down on a lemon. His teeth were stained with tannin from copious tea-drinking.

In his thirties Papa had a sense of fun that I only heard about second-hand: at work-related parties he surprised staff and clients with elaborate dressing-up disguises. His repertoire included a goggled winter sports tourist overburdened with luggage, skis and skates; a bewigged judge; a cardinal; and in a particularly spectacular homage, he once transformed himself into Shakespeare's Richard III by hiring Laurence Olivier's original costume and adding a fake plastic nose and a wig.

Hardly interested in sport, and a moderate drinker, he was a polished raconteur and joke-teller, urbane, worldly, sophisticated and generous with compliments and cigarettes. He could recite Shakespeare, quote Churchill, speak several languages fluently. American women fell for his cultured European manners and smooth eloquence. The female colleagues and clients who became close associates were not self-effacing, quiet, pretty women; he preferred those who were strong and independent. He referred to any women he liked as girlfriends, as if they had all been conquests at some stage. Unapologetically, defiantly sexist, he also used the term 'broad' like a character out of *Guys and Dolls*, in the same way as some men today might refer to a babe. All of this makes him sound rather brash, and a little vulgar, which he was, although he was never coarse or crude.

When my parents met, my father was not yet the workaholic he was to become. He had quit a job as a well-paid bureaucrat for UNESCO to start his own travel business, and hired my mother as his secretary on the strength of her bi-lingual skills. Their first date was a Berlin Philharmonic concert, which set the tone for their courtship: grand, formal and serious. On their second date they watched the Coronation of Queen Elizabeth on television, which would have suited my father's taste for pomp and ceremony more than my mother's republican sentiments. Decades later, attending a royal function, she refused to curtsy as protocol required when the monarch filed past.

Jacqueline and Harry got to know each other better over intimate dinners at favourite bistros and cabaret at the chic nightclubs. Including, I now realise with a sickening chill, the

Lido, where my father loved the magic acts and spangled and feathered showgirls, little suspecting that his future wife had been violated upstairs. I remember how whenever my father spoke fondly of those champagne soirées, my mother would murmur that she preferred to go to the Crazy Horse, the Lido's rival.

Jacqueline was seduced by his vigour and appetite for life, his enthusiasm for food, music and travel, and his grasp of world affairs and his erudition. She felt he was safe, reliable and worldly. He must have enjoyed making her feel that he could look after her, and felt proud to have such a glamorous woman on his arm, little realising how fragile she was beneath that *soignée* surface. These were superficial reasons, masking what probably drew them together at a far deeper, subconscious level, but that they did not, could not, would not, express to each other in those early days of attraction, or subsequently, when disillusionment and bitterness set in: a deep-seated need for stability, a shared wound of robbed childhood, loss, immeasurable sorrow and helpless anger. A magnet of tragedy that drew two fathomlessly incompatible elements together. What does it mean that Jacqueline never told Harry she had been raped? An incomplete intimacy? Shame? Or a desire to put it behind her? These are questions that, as a daughter, I never had the courage to ask.

⁓

Leaving France was never an issue, as my father seemed utterly at home there and as besotted with the place as with my mother. So it came as a total surprise when he decided to relocate to Britain to start a new company. He had originally come to Paris to wait out his divorce, following an impetuous marriage that had lasted just ten months. It took two years for the decree nisi to come through, during which time he met and courted my mother. They married in 1956 at Marylebone Registry Office and honeymooned in Majorca, where their low-rise hotel was the only one on the beach.

Back in London, my father threw himself into his work with endless stamina, travelling frequently. My mother did secretarial work for him. Sometimes they took ephedrine when they had to pull an all-nighter to meet a deadline on scripting a proposal for prospective American clients.

Jacqueline admitted to having no particular professional ambition, having failed to find work that could accommodate her anxious disposition. Before my father hired her, she worked as a ground hostess for high-status airline Pan Am at Orly airport. Being employed by an American company was considered the epitome of post-war glamour, and the company's smart sky-blue uniform was individually made to measure by a tailor. There were travel perks and parties in planes parked in their hangars. But although my mother enjoyed the camaraderie of her colleagues, she found the paperwork stressful, forever getting the indigo ink from the Gestetner and Roneo copying machines all over her hands. Worst of all was keeping the passenger manifest up to date and running to the plane with it at the last minute. Naturally disorganised and with virtually no training, she was often in a panic so that it was inevitable she would get things wrong, which meant that she sometimes sent passengers to one destination and their luggage to another.

She could not wait to give up work to become a full-time housewife and mother. But away from the first-floor office in Marylebone High Street, my mother must have been lonely. She knew no one, did not find Brits especially friendly and was having difficulty getting pregnant, which was her ultimate aim. The privations of rationing still existed in Britain. Jacqueline missed butter, cheese and market produce, and was shocked that Britons ate swedes, which the French normally only fed to pigs. The drab austerity of the post-war years was seemingly endless.

Through no fault of his own, my father was away on business when I was born two weeks prematurely (and I have been arriving early ever since). When we finally met, still in hospital, where my mother had developed complications, he was too afraid to hold me. In formal studio portraits taken a few months later, I look as startled as an owlet fallen from the nest. He is nowhere to be seen and rarely appears in any of the red leather-bound photo albums that document every moment of my evolution.

But he must have been delighted because he did something truly out of character: he wrote a poem, his first and last as far as I know, to mark the occasion.

*Poem on the birth of a daughter*
Caroline Françoise Leonore, *c'est moi*:
To be a good *petite* pumpkin, I've promised mama
And with a bit of luck, *je crois*
I plan to charm even papa
I suffer from the disability

Of developing his facsimile
But mama says it doesn't matter,
His rocking influence she'll shatter
With a view to my becoming
A young lady smart and stunning
Here we have a happy home
Where my mama does set the tone
Both my parents me adore
So we'll have lots of fun galore

Having given her much trouble
I shall always harder struggle
To endeavour to beguile
My mama's Mona Lisa Smile

This collection of words is as awkwardly sincere as a hastily assembled bouquet of mismatched flowers. A connoisseur of language who prided himself on his vocabulary and syntax and could recite Shakespeare by the yard, my father would have known that this was pure doggerel. It does not scan properly. Its clumsy construction, as wonky as a makeshift table cobbled together by an amateur carpenter, is at odds with his customary elegant turn of phrase and sweeping, if pompous, cadence in letters and speeches. Its sentiment is sickly sweet, its naïvety gauche and simple in its optimism. And yet—something moves me about his pride, his hopes. The higgledy-piggledy verses suggest joy, the smattering of French words a sure sign of euphoria. I wonder about him choosing to write in the voice of the baby, who speaks as if she already knows she has her parents wound tightly around her little finger.

Once I was brought home, Maman devoted herself to her role as full-time wife and mother with unqualified pleasure. She applied herself to homemaking and expressed her creativity through her talent for *la cuisine*, using her skills to lure my father home. My father salivated with anticipation for her *boeuf en gelée*. He would beg her to make his favourite Viennese *zwetschgen-knödel*, plum dumplings rolled in breadcrumbs, cinnamon sugar and melted butter; sigh for her Yorkshire pudding; devour her *mousse au chocolat*; and ask for second helpings of every dish. Maman became an unrivalled kitchen goddess. Keen to show off his wife's matchless beauty and talent, my father boasted to his colleagues, bringing them home for meals and equipping her with all the latest gadgets and accessories: a hostess trolley and hot plate, a fondue set, state-of-the-art mixers and a rotisserie oven.

My mother, however, hated playing the corporate wife for my father's business associates. Though she shone in the kitchen, she was bored and ill at ease at the dining table. Partly because my father, though he worshipped her cooking, was a tyrant about preparations for dinner parties.

If the kitchen was my mother's domain, my father invaded it with the brutality of a tank commander when it came to table setting. He planned as if preparing for full-scale battle. Out came his arsenal of weaponry: squadrons of glassware and crystal, which he insisted on washing in scalding water and then polishing till they sparkled. Inspecting cutlery as if it were troops, he ran a dishcloth between the tines of every fork before he was satisfied.

By the time he had fussed over whether individual crystal salt cellars had been refilled, the number of serving utensils and the starched crispness of the napkins, my mother was usually in tears. When guests arrived, she was such a nervous wreck she could hardly speak or she would sulk through the meal, glaring stonily at my father as guests praised the food through a cloud of cigarette smoke, lighting up between courses. They talked only of business, never including my mother in the conversation. She dismissed them all as philistines. It was a torment.

My role on these occasions was to curtsy at the door when introduced, take people's coats like a maid, and hand around the nibbles and cigarette boxes I had been previously instructed to top up while guests enjoyed their pre-dinner drinks. I hated the falsely jovial bonhomie my father displayed to these suited strangers who stayed too long. Why was he so agreeable and pleasant to them and so vile to us? I despised his gracious hospitality, knowing how much he had bullied my mother in the lead-up to his performance. She often went to bed before guests left or retreated to the kitchen, where she had set up a portable television to keep her company.

Once she left work to become a full-time housewife, my mother rarely visited my father at his office. I never enjoyed going there either. His manner was always imperious and peremptory, his tone either preoccupied or irritated. Staff acknowledged us with barely a smile. We always seemed to have arrived at an inconvenient moment or when a crisis was erupting. As a boss, Papa had the reputation of an ogre. His turnover in secretaries was so rapid that he could not remember their names and referred to them generically as 'cows'. Sometimes he would bellow 'COW!' through the glass window that separated his office from his staff. At home I often heard him shouting down the phone, 'I don't pay you to THINK, I pay you to FOLLOW ORDERS!' at some hapless employee who was just learning the ropes and was presumably stranded at an airport or hotel facing an unexpected disaster.

The permanent pall of cigarette smoke in his brown timber veneer office stung my eyes. Like a captain on the bridge issuing updates on a change of course over a tannoy, he shouted commands into the pyramid-shaped intercom on his desk, as if disaster were imminent and there was a large iceberg ahead, interrupting himself to speak a memo into his dictaphone. Everyone seemed to be on high alert. We never stayed long. The only perk was being able to raid the stationery cupboard, taking home boxes of staples and paper clips.

A military-style stickler for punctuality and order, my father expected his home to run on fixed routines. Dinner was always at 7.30. If he was late, stuck in traffic, we waited like staff for the master, without the benefit of a mobile-phone update. Everything was timed to be ready for his arrival. If he'd had a bad day, he would say, 'Fix me an aquavit,' before even crossing the threshold. I had the routine down pat: running to the hall cupboard lined with shelves of glasses and bottles to select a shallow eggcup of smoky Danish design, quickly pouring out just a thimbleful of the liquor. Having barely removed his overcoat, Papa would down it in one shot. The colourless fiery water took effect almost immediately, taking the edge off whatever tension threatened, causing his shoulders to drop slightly. Sometimes nothing could quell the storm: if his mouth was twisted in a distorted downward grimace when he rang the doorbell (despite my mother's repeated requests, he never used his keys, preferring to be formally welcomed like a visiting dignitary), it was wise to say nothing at the table and let my mother's culinary prowess work its magic.

If I was already in bed and heard his heavy footfall up the stairs, I prayed that he would not come and kiss me goodnight, as he tended to smother me in a crushing embrace that felt violent rather than loving.

With my father often away on extended business trips, my mother might as well have been a single parent, although she did not have to worry about money. If she missed him, she never said so. Instead, we became so girlish in our cosy complicity that I imagined we were sisters. (In pre-adolescence I developed a habit of introducing my mother as my daughter to shopkeepers. Although she found it amusing, I now wonder if I had already intuited that she lacked a mother of her own.)

These were placid times of companionship and harmony. Later, my mother would say that they were some of the happiest days of her life, when she had the home she dreamed of and the child she longed for. She felt safe and fulfilled. She wielded little or no authority and I rarely gave her cause to do so. I was, on the whole, as obedient as a bonsai tree. Brooding moodiness came later. When Papa was away, the atmosphere in the house loosened, and we celebrated our temporary freedom by eating with undisguised glee the food he disliked: Couscous! Sorrel soup! Curry! We counted down the days until his return with a mixture of unspoken guilty dread and anticipation: we both knew there would be lavish gifts. But we also knew that our freedom would be curbed as life returned to a stricter rhythm.

# CHAPTER 3

# The Kennedys and me

President John Fitzgerald Kennedy's daughter and I share not only a name but an exact birthday. Both our mothers, elegant and darkly beautiful with similar strong eyebrows, were called Jacqueline. Coincidence? At the ripe old age of five, my deductive powers told me otherwise.

JFK was more present to me than any relative. There were no pictures of grandparents, aunts or uncles in our home but there was a black-and-white portrait of Kennedy in profile in the sitting room and a life-size bronze bust of him in my father's study. Sometimes on Sunday mornings, if he was writing a speech to give at a conference, he would play recordings of JFK's most stirring addresses to summon up oratory inspiration. Everything the president said or did was discussed by my parents at dinner in the sort of admiring and affectionate tone you might use about a favourite family member. They talked with indulgent condescension about his plan to send a man to the moon as one might of an eccentric uncle who enjoyed tinkering with vintage cars.

On 22 November 1963, just days before my sixth birthday, I came out of school to the courtyard where mothers assembled to pick up their children. My mother was crying. It was the first time I had seen an adult shed tears. It frightened me like nothing ever had. It had not occurred to me that adults had anything to cry about: they were in control of everything. Even more unsettling was that the other mothers around her appeared to be crying too. With unfamiliar dread I took my mother's hand and asked, 'Is today the end of the world?'

'Yes,' she replied, without any further explanation.

I rode home in the car drinking in every last detail of the streets around me, thinking to myself that I must observe everything carefully so that when the world ended, I would remember it all. (Presuming, illogically, that I was somehow going to survive the apocalypse and bear witness: was this a precocious foreshadowing of the journalistic impulse?)

When my father came home that evening, he too was in unprecedented distress, sobbing, a sight even more frightening than my mother's crying. After dinner we watched television and I learned not only what had happened but saw faces around the world that looked as distorted and tear-stained as my parents'. I went to bed expecting no tomorrow.

But the next morning came. Without any discussion, my father drafted a letter to Mrs Kennedy on my behalf, expressing my sadness at her loss. Why from me and not from him? What had I done to be designated as mourner-in-chief and official emissary of his sorrow? No one told me.

Pressing down hard and close to the nib, I signed my name for the first time as opposed to merely forming capital letters, making sure not to smudge the ink with my elbow, a risk of the left-handedness my mother was keen to discourage. Months later I received an envelope from the White House edged in black containing a printed card from Mrs Kennedy thanking me for my kind wishes.

After that, my father sank into a sombre mood as each anniversary approached. He timed his annual business trip to the US so he could make a point of going to Arlington Cemetery to pay his respects on 22 November without fail. It was the most sacred date in his calendar. Even twenty years later, any correspondence he wrote on that day, no matter the subject or the addressee, was headed 'a day that will live in infamy', which must have baffled recipients. His grief did not diminish over time: faced with this unprecedented manifestation of sorrow, my internal logic told me that we had lost a member of our family.

Prone in my solitude to imagining the wildest scenarios, I deduced I was JFK's real daughter, swapped at birth for the pretender bearing my name. My earlier habit of spying on my parents now had a special focus: I watched for the slightest slip and betrayal of their devious plot. There was compelling evidence, like the day in 1967 when, in an unprecedented act, my parents took me out of school. This never happened.

We drove to a place called Runnymede, where we stood for hours in sweltering heat to catch a glimpse of Mrs Kennedy, all in white, accompanied by impostor Caroline, dressed to match her mother (I took this as another sign, since Maman and I often dressed alike. I never rebelled against the copycat outfits as I aspired to her elegance). The Queen dedicated a piece of Britain on which Magna Carta was signed to the memory of a fallen friend. Surely the only excuse for such an uncharacteristic breach of school attendance must be a secret connection, otherwise why weren't my classmates there too?

I documented all such details in my diary. When Bobby Kennedy was shot in 1968, I saw his lithe body lying in a pool of blood on television and felt a disconcerting sensation like a distant detonation. Our house plunged into fresh, raw sorrow, cementing my belief that our link to these two handsome brothers with their lustrous heads of hair and toothy magnetism could only be explained by a blood tie.

As hormones flooded my precociously pre-adolescent body, I wrote overheated letters to my best friend Antonia, who had moved to Hong Kong, documenting my theory and evidence with forensic method. She validated and encouraged my suspicions, contributing her own speculations, which included the inspired hypothesis that the state of Carolina had been named after me, a lasting memorial to the terrible deception at the heart of the

American nation. Little did they suspect that the president's real daughter was growing up captive in Wimbledon.

Eventually, our correspondence was intercepted, as all such incendiary espionage documents must be. I was unmasked, my cover blown. Surely now my parents would confess?

They did no such thing. Instead, they turned on me. How could I come up with such a hurtful, disrespectful scenario? I was sent to my room without dinner. My mother locked herself in her room, where I could hear her sobbing like a mewling kitten. I was forbidden to write to Antonia for a year and all my subsequent letters to her were vetted. Within months, the censorship made us self-conscious and stilted, killing the friendship stone dead.

I was baffled by the extreme overreaction and felt righteous with indignation. Surely I was the one with a grievance, I was the one who had been told a lie and deserved an explanation. None came. There was only the accusation that I was a wicked, ungrateful, bad child. It was not until a decade later that I understood the pain I had unsuspectingly caused with my all-too-classic adoption fantasy.

Fifty plus years after that fateful day, Jackie's card is propped beside my desk together with a photograph of my parents in their glamorous youth, radiating wholesome hope and vitality. My father has a full head of hair. My mother has killer cheekbones. Both are looking squarely at the camera, fully aware of their charisma. They could almost be Kennedys.

# CHAPTER 4

# A serious child

After the Kennedy episode, I turned inward, subjecting myself to rigorous self-scrutiny and fault-finding. Serious by nature, eager to please, I committed myself to a program of personal improvement. At the age of ten, I listed my new year's resolutions in my diary: to stop biting my nails and take more care of the dog. Nothing too bold or daring there.

In the space where I was asked to fill in my chosen motto I wrote '*Liberté, Egalité, Fraternité*'—proof that my French heritage and schooling were making a mark. My mother's insistence that I be sent to a *Lycée* paid off: I became bi-lingual without even noticing it. And as I read *Le Petit Prince*, sang '*Sur le Pont d'Avignon*' and recited *Les Fables de la Fontaine*, I fell in love with the widening spectrum of meanings that two parallel streams of words could express, and the ambiguity of the gap between them. As a hobby entomologist, I had enjoyed pulling the wings off bees to examine their jointed transparency; now, an amateur etymologist, I discovered words could not be pinned like insects.

The sensual heat of French suited my temperament. I preferred the stirring, bloodthirsty words of 'La Marseillaise' to the altogether more reverent 'God Save the Queen' we sang at Brownies, probably because the opening line mentioned children: 'Allons enfants de la patrie . . .'

Ours was a news-hungry household, whether it came in print, or on radio or television. The issues of the day (Vietnam, the 1969 miners' strike, the possibility of a European Union) were discussed in detail at dinner—or rather, my father delivered extended commentary on them while my mother interjected occasionally. As absorbent as a paper towel, I soaked it all up.

Reading the newspapers was a family ritual, especially on Sundays, when I would wait to hear them drop through the letterbox with a heavy thud and run down to read them, lying on my stomach on the hall carpet, before they got mussed and disordered by my parents.

I liked to get in early for another reason: due to shared chronic sinus conditions, my parents were both formidable nasal trumpeters. My father was the louder of the two, the bassoon to Maman's French horn. Despite a plentiful collection of extra-large Swiss-cotton handkerchiefs, he never seemed to have one to hand, or understand how to use it. My mother carried handkerchiefs everywhere, balling them up into the sleeves of her sweaters and cardigans so that they looked like bulging tumours on her arm. When fully roused by allergy into serial sneezing, she swapped her brass instrument for the vocalising acrobatics of an operatic coloratura soprano, never attempting to muffle the volume of her nose's irritation in the name of discretion or consideration for others. On the contrary, she turned each attack into a performance: a trill of her sneezes sounded like the Queen of the Night's impossible ascending solo in *The Magic Flute* compared to my father's guttural hawkings of phlegm. After the sneezing had climaxed, my mother shifted into vigorous nose-blowing, her rapid-fire alternate nostril exhalations sounding like the quacks of an agitated duck. By puberty, I had joined the snuffling orchestra due to severe hay fever. We were a snotty lot.

Like most only children, I was a precocious reader. Aping my parents' fascination for tragedy and disaster, I recorded events and facts with a strong preference for anything remotely catastrophic or morbid, noting whatever gruesome details I could harvest from the six o'clock news. Every calamity was meticulously documented, including the number of casualties and bodies recovered.

The first real tragedy to imprint itself on my consciousness was the Aberfan landslide, in 1966. I was eight years old. When a colliery spoil tip in the Welsh village collapsed, it killed 116 children and 28 adults, just minutes after the school day had started. I noted those figures with methodical and grim fascination. The fact of children dying at their desks, mid-lesson, struck me forcefully, as did the terrible detail of them being buried alive in the slag. We held a minute's silence in their memory in class the next day and were asked to donate our pocket money to a relief fund.

Plane crashes were of particular interest, because my father's business hinged on the new concept of chartered air travel for groups, so he was always concerned about which airlines had suffered losses. I recorded and updated body counts ('Four more bodies found from wreckage at sea') with pedantic and ghoulish diligence.

Our first bomb scare at school during the IRA's heyday (as the institution of choice for the *corps diplomatique* we were an obvious target), prompting a slow and inefficient evacuation, was duly noted—the first of many.

The explosion that crippled the lunar module on Apollo 13 provided gripping drama, seen live on television, culminating in the nail-biting re-entry into the earth's atmosphere. This dangerous procedure was accompanied by a longer than usual communications blackout, during which the entire Western world seemed to hold its breath for six minutes wondering whether the crippled craft would burn up due to heat-shield damage. I was no space geek, but it was impossible not to be affected by the fate of the three astronauts and their ingenuity in attempting repairs that meant the difference between life and death. I seem to remember writing them a letter to welcome them home and getting a printed card from NASA, but I doubt I did this under my own initiative, as I was only twelve at the time.

On a lighter note, I also recorded all the songs by Lulu vying to be chosen as Britain's entry to the Eurovision song contest: 'Bet Ya', 'March', 'Come September', 'Boom Bang-A-Bang'.

Why were my parents so hungry for the headlines? I now think this was a form of hypervigilance. That having lived through terrible events of which I suspected nothing, they were always on the alert for the next crisis that could trigger a state of emergency, the panic buying of currency or the stock-piling of food. They were looking for signs, warnings, indications of unrest and instability. Both of them, I would later learn, had lost everything and were determined never to let that happen again. My father in particular set great store by insurance and security: everything in our house was locked or put away in a safe. And I was never in doubt as to the most valuable property of all: me.

The sense of being a one-off and irreplaceable was drummed into me from the beginning. 'You're the only one we've got,' my father repeated over and over by way of explanation for every restriction. It was my responsibility to keep myself out of harm's way, to recognise potential danger and risk and to stay safe. To avoid situations where uncertainty or the unknown were factors and to steer clear of people who were unreliable or in any way irresponsible (though I had no real notion of what such people might look like or how they might behave). The rule was 'trust no one', but that jarred with my own curious and sociable nature. Later, this was the cause of endless friction when, like any teenager, I tested boundaries. I refused to see the world through a lens of wariness or suspicion, verbally scorning and pitying my parents for their cautious overprotectiveness. Challenged as to its cause, they remained evasive and Sphinx-like. This lack of explanation frustrated me but my father remained obdurate. 'Papa knows best' was inadequate but invariably shut down all argument.

If only the focus were not entirely and exclusively on me. If only there were other children around to distract and dilute their attention. There being none, I deflected attention by asking questions about anything and everything. The tactic seemed to work. My father in particular loved explaining a headline or a news item in detail, and encouraged me. Positive reinforcement. The message lodged itself unconsciously in my brain: asking questions was good.

Meanwhile, I furnished myself with imaginary sisters (I saw no point in boys for far longer than my peers) from books: Mary in *The Secret Garden*; Jo, of course, from *Little Women*; Scarlett O'Hara from *Gone with the Wind*; and Cassandra Mortmain from *I Capture the Castle*. These headstrong creatures nourished my spirit of stubborn defiance and stirred a yearning for freedom. I was praised for being able to sit quietly reading for hours, but under the guise of self-contained compliance I was secretly studying disobedience from the best of them.

As the blank pages in my diary attest, during holidays my social life outside school was immensely limited, aside from Saturday morning at the Brownies. There, I found the endless attention to learning various knots frustrating because of being left-handed but enjoyed the wearing of a uniform—a novelty to me, as French schools do not have them—despite its unflattering colour, somewhere between rust and cocoa powder. I liked polishing the trefoil-shaped toggle that held my scarf and making sure my shoes shone for inspection by Brown Owl. But I made no lasting friends there. My mother picked up one girl every week because her house was on the way, but she was even shyer than I was and smelled off-puttingly of tomato sauce with a ferrous hint of blood.

At school I recorded who sat next to me, switching loyalty between a coterie of girlfriends with fickle and opportunistic callousness, always repeating the same pattern: a threesome, the shape I was most familiar with. Inevitably, there were fractures leading to a pairing and a sudden rejection: I was fascinated by how quickly these relationships could split and reform like the amoebae we studied in biology.

As methodical as a bookkeeper, I entered my good marks for dictation and my non-attendance at sport, which I contrived through various faked ailments. On Monday mornings I regularly drank a cup of warm soapy water which I made by dissolving Lux flakes to make myself vomit—anything to avoid the terrors of *la gymnastique*, particularly the ordeals of the vaulting horse or rope climbing. My mother, also not a sporty type, obliged in writing notes to excuse me.

My only other attempt at dishonesty failed miserably when I faked her signature to confirm that she had witnessed the abysmal mark I had got in a maths test. I pressed through the paper too hard and made a hole in the middle of her elegant script, arousing suspicion. The school called home. A frightening lecture followed during which my father told me I could go to jail for such things. I duly waited for someone to come and take me away.

I was always waiting for someone to come and take me away.

When I was naughty, there were two options. In cases of truculence (who even uses that word today?) or disobedience, my father threatened to call Madame Karageorgevich. She was a terrifying witch-like crone who ran a convent institution strict beyond any imagining, somewhere cold and remote, in a never clearly stated country, though I imagined it bordered Austria, where I knew my father had spent his early childhood. Gravely announcing that he was going to call her, my father adjourned to his study. I would listen to his side of the conversation through the door—'Yes, she's ready now'—pleading to be forgiven. He would then negotiate terms with me to avert imminent despatch.

Madame K was entirely my father's creation. My mother never mentioned her name or bought into this gothic Dickensian scenario. Later, when I learned the story of her own childhood, it dawned on me that having endured removal from her home, she understood that this was not a punishment to deploy lightly.

When I was particularly rude or naughty I was punished with a beating administered with a finely stitched calf's leather slipper from a pair my father kept for travelling. At the appointed time, I had to present myself to my father's bedroom and lie face-down, bare-bottomed, to receive five blows. My mother maintains that this only happened once, but I think it took place several times. What hurt more than being struck was my father asking me to kiss him when it was over, as a sign that all was forgiven and forgotten. It was not. It never occurred to me that all children were not treated this way. Not until much later did I understand that this behaviour could be described as abuse, perhaps because my father affected an almost exaggerated calm throughout, giving the occasion a formal solemnity and legitimacy. My mother stayed downstairs, well out of earshot as I bellowed with indignation into the pillows that smothered my cries.

I don't want to excuse my parents' strict discipline but corporal punishment was rife in those days. Caning was not part of the French method, but as a chatterbox in primary school I regularly had my mouth taped over. In secondary school a sadistic Latin teacher slammed the tops of our hinged wooden desks on to the hands of those who could not master their declensions. Serial offenders had their ears twisted till their eyes watered while being dragged to the blackboard for further humiliation. No one ever reported him.

In childhood, I never questioned choices made on my behalf. I had no idea that others my age made decisions for themselves. I had a black sausage-dog stuffed toy with a bell for a nose that I slept with. My father called him Mr Krushchev, after the Soviet leader of the day. I had no idea why and never gave him an alternative name of my choosing. Similarly, when we went to pick my puppy at the breeder's, my mother named him Sasha to satisfy her Slavophile taste and I did not argue.

When I entered puberty and began to assert myself and attempt to make my own choices, I was put sharply in my place. Nothing belonged to me, including myself. If I was in a bad mood and took it out on the furniture with a stroppy kick at a chair leg, my father would turn apoplectic, reminding me in a sudden fury that I had not paid for it and it was not mine to abuse. 'That is MY PROPERTY!' he yelled, livid and spitting. 'YOU are MY property! Everything here belongs to ME! Is that UNDERSTOOD?'

In the calmer aftermath of these episodes I was called in to my father's study for a lecture about my attitude. I was always required to apologise for my deficiencies and promise that I would do better. Thus chastened, I drew up elaborately formal contracts between myself and my parents. In one such officious proposal I typed out when I was thirteen, I guaranteed to keep my room tidy 'but not dust or hoover', polish my shoes at weekends 'but not during the week', make breakfast once a month on Sunday, and set and clear the table for breakfast and dinner on weekdays. I thought that if I drew up these agreements we might secure a truce, but there was no chart to predict the emotional tides that ebbed and flowed in our little hermetically sealed biosphere.

Our triangle was elastic. When stretched it distorted this way and that, pulled by opposing forces. Most of the time I sided with my mother, cuddling on her lap well into my teens and giggling at her capacity for childish silliness: she was a champion face-puller, only too ready to distort those gorgeous symmetries into grotesque grimaces. At dinner if she was bored by my father's lengthy ruminations, she would suddenly interrupt with a demonstration of how easily she could touch the end of her nose with the tip of her tongue while simultaneously wiggling her ears, to deflate my father's self-important assertions. She had no respect for his pompous sermonising.

But if I was out of sorts or just feeling contrary, I ganged up with my father and patronised my mother insufferably, insulting her for being just a housewife, mocking her litanies of complaint and domestic woes when a plumber or some other repair man had failed to turn up. I belittled her hobbies, yawned at her accounts of the gardener's visits, and mocked her early adoption of yoga, her mastery of ikebana flower arranging and her attempt to learn pottery with scornful ridicule, aping my father's condescension and teasing.

If he was in a good mood and on a roll at dinner, we would ignore her and discuss history or the news as if she were a servant we tolerated sitting at the table but never invited to share her views. She could, if given the chance, more than match my father, who regularly sprinkled literary references throughout endless pronouncements on the events of the day. Quotes flew thick and fast as we ate. Hers were from Ancient Greek and Latin philosophers, Molière, Racine and Corneille—texts she studied at school, despite failing her Baccalauréat not once but twice, out of a bloody-minded stubborn refusal to work. No one noticed her rebellion. Too late, she realised the self-sabotage, making up for it in adult life with furious intensity as a reader in several languages.

When dinner was over, I left my mother to do the dishes without a second thought while my father disappeared to his study or to watch television. With a daily housekeeper and a steady string of Swiss au pairs to look after me and take care of cleaning and chores, my mother was free to fill the house with her exquisite flower arrangements, sculptural branches, tendrils of moss, single blooms and buds expressing nature's cycles according to the rigorous discipline of the Japanese aesthetic. Like her cooking, they were her declarations of creativity and love, but I don't remember ever complimenting her on a single one of them. I was an unappreciative, ungrateful, obnoxious snob. Now

I wince with shame at the memory of this horrible behaviour, for which I wrote her a letter of apology some years ago.

The strain of taking sides took its toll. By the time I was twelve, something in me had been broken. It was as if an internal string had fallen out of tune and could not be tightened back to harmony. I was in a permanently discordant state.

An intense melancholy took hold of me and I did not know what to do with it. When my parents were out, I drifted from room to room in our house, opening cupboards, inhaling the rich aroma of Calèche in the pile of my mother's neatly folded Hermès silk scarves, examining the racks of polished and neatly shelved shoes held in shape by springy metal trees. Sometimes I went into my father's study and took the very sharp scissors from their tooled maroon leather holder and wondered about stabbing myself with them, poking myself experimentally in the stomach, feeling their dagger point through my clothes.

Self-absorbed and solitary, I was frightened by my own sadness. In an attempt to be scientific, I decided to monitor it, drawing up a chart that I annotated daily, marking dots on a grid to map my moods: was there a pattern that I could predict or anticipate? Could I be less vulnerable to the gusts that seemed to buffet my spirit? The lines on the graph pointed downwards with few spikes.

One day I emptied the sadness into a poem. It poured out in one draft, as smoothly as milk from a jug:

Sitting by a lonely stream
Looking at my reflection

I see my years of sadness
And feel a great depression
Thinking that ten years are wasted
Never to come back
But if I look a little closer
I remember a merrier thing
Like dancing through the daffodils
Every single spring
But that too long ago has gone
And now there is but water
Where I saw my years of sadness
And the happy ones just after

A gust of confidence impelled me to send it to the Brownie magazine, which informed me a week later via a printed card that it would be published in the next month's issue. The string inside me twanged with an unfamiliar sensation. Joy.

When the poem was published I stared with complete fascination at my name printed beneath it. I could not tear my eyes away from those letters and their connection to my self. Here at last was something that belonged to me and only me. That had not been bought for me and could not be taken away.

Mine. All mine.

# CHAPTER 5

# Second-hand fame

'Your mother,' my father would frequently announce like a king issuing a decree, 'is the most beautiful woman in the world.' In a good mood, he was prone to making hyperbolic pronouncements. Indifferent to compliments from a man capable of spitting insults at her, my mother responded with exaggerated eye rolls, dismissive shrugs or a grimacing grin that mocked his flattery.

I was too young to understand how her handsome looks eclipsed more conventional notions of beauty. There was too much of the eagle in her face. And besides, I liked to argue for argument's sake: my father encouraged verbal jousting and the banter of rhetoric. 'What about Audrey Hepburn? Sophia Loren? Elizabeth Taylor?' I challenged with irritating gnat-like persistence. My father shook his head at the mention of each screen goddess. 'Too made up', 'Vulgar', 'Cheap', he replied with unwavering devotion, consistently dismissing all the obvious contenders I could name.

Beauty was a valued attribute in our home. We critiqued people's appearances anywhere we went, from theatre foyers to airport lounges. 'Nice pair of legs,' my father would say appreciatively and our heads would swivel to where his nodded. '*Regarde comme elle est moche, celle-là*,' ('Look at how crummy she is') my mother would say with uncharitable spite of someone with plain features or '*Dis donc, ce qu'elle est mal fichue!*' ('Goodness, she looks lousy') of someone poorly groomed or dressed frumpily as if such a thing were a crime. Her judgement was merciless.

My appearance was subject to constant comment and scrutiny. My mother documented every haircut and new outfit with her cumbersome Leica and later, an even more professional Nikon. The portraits continued even when I became too sulky to smile as first puberty, then adolescence, hit like long grumbling storms. There are hundreds of photographs of me brooding soulfully in velvet capes and romantically ruffled dresses, my gaze often clouded with resentment or averted as a sign of non-cooperation. She might, by then, have called herself a war photographer, so hostile was her subject.

In early childhood I was a severe thumb-sucker who then graduated to chronic nail-biting like my father. He marred his carefully groomed appearance by chewing his nails to the quick till they bled, turning his sausage fingers into mutilated stumps. I felt ashamed of how his hands must look in meetings and when he signed documents, but he never seemed embarrassed enough to hide them or to attempt to stop. The double standard that allowed him to tell me off for our shared habit while doing nothing to correct it in himself infuriated me.

On Sunday mornings, he would call me into his dressing room for an elaborate, weekly, humiliating and slightly creepy ritual inspection and manicure. I was instructed to soak my hands in warm soapy water, and then he would tidy my hangnails with a pair of shaped cuticle scissors before slathering my fingers with cream, shaking his head in disapproval at the damage I'd done. My objections that his self-mutilation was far worse were ignored. He painted my fingers with a disgusting clear liquid to act as a deterrent, offering me a pocket money reward as an incentive to grow my nails. It failed.

When my skin erupted in aggressive acne due to the inevitable pubescent hormonal surge, there was nowhere to hide my embarrassment and no one thought it might be tactful to ignore my condition. On the contrary, it was discussed in detail over dinner, making my already agonising self-consciousness worse. My father knew a world-famous dermatologist I should see. He brought me skincare products from America that might help. He meant well, but still commented on every new pustule.

While the acne raged, my teeth became a second focus of unwanted attention. Crowded and irregular, they required orthodontics. I hated the feeling of the ugly clamps when I ran my tongue over them. My mouth felt like a prison. The stainless steel braces and wires made me lisp, food got caught in them and they inhibited my willingness to smile, making me seem even more sullen than usual. At night, I had to wear an additional external brace resembling a scold's bridle, that medieval torture muzzle specifically designed for women. The metal boomerang on an elasticised headpiece made lying on my side uncomfortable and the thought of sleepovers with such a contraption inconceivable. I withdrew further into myself, my schoolwork and my books.

My chompers had already given me plenty of grief. When a milk tooth canine fell out but nothing dropped into its place, an X-ray revealed that the tooth was hiding in my cheekbone, impacted somewhere near the edge of my eye socket. I lived with the gap for a couple of years until I turned thirteen, when our Harley Street dentist, Dr Preston, suggested that rather than scar my face to extract the tooth, he would attempt a world first: he would make an incision in my palate and drill through the bone, attaching a wire around the rogue tooth, gradually winching it down into place with a winding mechanism much like the key on a sardine tin. The surgery would be performed under local anaesthetic.

On the appointed day, I woke up with a gnawing pain low in my belly and the bedsheets stained with rusty red smears. My period had decided to start that day of all days. A brisk explanation from my mother was all there was time for, together with a bulky sanitary pad. The surgery took much longer than expected and was extremely painful because the anaesthetic wore off. When Dr Preston attempted to top it up with booster shots, his bifocals magnified the needle to grotesque proportions, prompting me to slide away from him down the dentist's chair in whimpering terror. My mother sat in the room with me through the whole ordeal, clenching her fists and her jaw to remain composed, not daring to come near me and see the carnage for herself. But I could hear everything and see too much. Most traumatic was noticing tiny flecks of bone fly up from the drill and stick to Dr Preston's glasses. I was bleeding from both ends. For years after, when I lay in the bath, I would suddenly see the water turn red, as my brain replayed the trauma. Towards the end of the surgery, tears ran down Dr Preston's crevassed cheeks as he repeated, 'I'm sorry, I'm sorry,' for causing me so much pain.

The ordeal did not end there. The winching mechanism required tightening every few months, causing a temporary sensation of pressure and pulling. But, miracle of miracles, the procedure worked: two years later, a perfect canine appeared, its ivory tip heralded as it broke through the gum with all the jubilation of the moon landing. My father sent Dr Preston a case of champagne.

But I was not out of the woods yet. By the age of fifteen I was anxious to distract attention from the angry skin and heavy metal jaw that had shrivelled my self-confidence. To make matters worse, two of my closest friends at school were exceptional, head-turning beauties with ocean-coloured eyes, flawless complexions and California Girl manes of lustrous hair. Seeking to compensate for the features that so mortified me, I decided to treat myself to a new style at the hairdresser to boost my morale. Asking my most worldly and sophisticated girlfriend (her mother was a glamorous society fixture) where she had her hair done, I gamely booked myself in to Leonard's, then the poshest coiffeur in London. I made an appointment for a Wednesday afternoon after school, taking along a photograph I had cut out of a magazine of the kind of curls I wanted.

I was assigned a seat, the only schoolgirl in a sea of Sloanes and model types, and showed my photograph to a stylist. The look, she explained, would require a perm. She set about mixing and applying a solution to rollers curled tightly on to my scalp and left to set. I settled in to reading a glossy magazine. After a time, the rollers were removed, my hair was shampooed and a second stylist took over from the first one, reapplying solution and a second set of curlers. Absorbed in my magazine I paid little attention. When I looked up, I recognised faces I had seen in the glossies being offered tea which no one offered me. The atmosphere was hushed, the air pleasantly scented with hairspray and perfume. I glimpsed Leonard himself—his hair dyed as black as a crow's wing and stiffly coiffed in a gravity-defying upward bouffant style, his skin unnaturally tanned—skinnily swanning between clients in a black turtleneck and tight black flares, kissing cheeks and waving his scissors like a cigarette holder.

When the stylist came back to remove the curlers, I looked up expectantly. Something was wrong. My hair was coming out in tufts. Very soon all that was left on my head was a singed orange pubic fuzz. The stylist disappeared. Another one came, swept the hair at my feet away, removed my protective gown and ushered me to the front desk where I was presented with a bill—yes, a bill for more than a hundred pounds. Mortified but proud, I wrote out a cheque without argument, in a stupor of shock and humiliation. 'You are welcome to come back for a free scalp treatment,' the receptionist said in a rushed whisper, eager to get me off the premises.

I rode home on the underground and saw my reflection in the windows whenever we entered a tunnel. *This is not happening,* I told myself. *It will all be alright tomorrow.* People stared at me with open sympathy across the aisle. I rang the bell when I got to our front door. My mother took one look at me, gasped 'Mon *dieu!*' and recoiled in horror. 'Don't move!' she ordered, before I could cross the threshold. She returned with camera in hand, instructing me to turn around slowly so that she could document my condition from every angle. Too numb to cry, I revolved in slow motion, barely able to speak or eat my dinner. Fortunately, my father was not due home until late, sparing me his comments.

In the morning, my mother stopped the cheque and I applied myself to attempting to disguise my condition for the school day ahead. I chose a pale blue silk scarf and knotted it peasant-style at the nape of my neck. It stayed on for about a minute before a bratty boy behind me yanked it off and the class breathed a collective gasp of disbelief. That was when the tears fell hot on my cheeks and it sank in that this was not all some ghastly nightmare.

So now I had spots, a mouthful of metal and was virtually bald. Small wonder I excelled at my studies, seeking refuge in the sanctuary of my room where being a swot felt like something I could control. For the next two years, while others played sports on Wednesday afternoons, I sat under a heat lamp, my scalp smothered in a thick white cream, willing my hair to grow back. But it had been so severely nuked by the mistaken application of a double dose of chemicals (due to a change in shift between apprentices who had failed to communicate what stage of the process they were at during the handover), that when my hair grew longer than half an inch, it fell out. Over and over again, it just gave up the will to live. Any vanity I had was scorched along with it. Instead of fulfilling my secret hope of becoming as beautiful of my mother, thereby gaining my father's unconditional approval, I had found yet another way to disappoint my parents and myself.

~

Like beauty, fame had currency in my home. The word 'famous' was used by my parents with approval, whether applied to chefs, artists or politicians. They made it sound like an attractive quality worthy of respect. My father's tendency towards hyperbole meant that he often described someone or something he admired as 'the world's most famous' whether it was a conductor or a hamburger. Celebrity was something to strive for, and to be in its orbit was to be elevated into an exclusive realm of privilege and reward. It conferred immortality.

My first brush with fame is second-hand but I don't have any recollection of it, so I feel it does not count. There are photographs to prove it, but they do not jog my memory one jot, no matter how often the story is repeated. In the photographs I am just a toddler, one speck among other specks playing on a lawn at the home of Josephine Baker, the great American cabaret sensation who danced naked except for a scanty skirt of bananas. The pictures were taken at her home in the south of France while I was playing with the so-called Rainbow Family, children she had adopted from all over the world (long before Brangelina did the same).

At the time, my father was involved in the student travel business and looking for somewhere he could offer budget group accommodation to young American college graduates coming over on vacation. He heard that Baker, who was going broke thanks to her unscrupulous sponge of a husband, was offering to rent out her thirty-bedroom chateau in the Dordogne complete with its sumptuous formal gardens. We went to visit on one of our site-inspection holidays—the ones that always involved traipsing around a new hotel, sometimes as yet incomplete, and assessing rooms for future groups.

Built in 1489 as a Renaissance fortress, Les Milandes was where Baker indulged her idealistic and romantic but impractical dream of raising her brood of a dozen, some of them rescued from appalling circumstances. One had been found in a garbage bin. But she was never there, always busy on tour earning the money to keep the place going. Meanwhile, her bandleader husband, Jo Bouillon, and her staff of nannies robbed her blind, until she could no longer keep the children or the house. I was there in a brief halcyon moment before things went terribly wrong, but according to my mother the children were already pretty feral—unsupervised and bordering on neglected. Eventually Baker turned to her friend Princess Grace to help her out financially and rescue the children, finding new homes for them. Most have led troubled lives ever since.

In my forties, I found the story of Baker and her tribe poignant and intriguing enough to think I might write about it. On a trip to New York, it prompted me to visit a shabby restaurant upholstered in faded red velvet called Chez Josephine, on 42nd Street, run by her son Jean-Claude. He was distinctly unfriendly, suspicious and evasive, and refused to help me find and contact the other children, including his brother Jarry, who was working there as a waiter. In 2015, Jean-Claude took his own life, but the refurbished restaurant with its decor of Baker memorabilia is still a fixture of the theatre district.

My mother caught the fame bug early. While still in her teens, she had met her fair share of people who would become artistic luminaries. Through Arlette Varda, she became an acolyte in the orbit of Jean Vilar, France's Laurence Olivier, one of the great actor–managers of the twentieth century and the founder of the Avignon Festival. She was in his entourage at the inaugural festival, first minding his children, then as his assistant, mixing with the cream of France's actors including Jeanne Moreau ('She was imperious, she knew she was good,' my mother said). At the second festival she appeared on stage as a tree in *La Mort de Danton*. While she had no desire to perform, she blossomed in the fellowship of the company. It was perhaps her first experience of another kind of family: an ensemble. The troupe shared long convivial lunches where my ravishing mother more than held her own, according to Arlette, who took the company's production stills and watched Jacqueline develop a quick, sharp wit, parrying the banter and repartee of her country's most gifted performers. These were sparkling, carefree days that my mother would remember as the happiest of her life.

Perhaps her interest in fame was sharpened by her affair with Thérond, who was single-handedly responsible for the most intrusive long-lens stalking of celebrities in Europe at the time, making *Paris Match* the vanguard scandal magazine of the twentieth century.

When we watched French films together, she would suddenly exclaim, in the middle of a scene or watching the credits, '*Ah celui-là, je le connais!*' ('Oh, I know that one!') She speaks rarely of those days except to say that Jean Vilar propositioned her, which left her feeling betrayed. 'He said I could not come to rehearsals because my presence inflamed him,' she said with a smirk. When his wife Andrée, whom she adored, did the same, she was equally dismayed: 'One thing I am not, is a lesbian,' she told me emphatically at the age of eighty-five.

Her awareness sharpened by her theatre life, my mother developed a keen talent for celebrity spotting. We were holidaying in Spain where my father was attempting to slot his Jaguar into a particularly tight spot, when a man in short shorts appeared and began gesturing dramatically, miming hard steering to help my father slide into position. 'Isn't that Laurence Olivier?' said my mother. Olivier was my father's idol, a veritable god in his pantheon. A slavish, if not downright obsessive fan, my father had seen him as Shakespeare's Richard III no less than fourteen times, sometimes sleeping outside theatre box offices in queues for tickets. He had a photograph of Olivier in the role in his study at home. The chance encounter made his day, though Olivier slipped away before my father could thank him.

She was chuffed that our local GP, David Sacks, had a celebrity clientele that included Elizabeth Taylor. When it was time for me to be vaccinated, she suggested he administer the inoculations on the sole of the foot to avoid unsightly scarring on the more traditional arm or thigh. He duly obliged. Many years later, when I first met the awkwardly shy neurologist Oliver Sacks, I was able to break the ice by telling him that his brother had been the family doctor. When I added that his mother had been my own mother's paediatrician, he hugged me in delight.

The first person I ever interviewed was myself. Typical only child behaviour, you might say, but there was just no one else available at the time. I was maybe six or seven, in a hotel some-where, and had poured half a bottle of bubble bath into the tub and was now soaking in it, swathed in white foam I pretended was a fluffy fur coat, like one a starlet would wear. I had seen such things on television, so I knew they existed. The foam felt soft and luxurious, so I just started a fantasy conversation aloud, asking my alter ego questions. I replied that I lived in Paris, I was a film star, this was one of my many fur coats but the only one that was white, and my favourite food was a room-service club sandwich followed by chocolate mousse. If asked, I would probably still say that today.

I sustained this dialogue for some minutes before I heard giggling from the next room and realised that in getting carried away with my subject I had completely forgotten that my parents were next door, eavesdropping. Mortified, I ended the interview mid-sentence, pulled the plug and let the bubble bath drain away.

Star-spotting anecdotes, repeated often and with awe, left me in no doubt that any contact, however brief and impersonal, with people burnished by the flame of fame was to be encouraged. To be in the same restaurant or in their random presence anywhere was a mark of success, as long as they were from the world of the arts, media or politics. But not sports, which my parents had no interest in.

And not pop music, which my father regarded as an abomination. He had a cousin who worked for Berry Gordy, the founder of Motown Records, as the company lawyer, drawing up contracts for its stellar roster of performers. Papa was not impressed. When his cousin sent me a copy of the latest Supremes album, signed on the disc's label by all of the members of the group, my father broke the record in two and threw it in the bin.

My mother was less uncompromisingly highbrow. I once witnessed her tear the lyrics of 'Eleanor Rigby' out of *Harpers and Queen* in a Harley Street waiting room and fold them into her handbag because she liked them so much. When my father was away we watched *Top of the Pops* with shared pleasure.

Years later, Maman recognised a couple across the aisle on a flight to Bali as Mick Jagger and Jerry Hall. 'He really doesn't look bad for someone who has taken so many drugs,' she said, in a tone suggesting she was contemplating switching from her nightly application of Guerlain potions to his regime.

Fame was a presence at my school, though I was scarcely aware of it. When I mentioned a classmate's name, my parents often seemed to have a genealogical map of their origins like a social sat nav. According to their radar, Simon, probably the first boy I ever knew with one white and white black parent, was the son of a distinguished actor. A short American boy who had a ferrety face like a young Polanski and scowled at teachers turned out to be the son of one of the world's greatest writers of musicals. I did not like either of them the more for it, but my parents' preoccupation with lineage taught me that surnames were like a code to be cracked, that whoever you met had a history that connected them to others in ways that mattered, even if I could not quite see how. Later on I learned that my school was something of a magnet for the rich and famous, from Jacqueline Bissett to Madonna's daughter Lourdes, and that saying I had attended the French *Lycée* conferred snobbish cachet that ran parallel with academic achievement.

As a way of earning my parents' approval, I made an unconscious note to pursue fame as a goal. My ambition in life was to be in its orbit, no matter how small a planet in its galaxy. Long before celebrity became a pop-culture addiction, I believed its reflected sheen and lustre would act like a protective coating, shellacking me against failure and disappointment. But over time, as I saw it up close, its gleam tarnished.

# CHAPTER 6

# *Kindertransport*

My schoolfriends called their father 'Dad' or 'Daddy', but my father insisted on the European 'Papa'. I didn't like it. I wanted to be the same as everyone else. My mother was less fussed about whether she was Mummy or Maman, but Papa it had to be. As an adult, I called my father HB, as he was known to his staff and colleagues. He in turn called me a selection of nicknames, many of them obscure. I was his *Tochter aus Elysium*, from Beethoven's 'Ode to Joy', the climax of Symphony No. 9, sometimes just shortened to Tochter, but I was also Clonker (no idea why), Plum Pudding and, equally inexplicably, Ninotchka. If I was in a bad mood I was Sourpuss or Wagner's troubled daughter of the gods, Brunhilde. But mostly I was just Baby.

My mother's names for me were similarly exotic but obscure: Bécassine, a reference to her favourite French childhood cartoon character; Rostopchine, the name of a Franco-Russian aristocrat who wrote French children's books I adored; the idealised Cunégonde from Voltaire's *Candide* and Pocahontas, the Native American Indian princess, which was the name she almost saddled me with officially until my father put his foot down. If I was being belligerent, she called me *pouffiasse*, a French slang word for bitch, or *mégère*, the word for shrew, or Boadicea, the warrior queen.

~

Another difference: when I was about nine or ten I noticed that some of my schoolfriends were absent from class on the same days without bringing a note to say they had been ill.

'Probably Jewish,' said my father.

'What does that mean?' I asked, always keen on acquiring new words and definitions.

He explained that Jews were people whose religion meant they did not believe in Jesus Christ (with whom I was barely familiar, although I knew he appeared in the optional *catéchisme* classes I did not attend) and who therefore did not go to church but had special days for their own religious holidays.

'Are we Jewish?' I asked hopefully, since we did not go to church.

'I am, Mummy is not. So technically you're not,' replied my father, which was altogether too ambiguous for me. To add to my confusion, he then added cryptically: 'But of course you'd be Jewish enough for the Nazis, because you have a Jewish grandmother.'

'Who are the Nazis?'

'Not are. Were. The Nazis are in the past tense, Baby. It's a long story. Maybe when you're a bit older.'

That night, as I was about to turn out the light, my father came and stood by my bed and raised his hand as if he were about to bless me. 'Repeat after me, Baby,' he said, his voice gentle but charged with emotion. '*Shema Yisrael, Adonai Eloheinu Adonai echad.*'

I repeated the words until he was satisfied I knew them by heart. 'What does it mean?' I asked him.

'It means "I am the Lord thy God and you shall have no other God but me",' said my father without further elaboration. I took this to mean that I was to consider him an all-powerful deity with authority and dominion over everything. Which was pretty well the case.

Within a year or two of this conversation, prompted by a school project, I asked Papa to draw me a family tree. No sooner had he outlined the first branch than he broke down and wept—great heavings as he gulped for air like a fish on a slab—guilty that he could not remember the names of all his Hungarian and Polish cousins. These were children with whom he had played on family holidays, and he could see their faces, but their names were gone.

'Can't we ask someone?' I suggested, which only provoked more tears.

My mother whispered to me that they were all dead.

References to family were always made obliquely to minimise their emotional impact. That special silence, unique to homes traumatised by survivor nightmares, hovered over ours too. There was a perimeter fence around certain subjects, patrolled by invisible guards.

One day my father noticed the pencil I was using to draw with and flew into an instant rage.

'If I ever see you with a German implement of any kind again, I will DIS-IN-HERIT you!' he bellowed, separating each syllable for emphasis. I was not sure what that meant but it did not sound desirable.

The spare room in our house was not used except for storage, as we rarely had guests. It was always kept locked. One day while my parents were out, I unlocked the room and examined the bookshelves. There I found the fat blockbusters my father read on holiday. Like so many other adolescents I fell upon the famous wedding party sex scene in *The Godfather* and, while reading it, became flushed with excitement. Reading and a state of arousal became inextricably linked for me at that moment. Perhaps I chose to make reading central to my life, believing it might trigger such heightened sensations on a regular basis (which it does, though of a different nature).

But another, much darker association was forged in that room: mixed in with the trashy best-sellers were books with pictures of men in striped pyjamas, looking haunted and skeletal, pictures of piles of corpses, their limbs flung this way and that like rag dolls in the disarray and abandon of death, pictures of mountains of suitcases, and piles of shoes, of cell-like rooms captioned as gas chambers. I read a little, snatched a few phrases here and there, recoiled at the horror and wondered: Who were these people? Was there any connection between them and my father's dead relatives? Why did they look like that? Why were their ghastly images kept here, together with the books that caused my heartbeat to rise? In that incomplete awareness, was a connection made between sex and death? I never mentioned the room to my parents, never asked about those images. Instinctively, I knew not to.

Some stories keep you warm, like a blanket that wraps you up in comfort, security and identity. Like scraps of fabric saved to make a patchwork quilt, I only have fragments of information. Trying to stitch them together when none of them are evenly shaped or of the same weight makes for an awkward cloth full of holes, as if moths had got at it.

This much I know: immediately after *Kristallnacht*, when the Nazis burnt and destroyed synagogues across Germany and Austria in November 1938, my grandparents realised that the safety of the family was at risk. Because they were Jews.

Alexander and Laura Baum lived in the heart of Vienna, above a restaurant called *Drei Husaren* (Three Hussars) in Weihburggasse, not far from St Stephen's Cathedral which today looks like a very smart bourgeois part of town. But Alexander Baum was not a wealthy man by any means. Solidly middle class, of leftist leanings, he earned a modest living by stamping out small price-tag labels for jewellers using a machine he kept in the bathroom. His wife threaded the labels onto fine cotton and delivered them to shops.

As a cultured, well-read man who loved music, literature and the theatre, Alexander mingled on the periphery of those worlds; his association with Karl Kraus, the biting satirist and dramatist, whom he helped assemble his subversive magazine *Die Fackel* (*The Torch*), would later cost him his life.

In the ten years he shared with his son, he passed on his enthusiasms so effectively that they would last a lifetime. Later, my father would write whole paeans to me about artists to whom he was first introduced at this stage of his life and whom he venerated forever. Conductors like Wilhelm Furtwängler and Arturo Toscanini gave my father an example of what it meant to lead with complete authority that he would later emulate in business.

Even at the tender age of ten, he revered pianist Vladimir Horowitz. Many years on he wrote to me in one of his more sentimental moments of nostalgia: '*Horowitz once removed a bee sting at the tip of my left index finger when, at the age of five, I visited the villa where he was staying with my father; ever since, my left index finger has been holy and if you look carefully, you'll spot the halo that surrounds it.*'

Alexander was a strict old-school Prussian disciplinarian; family folklore suggests that my father inherited his short-fused temper. Laura was apparently an excellent cook, famous for her strudel pastry, as fine as gauze: my father claimed he could read through it. He talked reverently about her roasted goose and her *knödel*, potato dumplings filled with plums or apricots, whose stones she replaced with a sugar cube that melted during poaching. She was so fussy and exacting about ingredients that on the rare occasions the family dined in restaurants she would insist on going to inspect the kitchens to check how fresh the produce was and how well it was being prepared.

My father's favourite uncle, Ludwig Schiffer, was a distinguished partner in a law firm. Before the rise of the Nazis, the family socialised with Arthur Seyss-Inquart, a prominent lawyer with his own practice, who would go on to become Hitler's Austrian Minister for the Interior for just two days before the Anschluss merged Austria and Germany. Later he imposed a reign of terror over the Netherlands, sending thousands of Jews to their deaths before being tried and executed at Nuremberg.

But in pre-Hitler Vienna, Seyss-Inquart's anti-Semitism did not prevent him from associating with Jewish colleagues, not only in their offices but at home. On one such occasion, someone took a photograph of him pushing my father, who must have been about five or six years old, on a swing. In the light of subsequent events, this photograph has assumed mythical status in family lore, but of course, no one has a copy of it today.

Uncle Ludwig was sent to Dachau for six months, possibly by Seyss-Inquart. The story goes that his formidable wife, Olga, dressed in her best fur coat, went to see first Heinrich Himmler and then Seyss-Inquart, whom she reputedly slapped across the face for his act of betrayal. Why she got away with this is a mystery. Ludwig was released and he and his family emigrated to America. But that was much later.

In 1938, Alexander and Laura Baum saw the writing on the wall and decided not to delay. After hearing about a rescue operation to take Jewish children out of Eastern Europe through the Red Cross, my grandparents lobbied the Jewish emigration authorities, which had been established earlier that year under the command of SS captain Adolf Eichmann. They secured places for my father and his sister Franzi on the first convoy of children to leave Vienna.

Who told them what was to happen? When? How? Were they sitting at the dinner table? Was the mood sombre? Did Laura fight back tears? Was Alexander stern or reassuring when he told them they were going on a holiday to England? That they would join them later? Did the children get to ask any questions, like how soon will you come, or were they too obedient to ask anything at all except what could they take with them?

Uncle Ludwig, recently returned from his concentration camp experience, interceded personally to secure an export permit so that my father could take his most precious possession, his stamp collection, with him. On 7 December 1938, a date that stuck in my father's mind forever, they went together to a Nazi office to obtain the required official document. Four days later, my father and his sister left Vienna.

The rescue operation became known as *Kindertransport*. While *Kinder* means 'children' in German, I like the fact that in English, the word implies the kindness it demonstrated so tangibly. It was the ultimate manifestation of compassionate action, bringing together Quakers, Christians and Jews with a shared purpose. Many were exceptional individuals who showed great personal courage as volunteers travelling to Prague, Berlin and Vienna to organise the train convoys that brought thousands of children to a safer life in Britain. They had been galvanised into action by the incessant lobbying of the British Jewish

Refugee Committee, which prompted a debate in the House of Commons that led to an agreement allowing a limited number of children under seventeen years of age temporary residence. Ten thousand were saved from their fate.

The logistics of *Kindertransport* were a remarkable demonstration of cooperation and collaboration between unlikely partners, including the Nazis themselves, who supplied the trains. The children undertook their journey in sealed carriages, according to orders from Nazi command that echo the sinister conditions of those who travelled on cattle trucks to the death camps a few years later.

Each child could only take one small case (some managed to smuggle violins in their bags) and the Nazis imposed a rule that parents could not accompany their children on to the station platform to say goodbye, although my father disputed this, remembering that both his parents said their farewells at the train. Perhaps the regulations were tightened later. When I imagine this harrowing leave-taking—those last hugs and kisses and banal admonishments to be good which parents feel duty bound to mouth in such circumstances—I console myself with the fact that Laura and Alexander had no idea what lay ahead. How much more unbearable it would all have been if they had known.

I don't know whether my father knew any of the other children in his compartment or not, whether they played games, sang songs or found other ways to pass the time, whether the sealed compartments were claustrophobic, whether they could see out of the windows and work out where they were. I do know that initially my father was separated from Franzi and that he pleaded with one of the nurses or nuns (he can only remember them as women dressed in grey, and is unsure of their status, but I think they must have been Red Cross volunteers) to help him cross the alarmingly unstable section between two carriages so that he could be reunited with his sister. From then on, they stuck together.

When the train reached the Hook of Holland, Dutch families were waiting on the platform to pass the children cheese-filled bread rolls and pieces of chocolate. They then crossed the North Sea—which must have been my father's first experience of travelling by ship—and disembarked at the port of Harwich, where they were photographed by the waiting British press, wearing their ID number tags around their necks like labels on parcels.

In these images, some looked cheerful, others stricken: most had never been separated from their parents before. From there they were taken to a holiday camp owned by Billy Butlin called Dovercourt Bay in Essex. The camp was brand new, and Butlin had offered it to the relief campaign as a generous gesture. But it was winter, and the weather was wet and cold; my father remembers the place primarily because of the mud between the barracks-style accommodation blocks that housed six hundred children.

Staffed by Quakers, including students on university vacations, the place had a canteen and a post office, and charities and various businesses donated items to the refugee children: one day Marks and Spencer delivered hundreds of pairs of much-needed gumboots.

On Sundays, visitors who were prospective foster parents could come into the camp and view the children while they ate lunch in the canteen. If a child appealed to them, they were allowed to take them on an afternoon outing as a sort of trial run, to see if they were compatible. My father got his hopes up when he and Franzi were taken out by a smart couple in a Rolls Royce, who lived nearby in a rather grand mansion, but they were returned at the end of the afternoon without any follow-up. Younger children were more appealing and easy to place, so Harry and Franzi, who insisted on not being separated, were harder to find a home for. What can it have felt like to see other children leave and to be left behind?

Children who were taken to London on subsequent *Kinder-transports* arrived at King's Cross Station, where they went to a large gymnasium divided by a rope. They stood on one side of it, and prospective foster couples stood on the other. When the child's name was called out, they stepped forward to the rope and met their new families. There was no vetting, no checks on suitability or circumstances.

After a week at Dovercourt Bay, Mr Blodek, one of the camp's army of volunteer guardians, took a group of about thirty children to Bath. Late one night, Harry and Franzi were delivered to an imposing house covered in ivy on the outskirts of town.

Writing about it many years later for a *Kindertransport* anniversary newsletter, my father heightened the theatrical, Dickensian atmosphere of the place and its owner, turning her into his very own Miss Havisham:

My sister and I were assigned to a certain Mrs Tanner, who was as nutty as a fruitcake and lived in a twenty six room house called The Cottage, with no electric light, no heating and no domestic staff.

On our second day, my sister tried to make some coffee, and found a dead mouse in the coffee grinder. The only food in the house was a supply of tins of Heinz baked beans, which we thought a great treat and some home grown artichokes, but we had no idea how to eat these. Our Christmas presents were a tube of Rowntrees fruit drops each.

But the Cottage did have its compensation in that Mrs Tanner owned not one, not two, but three Bechsteins: one in the hall on the ground floor, a second in the drawing room on the first floor, and a third in her bedroom on the second floor. She was an accomplished pianist and would start, dressed only in a wafting negligé, usually with some Liszt or Chopin on Bechstein number one; then, suddenly, she would stop, and accompanied by a manic giggle rising in tone with her increasing lunacy, she would run upstairs to Bechstein number two, and continue at the precise points where she had interrupted herself; after a few more minutes of playing she would ascend to Bechstein number three for the grand finale of her performance. We could hardly complain of a lack of high class entertainment.

There was a collection of rather handsome suits of medieval armour positioned on the landings of the staircase leading to the upper floors, but when I ran past one of these, the vibration caused one knight's visor to snap shut suddenly and the lance he held in his right hand fell clean across my path so that I was convinced he was alive. I ran out of the house screaming blue murder, with Franzi following, until we reached Bath, where we took refuge in the home of one of *the other Kinder. In the morning, we phoned Mr Blodek and told him we could not possibly stay with Mrs Tanner. We begged to be allowed to return to Dovercourt Bay until they could find another home for us. Mr Blodek was sympathetic and kindly arranged for us to be repatriated to the camp. We learned later that Mrs Tanner had been removed to a home for the mentally ill.*

Back at square one, and waiting to be re-fostered, my father went to the camp post office daily, hoping for a letter from home. He was also allowed to call his parents but I have no idea how often he received news from his family or what they told him of what was happening to them in Vienna. His regular appearance attracted the attention of David Hughes, a seventeen-year-old Quaker in his first year of studying geography at Cambridge, who was volunteering there during the term break. He spoke German fluently, having spent the summer of 1938 cycling all over Germany, and soon extended his friendship to my father.

'I remember a quiet, neatly dressed small boy politely asking for stamps, his head not much above the level of the counter,' David Hughes wrote, when I asked for his first impressions of my father.

In January of 1939, David Hughes sent a letter to his parents, John and Mary: *'The main thing is these children must be taken in somewhere. There are two I have noticed in particular, a boy of 9–11 and his sister of about 16. The boy, Harry Baum, is brilliant, naturally well-mannered, and you fall for him immediately. Both of them have an exceeding charm and grace . . . these kids are among the most outstanding in the camp. The children were given a test in German today on general knowledge and Harry came out top. I am convinced that he could walk away with a scholarship after six months of English.'*

That letter sealed their fate. Thirty-six hours later, Mary Hughes wrote a one-word reply to her son: 'YES'. Although of modest means, and already stretched to the limit by appeals for help from extensive aid networks, the Hugheses took Harry and Franzi into their home without hesitation or conditions.

Describing them in her diary as 'shy and apprehensive' after their first experience, Mary seated them by the fire to warm up after their journey and made them feel immediately welcome as the first *Kinder* to be received in York. Others were to follow.

My father later wrote: *'Our circle of fellow refugees soon expanded. The generosity and kindness of the city knew no bounds. We had unlimited access to the cinemas and theatres and to public transport, free of charge.'*

The hospitality is ironic, given York's notorious past as the scene of ferocious pogroms against Jews during the times of the Crusades. But my father was as unaware of that distant violence as he was of what was happening in Vienna. He found himself in the bosom of a loving family, his school fees paid by donations from strangers across the community.

The Hugheses were cultured and well travelled. Educated at Oxford, John Hughes had served as president of the prestigious Swarthmore College in Pennsylvania, the heartland of American Quakerism, for two years. Mary Hughes was not only a genuine royal Stuart but a direct descendant of Robert the Bruce, the King of Scotland. Her mother, known only as Granny Stuart, made a lasting impression on my father: *'She lived in a large house in Harrogate with a staff of five, including a chauffeur, and always wore a toque, just like Queen Mary, even when she was in her own home. Whenever we went to tea there at the weekend, she would organise all the staff to form a receiving line and they would be introduced to us as if we had never met before.'*

I wonder if the Hugheses spoilt my father just a tiny bit, even though material possessions were never a priority in Quaker life. I hope so. Quakers are not renowned for their cuisine, and coming from a Viennese home, Harry and Franzi would have missed Laura's cooking acutely. But even in wartime, Mary Hughes made an effort in the kitchen, recording in her 1941 diary that she served the children damsons and custard, Bakewell pudding and, as a special treat for Christmas, a goose, prepared, as his mother used to, roasted and stuffed with apples.

Harry was thrilled to receive a Raleigh bicycle as a birthday present, and became such a daring and speedy rider that the police eventually banned him from city streets for being a hazard to public safety after he clipped a pedestrian. Mary Hughes's diary paints a picture of a young man I do not recognise, brimming with physical vitality, riding to the Lake District with schoolfriends during holidays. A couple of years later he spent a summer holiday exploring Scotland with a chum on a tandem. Mary records him being a willing and diligent helper in all domestic chores, even digging in the kitchen garden, which is hard to believe. He never set foot in the garden at home.

Like the Baums, the Hugheses loved classical music and choral singing; the house was frequently filled with Bach and Beethoven, which must have provided a great sense of comfort and continuity to both Harry and Franzi. They all attended concerts at York Minster. As Mary Hughes noted approvingly in her diary, 'No wasting time on jazz for Harry.' From that time forward, his tastes were set to the highbrow end of the scale and never wavered.

As David Hughes predicted, Harry soon won a scholarship to Bootham, the top Quaker school in the country. Located within the medieval walls of the fortress city, Bootham was a liberal and progressive public (that is to say in Australia, private) boys' school where students were allowed to call teachers by their first names. I am trying to imagine how my father managed to thrive there when he had only just acquired English, but he must have had some inspirational teachers who gave him a lifelong love of history, which became his passion and in which he soon achieved top marks. He became a prefect at the school and was instrumental in establishing its debating society. Holidays were an opportunity for high-culture pursuits including his first visit to Stratford-upon-Avon, where he would become a lifelong patron of the Royal Shakespeare Company.

The Archbishop of York at the time was Dr William Temple, a committed social reformer who was also a member of the Labour Party and who later, with Rabbi Joseph Hertz, went on to found an anti-bigotry group known as the Council of Christians and Jews. Dr Temple also had close links with the local Quakers (including John Hughes, one of his contemporaries at Oxford), although he earned their dismay by refusing to condemn the carpet-bombing of German cities by Allied forces.

I have no idea whether only occasionally or on a regular basis, but my father says he remembers being invited to sumptuous afternoon teas at Bishopthorpe, the prelate's palace, on Sundays, when he feasted on strawberries with cream. Rather than merely enjoying this as a treat, my father, always strategic, used these occasions as an opportunity to lobby Dr Temple, whom he was invited to call Uncle Bill, to help him get his parents out of Austria. Dr Temple duly obliged, and after writing letters to sponsor her, he managed to secure a visa for Laura Baum to work as a domestic servant, which was the only kind of work the British government permitted the parents of *Kinder*, so that they could not be accused of depriving British nationals of jobs. She arrived in July 1939.

Alexander should have joined his family in September of that year, also with a visa secured by Dr Temple, but the outbreak of war made this impossible. He disappeared without trace. For many years, we presumed he had died in a concentration camp, along with most of my father's other relatives.

There is no question in my mind that my father felt he had failed personally in saving his father. I also believe that, though this was never overtly expressed, in some way he resented his mother for getting out instead of his father. Alexander loomed larger in his life, absence magnifying his impact. Perhaps the reason that music always made my father so emotional was that it conjured up the parent who took him to concerts. Certainly I have never seen anyone listen to a symphony with more intensity, as if communing with a higher power.

I grew up with no relationship to my grandmother, barely knowing or visiting her. She was hardly mentioned. I assumed she was dead so that I was shocked when, one evening in my teens, we received the news that she had just passed away in New York. My father did not attend her funeral and I don't believe he ever visited her gravesite.

Only a couple of years ago, my father announced, out of the blue, that he believed his father had died in Minsk, now the capital of Belarus. He suddenly claimed to remember receiving a postcard from his father somewhere near there.

He also told us that the Red Cross tried to inform him of his father's deportation. Alexander was arrested by the Nazis supposedly for possessing a complete set of *Die Fackel*, Karl Kraus's magazine. The Red Cross reported, in a letter sent in October 1946, that he was sent to Minsk on 29 December 1941, but my father never received their communication—he was by then a student at Manchester University and the Red Cross did not track him down there.

But as he had never mentioned it before, my mother wondered if he was imagining things, as my father was unable to explain where he was when he got this news. By then in his late seventies, he wanted to go to Minsk and look for traces of my grandfather's final resting place, a journey for which he was not physically equipped. Hoping to prevent him from undertaking such an arduous journey, my mother undertook her own research and correspondence with Jewish organisations and got a prompt reply. It confirmed that there were at least ten deportations of Jewish males from Vienna to Minsk between November 1941 and October 1942.

As to their fate, Yuri Dorn, the coordinator of Jewish Heritage in Belarus, wrote without attempt to gloss over the starkness of the facts: *'First the trains went to Vilovysk [Volkovysk]. In this town people were moved to trains used to transport animals and then they were moved to the ghetto in Minsk. This trip lasted seven to eight days. There was neither food nor water. Ten per cent of men died on the journey. When they arrived in Minsk, professionals such as tailors and shoemakers were selected and sent to a concentration camp called Maly Trostinetz [Trostenets], about 12 kms from the town. Others lived in the ghetto, where there were 7300 Jews from Austria and Germany. They were killed in 1942–1943. The professionals who had been selected for Maly Trostinetz and their families were shot and burned at the beginning of 1944. No lists of the victims' names were preserved.'*

It is believed that the Jews were buried in a mass grave. It had taken my father sixty years to dredge this episode out of his subconscious. What else might have been lurking there?

# CHAPTER 7

# Return to Vienna

After the war, my father was naturalised—a dreadful term that sounds chemical, like the pasteurisation of milk. Once he became a British citizen, he returned to Vienna to help with a process known as de-Nazification. Like other German and Austrian refugees keen to help rebuild their countries and eradicate the cancer that had destroyed them, he joined the British Intelligence Corps. Wearing its uniform, he took part in a naïve but well-intentioned Allied initiative to rid German and Austrian culture of every remnant of Nazi ideology in all spheres of public life.

The task was much greater and more difficult than anyone had anticipated, compromised by the poor language skills of most of the non-native recruits and the lack of impartiality of those who, like my father, had Jewish relatives. But the mission was urgent if Germany and Austria were to be rebuilt physically and psychologically, so deficiencies were overlooked.

My father was assigned to the university in Vienna, where he rooted out academics who harboured vestigial loyalties to the National Socialist regime. I do not know how many people he reported but I expect that he was methodical and ruthless. He had a lot to avenge.

Many years later he told my mother and me a story about those days which I have no doubt he embroidered. As with so many of these anecdotes, it cannot be verified. Nor was there any context for this episode. So I don't know where he was staying, or for how long, whether he worked on his own or with others.

I am trying to imagine the overwhelming and complex emotions that must have been swirling around in this young man's head, returning to his native city for the first time since the end of the war, fully cognisant of all the horror that had occurred. He must have been in a state of inner turmoil I can only liken to post-traumatic stress. But my father rarely talked about feelings, so I am only guessing.

One day, after he had finished his work, he decided, on impulse, to revisit the family home, to see what remained of it and who was now living there. He made his way to number 4 Weihburggasse and knocked on the door of his former apartment. He heard approaching steps, then a pause, presumably while someone looked through the spy glass to identify their visitor. There was another pause, then a muffled sound and a heavy slump, like the sound of a sack being dropped.

He rang the bell again. Now more steps, and this time a horrified shriek on the other side of the door. When it opened, he recognised his family's former neighbours, the Tulicheks.

According to my father, Mr Tulichek had been an early adopter of Nazi ideology and had become some kind of self-appointed block warden, doing the party's bidding. In this capacity, accompanied by other Nazis in civilian clothes, he had methodically requisitioned a large number of the family's possessions, including all the silverware. My father remembers sitting on the floor of his home with Franzi, itemising every fork and spoon before everything was confiscated. Embracing the Nazi-sanctioned compulsory acquisition, Mr Tulichek paid a pittance for the family's Blüthner baby grand piano and Alexander Baum's substantial library, which my father estimated at two thousand leather-bound volumes of literature, philosophy and art, together with bookcases and fine rugs. It was all done perfectly legally, with copious handwritten receipts issued for everything.

When Alexander went into hiding and Laura fled to England, the Tulicheks seized the opportunity to move into the Baums' larger apartment. Now Mr Tulichek lay on the ground, presumably felled by the shock of seeing my father, while his wife bent over him.

My father claimed Mr Tulichek was dead. He may have wanted that to be the case, but I believe that Mr Tulichek had fainted. My father did not stay long enough to find out. He took in the scene with a sweeping glance, recognising the hallway rug and other pieces of furniture. He made no attempt to enter the premises or to claim anything that was rightfully his. Turning on his heels, he left without a word.

I have so many questions: such as would my father and his sister have been entitled to reclaim the apartment after the war, when restitution programs were put in place? Later, they joined a class action and received a pension from the state to compensate for loss and damages. My father refused to take what he considered blood money and gave it to his sister. Neither showed any desire to return to their country.

By that time, my father's assimilation into British life was in its first flush of promise: he'd won a scholarship to Manchester University from which he'd graduated with a First in history. He spoke the language without a trace of an accent and he had a new adopted family whom he loved and who loved him in return. He made the decision to turn over a new leaf and not to look back. Meanwhile, Franzi qualified as a nurse and moved to America with Laura and a fellow *Kindertransport* refugee whom she married and had children with. Once she left England, she and Harry were never close again.

⁓

Fast-forward to London in the late 1970s: at university I had a brainy boyfriend whose mother was a chilly, snooty Austrian. When the relationship got serious, he invited me to stay at the family schloss in the Vienna woods. During our holiday, we made the rounds of his semi-aristocratic relatives in their Viennese homes of faded gilding and chandeliered splendour. Almost in passing, he told me not to mention that I was Jewish as we attended stiffly formal teas with aunts who spoke no English. Stunned, never having considered this label might still carry any kind of social stigma, I smiled politely, nibbling at my *linzertorte* or *krapfen*. But it seems that my olive skin and surname were enough to make my racial heritage suspect. The aunts' lips were pursed, their heads barely nodding to me with frosty hauteur and disapproving condescension. On our return, we showed my parents our holiday snaps over dinner. One featured a roof tiled with the name of the family business: Schenker.

On seeing the name and learning of the connection, my father got up abruptly from the table, his face ashen. We waited in pained silence, but he did not return, leaving his meal unfinished. My mother delegated me to go and investigate.

I found him in his study, smoking himself into a fog and fury. It turned out that Schenker was the name of the removalist company that had, on Nazi orders, taken away his family's furniture. He told me to break off with my boyfriend immediately (I think he actually said, 'That is an ORDER'—one of his stock phrases). I did not comply, but the relationship was doomed.

One pleasing fact I later learned: when Arthur Seyss-Inquart was arrested in Hamburg, it was by a young member of the Royal Welsh Fusiliers with a distinctly un-Welsh name, Norman Miller (originally Mueller), who had left Nuremberg at the age of fifteen as part of the *Kindertransport*.

The last to mount the scaffold with nine other defendants, Seyss-Inquart, then 54, said: 'I hope that this execution is the last act of the tragedy of the Second World War and that the lesson taken from it will be that peace and understanding should exist between peoples. I believe in Germany.'

I have always felt uncomfortable in Vienna. The city feels trapped in an aspic of snobbery, its past still not fully acknowledged, its enthusiastic embrace of Nazism never completely disclosed. I remember being there once with my father when I was in my teens and him suddenly chasing an elderly man in the street and calling him a Nazi to his face for no obvious reasons except that he was the right age—the fact that he was wearing a loden coat and one of those Tyrolean hats with a feather in the brim seemed to provide an irrational trigger, as if the traditional costume were an SS uniform. The man raised his stick to protect himself from my father and I was profoundly ashamed of him for making a scene. Now, when I think about what my father must have felt walking those streets, I cannot blame him.

But what to make of the fact that, a few years earlier, he had taken my mother to dinner at the *Drei Husaren* without ever mentioning to her that he had lived directly above the restaurant? Was he testing himself to see whether he could withstand the pain of his memoires, and whether sufficient time had passed for the wounds to be cauterised? Could he enjoy the plush surrounds and familiar dishes without a bitter aftertaste? And on a subsequent visit, how could he sit serenely with my mother and me at the terrace of Sacher's, eating their famously dense but overpriced chocolate torte? Never one to choose where we stayed casually, he would have been all too aware of the history of the lavish Imperial Hotel as the former headquarters of the Nazis. So was taking a suite there proof that success is the best revenge?

I would happily never set foot in the city again. No amount of old-world charm or Hapsburg grandeur can make up for my malaise there. Even Mozart can't drown out the echoes of the chorus of *Sieg Heils* with which the good burghers welcomed Hitler.

My father could bring us to Vienna on a musical pilgrimage for a concert conducted by Herbert von Karajan, a known Nazi sympathiser, and enjoy it, because for him the orchestra was the orchestra of his boyhood, first heard with his father. The spirit of Furtwängler and Toscanini lingered in the ether when he came to pay his respects. For him, music was always a neutral, sacred space. After I had seen *Taking Sides*, a film about Furtwängler and his ambiguous role at the helm of the Berlin Philharmonic, my father wrote to me: '*I am sure that he was politically naïve like many "cultivated" Germans and could not envisage that the Nazis would develop into such monsters or that the German people would allow themselves to be duped to such an extent. I always thought that when he was conducting, he psyched himself into some kind of trance, and in the same way he must've been in some kind of trance when he imagined that he could simply ignore them by not participating in their activities. In kidding himself that he could register his non participation by simply bowing to Hitler and co at a concert instead of giving the Nazi salute, he failed to appreciate that his very eminence created a burden of responsibility he could not escape . . . there were many contradictions in his character . . . Geissmar, his secretary, was partly Jewish and everybody knew it, but nobody ever tried to touch her but his third and final wife, Elizabeth was well-known as an enthusiastic Nazi supporter . . .'*

Always impressed by any contact, however slight or random with greatness, he added: *'I once sat next to Furtwängler at the Salzburg Festival; the sleeve of the suit I was wearing brushed against his.'* No matter the circumstance, my father had the capacity to be endearingly, sentimentally star-struck.

I believe the impact of being separated from his parents on an impressionable, alert, brainy boy of ten shaped and defined my father's life forever. But he was never one for introspection, so I can't be sure. To me, it drove him to excel, prove himself, make a mark as if to assuage the guilt he may have felt for surviving when so many did not. It manifested in even the smallest details of everyday life.

Departures were always fraught in our family. Packing would go on for days before we left and anxiety levels would rise as the due date drew closer. Inevitably there would be a pre-departure row between my parents, when conditions just got too intense, my father becoming increasingly shrill and authoritarian, insisting on the exact moment when all suitcases must be closed, locked and presented at the front door. He would count them over and over as if they were children, to make sure none was missing, repeating the exercise at luggage carousels in stations and airports across the globe, sometimes yelling at the top of his lungs across crowded baggage halls to no one in particular 'THE SHOE BAG IS MISSING!' as if he could summon it back like a stray infant. Was this some kind of warped re-enactment of what happened in the fraught preparations for leaving the family home in Vienna? I never dared ask.

~

When I was in my teens and exhibiting the first sparks of desultory curiosity about anyone other than myself, my father told me about his *Kindertransport* experience as if it were a jolly jaunt. He made light of it. His tendency to exaggeration made him caricature individuals until they resembled grotesque characters from a gothic novel. He emphasised the sense of adventure and downplayed the fear of the unknown. There was never any talk of homesickness or loss.

Until I was in my thirties, I did not meet any members of the Hughes family, despite his reverential references to them. They were not invited to our home and did not attend significant birthdays. Why had my father drifted out of contact from a family he claimed to love and to whom he owed so much?

As if to make up for this inexplicable lapse, in 2000 my father arranged for a reunion with the Hugheses. Always aware of symbolism, he chose 3 September, the anniversary of the day the prime minister Neville Chamberlain told Britons they were at war with Germany. My father had listened to the solemn broadcast at home with the Hugheses, who, as Quakers, were committed pacifists.

We travelled up to York by train and walked to Bootham from the station, my father leading the way at his usual follow-the-leader jaunty clip. Outside the school two generations of Hugheses greeted us as if we had all seen each other the day before. The school was closed for the holidays but there was a caretaker on the premises who kindly allowed us in and we visited my father's classroom and the library before going to lunch in a private room at a nearby hotel. Over drinks beforehand, my father made a speech that started with his usual polished confidence.

But when he got past the formalities of welcoming everyone as the magnanimous host and recalled his boyhood with the Hughes, a dam inside him broke and the floodgates opened. One minute he was saying that the years he spent with them were among the happiest of his life and the next he was weeping uncontrollably and nothing could stop him.

He choked and hiccupped and no amount of 'There there, Harry, take a moment, breathe, sit down, have another drink,' could calm or console him. He simply could not contain the emotion he had unleashed; it flooded out, drenching us all. Eventually one of the Hugheses rose to respond and suggested we move to the dining room, hoping that a change of scene would release us all from the intensity of my father's outburst. It worked. He settled and the lunch was a gentle gathering of our strange and hybrid newly expanded clan. Like any family, we included the troubled young man who dabbled with drugs and could not hold a job and the introverted cousin who was hard work to sit next to, but our common fellowship was magnified, amplified when we were all mixed in together. No wonder the Quakers are known as the Society of Friends. That is what we were that day and that is what we remain.

I wonder how long it took for my father to discover the tattered remnants of his extended family. I was never aware of him searching for them. In my thirties we spent a harrowing day at Yad Vashem, the memorial to the Holocaust in Israel. My mother had to insist, with uncharacteristic force, that he take the opportunity of their unique database to look up his relatives. He did so half-heartedly and, after a cursory search, claimed they had nothing. The subject was closed.

The one story he did tell me, many years later, interrupted by tears, was the fate of his mother's relatives, the Shochets, with whom he had holidayed at their home in Jasło, Poland, as a child.

In 2003 he wrote to me, giving me as much as he knew of the family's history and providing a unique glimpse of the ambience of his stay in 1937:

*The family house was on 3rd of May Street in the centre of the village. It was comfortably middle class with quite a few children and staff. Family discipline was strict, with meals eaten in silence with only grown-ups talking. Children only spoke in response to a question from adults. All meals started with* kasha *(buckwheat) which I hated. If you did not eat your* kasha, *that was the end of the meal for you. If a woman, including a servant, entered the room, boys had to stand up. Meals were eaten with children holding a folded newspaper under their arms to learn not to assail their neighbours with their elbows. Drop your newspaper and that was the end of your meal. After lunch you had a rest and then went riding or drove a droschke. We would also go for long walks across the fields barefoot, even though the stubble from the crops was razor sharp. It was an exercise in mind over matter. In the evening we played gramophone records and wrote home to our parents. It sounds terribly spartan but we had a great time and loved every minute of it.*

The Shochet home was linked from the first-floor landing via a bridge to the family's factory, a large diversified printing plant that employed three hundred people and also manufactured files, envelopes and adhesive tape, exporting these goods across Eastern Europe.

Following the Nazi–Soviet pact of August 1939, Jasło found itself in Nazi territory. The two brothers who were heads of the family business, Ludwig and Poldek, called all their employees and their families together and told them that as Jews they could not remain in Jasło and had decided to flee into the Soviet zone. Any employees and their families who wished to do so were welcome to go with them, regardless of whether they were Jewish or not. They could take no luggage so as to maximise space for as many people as possible.

Most chose to go. Mobilising all the village trucks, they set off in a convoy towards the east, and were arrested by the Soviets who transported them by rail to Siberia. In 1941, my father received a postcard in York from his uncle Ludwig, saying that he was in a Siberian camp, starving. My father contacted another uncle in New York, who arranged to send food parcels but none of them ever got through. By 1942, though many had died of starvation and disease, there were more than two hundred members of the Jasło contingent still alive, and they decided to break out of their prison and walk to Palestine. This was a journey equivalent to walking from Sydney to Perth. They were recaptured by the Soviets and taken back to Siberia, where they were so hungry they ate cow dung to survive.

In early 1945 the group escaped a second time and began a fresh attempt to reach Palestine on foot. Although twenty-six members of the family perished, the Shochets succeeded and made a home for themselves there, at 27 Pines Street, Tel Aviv, re-establishing an identical factory to the one they had left behind in Poland, connected to the house by a bridge at the rear. My father's uncle Ludwig survived. The house was presided over by my father's regal Great-aunt Fanny, who had emigrated to Palestine in 1911. Through her network of friends and acquaintances, she managed to find food, shelter and employment for everyone who had endured the migration ordeal.

When my father visited without warning in 1951, he was welcomed by an astonished Fanny and her son:

*Down the stairs came my uncle Ludwig, wearing exactly the same jacket he had worn every day in Jaslo and presumably Siberia and on the march and he spoke to me in exactly the same tone as he would have used to me had I still been eight years old, as if the past sixteen years had not occurred, as if zillions of people had not been killed, 'Harry, warum hast Du uns nicht gesagt das Du kommst?' [Harry, why did you not tell us you were coming?]*

*That evening there was the same bustle of people, with children returning for dinner from the army and university. The same meal time discipline prevailed as had in Jaslo. It was the preservation of*

*this discipline which brought these people through all that misery*
*and suffering and pain and danger.*

I visited Israel for the first time during my gap year at the age of seventeen with four girlfriends, all of them from Jewish families. For the final days of the trip, my father treated us all to the luxury of the American Colony Hotel in East Jerusalem, then the epicentre of backchannel diplomacy and intrigue, but we were ignorant of that. Tanned and lean, our hair matted and tangled with sand and salt from Eilat beaches and the Sinai desert, we soaked in the deep baths like hippos and sprawled beneath the domed ceilings of our rooms with their elaborately tiled walls, feeling like oriental princesses on the lam. We gorged on the hotel's famous breakfast buffet before wandering the golden streets of the old city, haggling for trinkets and visiting the sights. (At one point a stallholder offered to buy me in exchange for three camels.) At no point did my father tell me that I had relatives less than two hours' drive away.

Fifteen years later, I returned to Israel with my parents. We spent a week there, including the visit to Yad Vashem. No mention was ever made of the Shochets.

I look up the Schochet compound address on Google Earth. It's a grand terracotta-coloured three-tiered structure, with shutters and a roof garden. It looks prosperous and splendid, a fitting sanctuary for those who made that remarkable journey, a monument to the endurance of the spirit. As I move the cursor to do all these things so effortlessly, I am swamped with feelings of regret and sorrow at how little I know, and how it is all too late. Or is it? I look up a couple of genealogy sites and wonder if any of my relatives live at that address today. And if they did, would they have the answers to any of my questions?

Many months later I meet a woman of my age, another journalist and writer, who tells me that, like me, she has a parent who left her native home thanks to *Kindertransport*. I am mildly interested, as I am each time I hear such an account: they all feature similar details, though each is subtly different in its tragedy.

The jolt comes when she tells me that her family also included a branch that walked from Siberia to Palestine. I am stunned: the way my father told it, the heroism with which he endowed the journey made it seem mythic and unique. I had no idea that this trek to freedom was the fate of others. Suddenly I feel destabilised, rocked by this information, even more so when she tells me that she went to Israel and met relatives she did not know she had.

A sudden ugly tide washes over me, like having a bucket of dirty water thrown on your head from an upstairs window. Envy: she managed what I had not, she found something I did not even know to look for until it was too late. Churned up, anxious, ashamed of my feelings, I find her on a walk a few hours later and confess the effect her revelations have had on me. She understands, and a fresh bond of kinship forged from a common past is made, there and then. Some families are connected by common blood, others by shared memory.

# CHAPTER 8

# Googling a murder

It was not until I was in my twenties that my mother told me why I did not have grandparents on her side of the family.

I had often wondered, but never asked. The radar of childhood picked up a current of sadness transmitted through silences and an absence of photos. I knew to avoid the force field of static electricity crackling in the air: lightning without thunder.

There were clues: in my teens, my mother took me to see a film she declared one of her favourites, *Jeux Interdits*. Made in 1952 by René Clément, it tells the story of a five-year-old girl, Paulette, whose parents have been killed by the Germans in an air attack. She is taken in by a family of peasants and soon becomes attached to their ten-year-old son, Michel. But eventually she is removed by gendarmes to a Red Cross camp and at the poignant, hankie-twisting end of the film we see

Paulette running away into a crowd, crying for Michel and for her mother.

When the lights came up in the cinema, my mother was in disarray, blowing her nose loudly and wiping her face of tears while asking me if I liked the film. The question was jarring: why should I like something that had so visibly upset her? Confused, I mumbled in the affirmative, not wishing to disappoint her in such an obviously fragile state. But the paradox baffled me. I had not yet heard the word 'catharsis'. Later, when I learned to play the soundtrack's mournful melody on the guitar, my mother always paused in her ironing or cooking to give the tune her full attention as if it were an anthem. Which, in a way, it was. An anthem to a robbed childhood.

The first time she told me about her family, it was in a clipped précis, like the short synopsis of a film or a fairytale complete with wicked witch: she had lost her parents very young, been taken in by one of her aunts whom she hated and never wanted to see again.

An invisible cordon roped off this information, discouraging further probing, just like her delivery of the facts of life—in a green booklet—in my early adolescence. A well-trained jellyfish would have picked up that the tone in which she said, 'If you have any questions, ask,' meant the exact opposite. So I knew that she was born in Paris, and that something cataclysmic had happened in her childhood, something more terrible and tragic than being raped, and that it was never mentioned. Even my father, who was not renowned for his tact or sensitivity, tiptoed around it.

I cannot remember what emboldened me to ask her for more details later on. Another film perhaps, or a conversation with friends? 'Ahhh, so *now* you want to know?' she asked accusingly, her voice full of needle-sharp accents, suddenly more French in its emphasis. (Whenever we argued, it was in her native tongue, whose rolled Rs, sibilants and plosives seem ideally suited to conflict. No matter that the rest of the world considers French the language of diplomacy, it was never so in our household.)

In my twenties, she told me that her father, Roger, a sailor in the merchant navy, had shot her mother, Lucienne, and then turned the gun on himself. In broad daylight, on a busy street. The dates and details are sketchy on what happened next to their only child, Jacqueline, but in a highly unorthodox decision for the times, my mother's maternal grandfather, Noel Duran, though divorced, was granted custody. A remarkable character who started life as an illiterate peasant, he had risen to the status of military magistrate and was also an active member of the Freemasons.

For the next six years, my mother lived happily with him. 'I adored him,' she says, her voice suddenly warm with affection. 'I remember that he made me the most delicious hot chocolate I ever tasted and cooked me fried cubed potatoes over which he melted Cantal cheese,' she said, licking her lips. When the war began, Noel rejoined the army and sent my mother to various families to look after her, but as long as she could return when he was on leave she made the best of her disrupted circumstances.

Then tragedy struck once again. Her grandfather was thrown from his motorbike in Blois. Being something of a mystic, he summoned my mother to his bedside and asked her to lay her hands on him. She did so. He died shortly after. My mother was eleven years old. Inconsolable, she blamed herself.

Jacqueline's own relatives were not keen to take her in: even her mother's sister, *tante* Marguerite hesitated, ashamed of the stigma of domestic violence. Instead, she farmed Jacqueline out to various foster families. One was a tax inspector's. When it was time for her to leave, the man refused to let her take her favourite doll, one of the few treasures her father had given her. Marguerite, it transpired, had fallen behind on paying for her bed and board, and the man insisted on keeping the doll in forfeit.

Whether through deliberate cruelty or by sheer bad luck, Jacqueline was passed around like a parcel. Anyone she felt affection for was forced to give her up for reasons that were never clear. As soon as she did well at school, she was moved. She became a disruptive influence—most memorably when she persuaded an entire classroom to squint at a cross-eyed teacher she loathed. How I love that little act of spiteful subversion for showing that her spirit had not been crushed. When she was placed in a boarding school where she was especially miserable and lonely, she bit herself until she bled.

Eventually Marguerite ran out of options and took her in. Apprehensive, pious and humourless, she made a point of only dressing in brown. When she noticed the red buttons on Jacqueline's winter coat, she removed them. Marguerite was on high alert for any signs of disruption: as the daughter of a violent man, my mother came with a reputation that preceded her as a potential trouble-maker. There had already been more drama and scandal in the family than Marguerite could tolerate. The last straw came when Marguerite's sister, Jeanne, a doctor, threw my mother out after she complained that Jeanne's husband had sexually harassed her.

While Marguerite was wary and suspicious of her unwelcome guest, her cardiologist husband Jean-Jacques appreciated my mother's intelligence and quick wit, which only made Marguerite jealous. Sensing the potential for conflict, my mother took advantage of it and played her aunt and uncle off against each other. In the full fig of teenage revolt, during the Occupation, she sought out ways to shock and provoke *tante* Marguerite—once threatening to knit a row of swastikas into a sweater. Adept at needling and sharp-tongued, she was, by her own admission, a handful.

These details, extracted in intermittent conversations over many years, were like small detonating devices; though my mother dropped them with seemingly casual indifference, tinged with defiance and pride, they exploded with bitterness and pain. Every inflexion told a story of enduring grievance, of growing up feeling unloved and unwanted, angry and anxious, mistrustful and fearful. Once when we were talking about some aspect of my father's family's fate at the hands of the Nazis, she turned to him, eyes glinting like jet beads, chin thrust forward at an angle of vehemence: 'At least what happened to you happened to others. What happened to me only happened to me.' As if suffering were a competition.

She remembered nothing of her parents, not their voice, not their smell, though she mentioned that in childhood her father sometimes appeared to her as a ghost and she did not find his presence frightening. When Marguerite gave her photographs of her parents, she cut out their faces with nail scissors.

In France, so-called crimes of passion were recognised until the 1970s as mitigating circumstances by French law. Although it bore all the hallmarks of a *crime passionnel*, Roger and Lucienne's murder–suicide was not one, because it was premeditated. Where did my grandfather, an amateur boxer, get the gun? We will never know, but he obviously had the temperament for aggression.

Years later a therapist told me that a killing of this kind rarely occurs out of the blue and is usually preceded by other kinds of domestic violence. It is highly probable that my mother witnessed her father striking her mother, but had wiped any recollection of it. Once I understood this, it made it easier for me to accept that she had been so passive when my father punished me with beating.

Her parents' murder–suicide was the defining moment in my mother's life. Forever after, she feared abandonment. She fought to save her marriage because anything was better than being left yet again. When I left England to live in Australia, she interpreted my departure as her cruel but inevitable fate, cursing her for a third time. Each time I left after an annual visit, she became almost ill with grief, as if part of her was being torn away. The guilt of causing such anguish was unbearable.

Now I am in my fifties and she is in her eighties. Last year, knowing only the bare bones of a story that caused her pain to relate, I felt the pressure of time draining away and wanted more information about how, where and when it all happened.

The story had, I knew, made the papers, because the shooting, unlike most domestic violence, had occurred in public. So I asked a friend in Paris to see what she could find in the archives. By sheer coincidence, her research yielded results while Maman was visiting me in Australia to celebrate her birthday. An email came through with copies of press clippings attached, providing details I had never heard, including eyewitness testimony from Lucienne's sister Jeanne, who had come to meet my grandmother for lunch outside the bank where she worked and watched the tragedy unfold.

*Le Petit Parisien* featured my maternal grandparents on the front page. The paper was a well-known *canard*, a kind of French tabloid scandal sheet that specialised in reporting lurid crimes. But another domestic tragedy soon eclipsed it when Violette Nozière was arrested for the attempted murder by poisoning of her parents. In the end, she succeeded only in killing her father, whom she accused of incest.

Nozière's trial was widely reported, because of sensational revelations that she had worked as a prostitute and was suffering from venereal disease. She was sentenced to death by guillotine but that sentence was eventually commuted, and when released from jail after eleven years in 1945 she married and then had five children. Later, her story was told in a stylish and sympathetic film by Claude Chabrol starring a young Isabelle Huppert.

That year, 1933, was a juicy year for violent and sensational crime in Paris. In perhaps the most disturbing case, the two

Papin sisters, who worked as domestic servants, were accused of murdering their employer, having first gouged out her eyes with their bare hands. Later, Jean Genet immortalised their sociopathic relationship in his psychosexual play *The Maids*.

By comparison, the mere shooting by Roger Legout, 29 (described as a mechanic and not a sailor as my mother had believed), of his wife Lucienne Duran, 23, lacked such warped details.

I kept my discoveries from my mother for several days, not wishing to ruin her birthday.

~

When I first moved to Australia thirty years ago, phone calls home were prohibitively expensive, inhibiting casual chitchat. The line was awful, with that awkward time delay that meant you always spoke over each other and missed half of what was said. My mother found those conversations excruciating: the technology only serving to underline how far apart we were. She came to dread calling and eventually stopped altogether except for birthdays.

But by the time Skype came along, my mother was eager for more regular communication and adopted it with enthusiasm. Both of us are grateful for the way it bridges the chasm of time and distance, allowing us to exchange the banalities of ordinary life with uncensored ease. First thing in the morning, London time, she switches on the video link, still wearing her floral nightdress, white hair unbrushed, eating a banana for breakfast just as I am about to start preparing dinner. She turns the volume up high to compensate for her diminishing hearing and leans in to see what I am wearing. We talk about nothing, that is to say, the news headlines, the latest series by her television darlings, David Attenborough and Jamie Oliver, the latest crime fiction she is reading. The easiest, least charged, most banal exchanges. My mother has never forgotten me telling her, in my bolshy teens, that her conversation made me tired. It was a casual insult aimed at her housewife's litany of daily woes about tradies who failed to turn up. My remark cut deep: she has been verbally tentative with me ever since. Now we revel in being able to exchange pleasantries about the weather, both of us aware that such normality eluded us for so long.

Once her birthday has passed, I tell my mother about my investigations and ask if she wants to read the press clippings I have been sent. Like a displeased hen, she expresses surprise with an indignant cluck, before seating herself at my computer, which she is adept at navigating: she checks email daily, has a couple of favourite food and knitting blogs, and prints out her boarding passes.

At first she squints too close to the screen until I enlarge the front page of the newspaper for her. Widened in almost cartoonish child-like curiosity, her eyes travel to the date below the masthead and then back to me in surprise. She had always believed she was two when her parents died, which helped explain her total absence of recall of either of them. But now, it turns out, she was actually five, making her lack of any memory of their presence much more explicable as post-traumatic stress. She had simply blocked them out.

I watch her features rearrange themselves in light of this new knowledge. She reads on, mostly in silence, occasionally muttering in disbelief, making those strangled, guttural noises of disapproval that are so unmistakably French and sound like throat-clearing exercises.

When she finishes she pauses, swallows, sinks a little in the chair before saying with a half-hearted Gallic shrug, 'I am still angry.' She does not say, 'It isn't fair,' but that is what I hear. Her life ruined in an instant, and for what?

There is so much to digest. Now I have an address—10 Avenue de la Grande Armée. Now I know that my grandparents had fought, that neighbours reported hearing a violent argument and female cries of distress coming from their third-floor apart-ment in Clamart, a south-western suburb of Paris that supplied the city with its peas. There, Roger had accused his wife of having an affair. Lucienne had taken their daughter to stay with relatives because she planned to go away.

Roger had discovered her intentions and gone to her work-place, the Pari Mutuel Urbain or PMU as it was known, a newly established horse-racing betting agency. Lucienne had arranged to meet her sister Jeanne Sachs at lunchtime. She had called Jeanne the night before, telling her that Roger was jealous, had accused her of being unfaithful with her brother-in-law and struck her. While he was asleep she had fled with thirty francs, leaving their daughter in the care of her mother-in-law.

When Lucienne emerged from her workplace, she and Roger began to argue violently about the money she had taken. Jeanne saw him draw a revolver and shoot her sister three times before turning the gun on himself. He died instantly. On his body was found a letter addressed to his mother, saying, 'Forgive me. Everything disgusts me. My wife cheated on me six months ago. I prefer to die and drag the woman I adored with me to her death.'

After giving a bedside statement to police, it took Lucienne three days to die of her wounds at Beaujon Hospital on the rue du Faubourg Saint-Honoré. It was chilling to see her quoted in the article, to read her actual version of events.

After a long pause my mother rises from my desk.

'I think I need to see for myself.'

'You can,' I offer, perhaps too quickly.

'What do you mean?' asks my mother, looking suspicious, as if she thinks I'm going to suggest we fly to Paris there and then.

'I mean we could look now, with Google Earth.'

My mother may be computer literate, but she has never used Google Earth.

'Perhaps the place where it happened is no longer there,' she says doubtfully, though she knows full well that the street in question is a busy thoroughfare and has driven past it many times. She is hesitating, now that it is possible to look immediately; she is stalling for time, trying to absorb it all. It is too soon.

'Maybe tomorrow,' she shrugs and retreats to her room for a nap.

The next day after morning coffee, Mum asks, 'Can we look?' Her eyes are shiny with anticipation, her body squirming and fidgeting with impatience in my office chair while, leaning over her shoulder, I key in the street name and number. The avenue is a spoke off the Arc de Triomphe: smart, prosperous, bourgeois.

The image comes up quickly, revealing a corner building. The ground floor, where my grandmother would perhaps have worked, had become a prestige car showroom. The pavement is broad and for the briefest of moments I wonder about the blood that stained it on that day: how much of it there was and how long it took to be washed away by rain and street cleaners. There is a café with a terrace just next door. For a moment I think, as if I am planning a normal outing, 'That's where we'll have a cup of tea when we visit,' before I correct myself: why on earth would we want to linger there, of all places? I wonder, too, how many streets bear the invisible scars of forgotten brutalities: unmarked graves we walk over heedlessly.

I show my mother how to get a 360-degree view from that corner and how to zoom in and look at the building and the area in front of it from every angle. But soon it makes us feel slightly seasick and we shut the program down. She does not ask to look a second time.

A few months later, we are in Paris together as part of a holiday in Europe. We eat and walk and look in shop windows and go to street markets and watch people from heated terraces, each contentedly nursing an overpriced Kir Royal.

Prompted by reading Edmund de Waal's *The Hare with Amber Eyes* about his wealthy ancestors, we plan to visit a house near the Parc Monceau that is now a museum dedicated to the life of a Jewish family who lived in similar Proustian opulence.

The Musée Nissim de Camondo is named after the last son in the family of wealthy banker Moïse de Camondo, who built himself a splendid palace at the height of the Belle Epoque, intending to leave it all to his son Nissim. But Nissim was killed in an air battle in 1917. Because his other children showed no interest in the arts, Moïse bequeathed his house and its collection to the Musée des Arts Décoratifs. Later, all his relatives died at the hands of the Nazis, leaving no descendants. Like the dodo, the Camondos became extinct.

The exclusive address is not far from where my grandparents' fate unravelled. If we are to visit, today is the day. I plan a strategy intended to look like a spontaneous afterthought. As the museum has lots of stairs and will be quite arduous, we make the trip easier by taking a taxi instead of the metro. As casually as possible, I mention that we will be near the Avenue de la Grande Armée, as if this were an unexpected bonus.

'Oh, I know, I know,' says my mother, huffily resisting being managed.

We visit the museum. Solemn, sad, a melancholy monument to gorgeous taste, the highest social position and dynastic tragedy from which wealth and status were no protection.

Afterwards we sit in a café, glowing with waxy round lights like multiple full moons, drinking dark hot chocolate so thick our spoons stand up in it, watching well-dressed children head for the park on scooters with smart parents dressed in long wool coats the colour of caramel.

'I thought perhaps on the way home we could ask the taxi driver to go past . . .'

My mother shrugs her ambivalent assent. 'Why spoil the day?' her gesture says.

I feel a little guilty for persisting but if not now, when? My mother is eighty-four and we may never come to Paris again.

We drive up towards the Champs-Elysées, which is festooned with Christmas lights and fibre-optic sparkles that shimmer gaudily in patriotic *bleu blanc rouge* up the trees. Approaching the avenue where it happened, I ask the taxi driver to slow.

'Would you like to get out?' I say to my mother, preparing to ask the driver to wait.

But my mother shakes her head very definitely. At the last minute, as we reach the corner she turns away deliberately, almost defiantly facing the opposite direction, resolute and unblinking, as if, after all these years, she could wipe away the facts simply by refusing to look.

And because I am so busy watching her, keen to harvest the moment for any shards of meaning, any emotional significance that might endow our stay with an extra layer of meaning and somehow bring us closer, I miss the chance to look until it is too late, the corner just glimpsed as we turn off.

Later, while my mother is reading (on her Kindle, *bien sûr*) in our Paris apartment, I try to understand her reaction. Reality may be sharper than any image and offer sensations—noise, smell, movement—that Google Earth cannot convey, but she had already seen everything she needed to see in a satellite photo on a laptop twelve thousand miles away.

# CHAPTER 9

# The dandy

In his heyday as a successful company director, Papa's wardrobe occupied double the space of my mother's in a purpose-built dressing room. Never a follower of fashion, he adhered to the more conservative dictates of fine tailoring, and for decades his suits were always cut the same: single-breasted with a double vent at the back. No turn-ups on his trousers, ever. Only the width of his lapels and the slant of his pockets varied by marginal degrees. He also owned 122 Hermès ties. They were a lifelong extravagance and he cared for them so tenderly that he sent them back to the flagship store in Paris to be cleaned, believing no one in London was up to the task.

On school mornings, we had a regular ritual: my father would call me to his dressing room to pick out a tie and pocket handkerchief to complement his suit and shirt. I ran my fingers through the heavy silk twill tongues to make my selection from geometric patterns of animals, knots, flags, stirrups, keys, pennants and heraldic emblems on brilliant backgrounds of burnt orange, crimson, magenta and French navy. Selecting from the matching silk squares, I learned to contrast the kerchief with the tie for greater impact.

Sometimes, Papa would ask me to pick out cufflinks from a suede-lined box on one of the polished timber shelves where he also kept clothes brushes, fine-denier silk socks rolled into a fist and neat piles of cashmere fringed scarves. I'd insert the cufflinks in his starched double cuffs. His initials in gold were favourites, matching other elements of his monogram mania: to him the B logo on Bally shoes was really B for Baum, just as the H buckle on an Hermès leather belt was H for Harry. As if to confirm his identity, he had his initials embroidered on all his shirt pockets.

Although he drew the line at bespoke shoes, he made annual trips to Hong Kong to be measured up for a dozen suits. In the 1970s, he favoured a fabric called sharkskin, which had a greenish sheen when it caught the light, resembling a ripe bruise.

On all but the rarest occasions, Papa dressed formally. The most casual he ever got was wearing a cashmere V-neck sweater or a brushed-cotton checked shirt at weekends. He never owned a T-shirt and despised jeans. His shoes were always city shoes, smart leather loafers and slip-ons that he even wore to the beach and in the snow if he had to, or, when he came to Australia and ventured, under duress, into the bush.

Sometimes on Saturdays, if we had errands to do in the West End, we would divert to Jermyn Street and window-shop the smart menswear vitrines, occasionally venturing into those dark, timber-lined, clubby dens so he could try on a jacket. I loved fingering the bolts of wools and worsteds, the obsequious deference of the tailors with the tape measures around their necks as they took their brisk measurements while trying to wheedle my father into ordering something made to measure: 'A new overcoat, Sir? A dinner jacket perhaps?' As I got older, I enjoyed the ambiguity of my identity on these visits, leaving the salesman to speculate: was I the gentleman's daughter or his much younger girlfriend?

Unusually, my father was as enthusiastic shopping for my mother as for himself, confident enough to do it even when she was not there. On his annual business trip to the US, he would spend half a day at New York's best department stores, gathering up bulk purchases of nylon stockings, bathing suits, nightdresses, housecoats and blouses, with varying degrees of success. He had louder taste than hers, choosing gaudy patterns that were large and vibrant, when she preferred smaller, less showy prints. He also favoured a touch of the military in details, like epaulettes and frogging for her coats and jackets. Over time she coached him and gave him precise instructions which he grew more and more adept at following. Sometimes he tripped up on size, for which he came up with an ingenious solution: a blow-up doll available in several sizes that could be inflated in front of salesgirls? Happily, such an item was not for sale.

When my mother was present on these sprees, he liked to play the bountiful patriarch: 'Darling (pronounced *Dah-link*), if you like it, have several . . .' was a common refrain, as he encouraged her to buy three or four pairs of shoes, or several cashmere sweaters or silk blouses in different colours. As a result, my mother always looked immaculate because her clothes suffered little wear and tear.

His one regret when it came to showing off the ornament of his beautiful French wife was not being able to afford to buy her a truly opulent full-length mink coat such as the luscious one that belonged to my flamboyant Italian godmother Luciana. An enthusiastic pioneer of bling, she wore her chocolate-coloured fur dripping with diamonds, even to the little trattoria down the street from her apartment in Venice.

On holiday with Luciana and her laconic Yorkshire husband, I was allowed to play dress-ups with her slinky sequined clothes and jewelled accessories. Accompanying it all with a raucous, macaw laugh and cigarette-infused rasp Luciana taught me can-can high kicks and not to be afraid of a full-length mirror, encouraging me to twirl unselfconsciously, striking vamping poses to work out my best angles. She was the closest thing to pure uncomplicated fun I had ever met in an adult and I adored her. When my parents were with Luciana, her effervescence infected the atmosphere. She was built for laughter with a whisky chaser.

Together in adjoining lavish hotel suites, Luciana and I rehearsed showgirl routines to perform as after-dinner floor shows for the benefit of my parents; childless, she was as much a child as I, refreshingly uninhibited by age when it came to silliness.

She told saucy jokes and sprinkled conversation with liberal, genuine '*mamma mia*'s.

I loved to stroke Luciana's mink, pretending it was a living creature. My mother didn't care that she did not own one, perfectly content with a shoulder-covering stole, which she wore less frequently as it fell out of fashion. As her sympathy for animal rights increased, she sometimes hissed at women wearing fur in the street or said '*dégoutant*' ('disgusting') loudly within earshot. Though she felt deeply guilty about a pair of sealskin boots, she continued to wear them as an act of penance.

Inexplicably, given his background, my father was enthusiastic about my mother adopting the traditional dress of Austria, which suited her voluptuous, narrow-waisted figure. The Tyrolean dirndl with its fitted low-cut bodice accentuated her ample bosom, while its full skirts concealed her wide hips. He bought her two: a daytime version in black with a white blouse and *hausfrau* red apron; and a full-length evening version in shades of deep mauve, offset by a necklace of amethysts and turquoise, which she wore to the opera, drawing many an admiring gaze.

Why, when he loathed manifestations of Austrian nationalism so that the sight of a loden coat was enough to make him froth at the mouth with rage, did he encourage her to dress like a chic version of Maria in *The Sound of Music*? It's not as if you'd catch him in *lederhosen* or a boiled wool jacket with contrasting piping, horn buttons and toggles. To this day, the question mystifies us both.

The dirndl was also inflicted on me, reinforcing the notion that I was a doll to be dressed in various costumes. I also owned a painted silk kimono, complete with tortuous Japanese socks with their separate big toe, and absurdly fiddly side fastenings and a stiff cinching obi girdle with a large bow at the back. My mother liked to photograph me in this get-up with my hair pulled into a geisha's bun, standing near her latest ikebana arrangements, waving a pleated and gilded fan, while balancing on the lacquered wooden shoes that completed the look.

Maman's dramatic bone structure made her especially suited to hats. She wore a mannish riding bowler, a blue felt trilby, a Cossack-style fur and an assortment of straw hats from Thailand and Mexico. I was less confident but was given little choice. Despite protestations and tears, my mother insisted that I wear a black velvet beret with pompom and grouse feather as a teen. With the beret tilted at a perilous angle and hooked under one ear, I felt that bloody feather was like an arrow telling the world to look at me when I least wanted attention. But later on I loved rummaging among Maman's hat boxes, finding the petalled and feathered confection she wore for her wedding. In my twenties I appropriated a fluffy fox-fur toque that made my head look like a chocolate truffle.

My mother's taste in clothes spanned classic suits and folkloric ethnic wear: heavily embroidered peasant blouses, full skirts, quilted Indian jackets. She loved colourful paisleys and geometric prints but also neat twinsets, fitted jackets and evening wear that showed off her voluptuous cleavage and slim waist. She was elegant and stylish, a *bourgeoise soignée*, rather than a sexy groovy mum (or what today would so inelegantly be called a MILF).

When younger mums embraced the latest Carnaby Street look, wearing tiny miniskirts with broad belts slung loosely over their hips, with newly Sassoon shagged hair and wet-look patent boots, my mother resisted the fickleness of fashion: her hemlines never rose above the knee. Like any Frenchwoman she knew what her assets were and maximised those while concealing the features she disliked.

Once a year, when we were in the south of France for the summer, my father would take my mother to have a couple of new suits and dresses made at Fernand Desgranges, a second-tier couture house that was more affordable than Chanel. There, he took an active interest in selecting cloth and approving finishes and trims. When it was time for the final fitting to fix my mother's hems, Papa would appropriate the seamstress's velvet pin cushion from her wrist and get down on the ground to mark his preferred length, as my mother turned slowly on a raised plinth. I found these sessions excruciatingly boring, but now they are vivid in my mind—the only time I ever saw my father comfortable on the ground (he was useless at picnics), his face tilted upwards in admiration of his chic wife.

When I was a toddler, he bought me extravagantly hand-smocked dresses, layered over stiff and voluminous eyelet-lace petticoats that stood out like ruffs beneath my skirts. While I was pre-adolescent, Ponds ran a hugely successful skincare campaign that played on the idea that mothers and daughters who used their cold cream looked more like youthful twin sisters. My father embraced the cuteness of dressing me to look like my mother, hunting out dresses to match the cut and colour of hers.

The most elegant came from an exclusive designer in Nice in a box that was taller than me, emerging from a cloud of tissue paper. A pale duck-egg blue shift made of exquisitely fine gabardine, with a slightly military look: six flat disc-like small gold buttons arranged across the chest in three rows of two, and a rolled two-stranded belt that tied at the back of the waist. It was like wearing a piece of the morning sky.

'Pure Balmain,' pronounced my father, who had seen a similar style from the great couturier in one of the French glossy magazines he occasionally bought and that we pored over, page by page, after dinner, criticising every garment. Courrèges and Cardin got the thumbs down for being futuristic and gimmicky. He was more of a Dior man.

Another outfit he bought was a candy-pink silk and linen shift dress with a matching coat that would have been perfect attire for the cocktail party circuit—only I was barely nine at the time. It was very Jackie Kennedy—all it needed was a pillbox hat to complete the look and a pair of slim long white gloves. I wore it with patent shoes and white ankle socks to the ballet and grown-up occasions, fully aware that I looked a picture in it, catching the envious glances of mothers.

Later on, Maman became adept at dressmaking. She expanded her sewing domain from the kitchen to take over the dining room, a stealthy way of announcing that there would be no more formal entertaining. She cut and fitted silks and tweeds on a tailor's dummy like a professional. Borrowing the technique from Chanel, she weighted her suit jackets with gold chains; copying a trick of the royal dressmaker's, she sewed pennies into the hems of her dresses to prevent them being blown up by the wind. She also made many of my clothes. Some I hated. Once she perfected the technique for knife pleats and made me a pale-blue kilt I detested so much I took a pair of scissors and cut a small but unmissable window into the front panel, leaving no doubt about my feelings. It was the first time I asserted my own taste and refused to be dressed like a doll. It seems unbelievable now, but until I was fifteen, she laid out my clothes for school and I wore them unquestioningly.

While friends were confidently shopping in Carnaby Street and at Biba, I was a late developer when it came to discovering my personal style. I wore goody-goody dresses with none of the sophistication I craved. Maman liked to see me in puffy sleeves, swirling skirts and fitted waistcoats like a member of an Estonian dance troupe. She made me blouses and summer dresses in Liberty floral prints that suited an English rose complexion but looked wrong against my olive skin, as if I were a gypsy who had raided the closet of a Cornish milkmaid. For my first ball she made me a dress with a sweetheart neckline and cap sleeves, and while its narrow fit emphasised my slim figure, it had none of the vampish appeal of the slinkier, more sparkling and flesh-exposing dresses my friends wore.

Being French, my school was very appearance-conscious. It was important to keep up with trends: the crazes for cheesecloth, wet-look patent leather, denim . . . Mortifyingly, anything for which I expressed a desire was subjected to a jury on family outings, with both parents present, sitting in judgement outside changing rooms. I had to model every item, my father insisting

I twirl so they could consider me from every angle. His verdict was always that everything was too tight. Shop assistants looked on in amazement at how intensely every garment was scrutinised and deliberated over. Sometimes I caught an expression of pity on their faces. Small wonder that these days I prefer to shop alone.

But back in the day, when my father was flush and proud of his success, he expressed it through showy materialism. Like many survivors of wartime privation, he was also a great believer in buying in bulk, whether he was purchasing food, jewellery, perfume or clothes. So he stocked up on duty-free on every trip, buying dozens of giant cartons of Benson & Hedges for colleagues and litre bottles of gin and Dior and Chanel fragrance to give as corporate gifts. My head teachers were always delighted to receive their end-of-year thank-you bottle of Je Reviens, L'Air du Temps or my mother's favourite, Calèche, a potent androgynous scent that smelled of hay and leather.

Our most memorable shopping binge was in Milan. Planned and executed like a smash-and-grab operation, our raid on the flagship stores of luxury brands on the Via Montenapoleone was targeted, efficient, lethal. Like professionals, we cased the street the night before, scanning the windows of the most exclusive boutiques for the booty we planned to secure. Then, like locusts chewing through a field of wheat, we moved with speed along the glass-fronted vitrines, pointing, nodding, choosing in a kind of retail euphoria similar to a sugar hit. At the end of it, we emerged laden with bags, leaving the shop assistants in a state of shock.

I now think that there was an unconscious second motive for this obscene spending spree. Just a few years earlier, my father's business had been nearly wiped out by a fraudulent accountant called Hamlett Isaacs. The fact that his protégé bore the name of one of my father's most cherished Shakespearean characters only made the wound deeper. When Hamlett stole a quarter of a million pounds to feed a gambling habit and a taste for expensive cars (which rang alarm bells for my mother but my father disregarded), he did more than take my father's money. He broke his spirit.

Every employee who stuck by my father through the tough years that followed agreed that he was never the same again. Humiliated, he never trusted anyone the way he had trusted Hamlett, for whom he had developed an almost fatherly affection. His dreams of expansion were ruined, and although the business recovered, it never achieved my father's grandiose vision. He referred to the episode thereafter as 'The Titanic'.

I was never fully aware of the extent of the devastation as I was at university at the time. I remember my mother saying they were receiving anonymous threatening calls in the middle of the night and urging me to stay away from home until things calmed down. (When one caller woke my mother, saying he was going to cut off my father's balls and hang him from a tree, she replied with admirably cool presence of mind, 'Jolly good,' which cannot have been the expected response.)

Wanted by Interpol, Hamlett was arrested at Heathrow airport attempting to flee to his native Pakistan; he served three years in jail before being deported. The bank, which had failed in its duty of care, paid compensation for its part in the affair. But Hamlett made a fool of my father, and Papa never forgot it. Occasionally over the ensuing decades, when he was in the doldrums and business was bad, he expressed a murderous fantasy to hire a contract killer to exact his own form of revenge. To me, that Italian shopping rampage was, unconsciously, my father demonstrating to the world that Hamlett had not won. But it would not be the last time that he would deliver himself into the hands of conmen.

# CHAPTER 10

# Mother Russia

By the time I reached puberty it would be fair to say I was confused: surrounded by material comfort, but told that nothing was mine; smothered with love, but also controlled, judged and punished. Conflict raged inside me. I daydreamed about getting away but my attachment to everything that was comfortable about my existence held me back. And I felt a loyalty to my mother, whom I felt the need to protect and defend as the victim of my father's bullying.

School provided welcome respite. I thrived academically and socially. At weekends, in search of relief from the claustrophobia of home, I spent more and more and more time at friends' places, amazed at how different the atmosphere was in other families: it was as if there were more oxygen in their air. Some I visited so frequently that I thought of them as surrogate families, able to supplement my own with siblings and grandparents, and my desire to belong to a bigger tribe drew me to multi-generational dynasties. I was intrigued by dinner conversation that was neither an interrogation nor a lesson. Teasing was good-humoured and mild rather than spiteful. Parents and grandparents told silly jokes or stories that had no particular point but lubricated an easy harmony. Children spoke freely. Interruptions were tolerated. Noise levels were higher. Discipline was not the be-all and end-all, table manners were slacker, and while the food could never match Maman's culinary repertoire, meals were more enjoyable if less abundant and tasty.

I found myself appreciating packet-made mashed potato, custard and strawberry whip just as much as our more cosmopolitan homemade desserts. Soon, to my mother's chagrin, I was requesting baked beans and fish fingers at home. We reached a compromise: I could have these as treats on nights when she and my father went out and a sitter or au pair was in attendance. (I never spent an evening, never mind a night, alone in my family home.)

Little did they suspect that the Swiss milkmaids who lived with us were capable of corrupting my innocence; one of them taught me how to smoke while my parents were away on a business trip. When our cover was blown by the smell in my room, she was instantly dismissed. Another had come to London under the pretext of learning the language only to confess that she had, in fact, come to get an abortion. She disappeared overnight after I overheard her sobbing out her real motives to my mother.

Becoming more socially adventurous and independent triggered a new conflict for which I was completely unprepared: my mother became jealous of my friends. It had not occurred to me that she might feel threatened by the bonds I forged with my peers. I was unfamiliar with the term insecurity, had never heard of self-esteem. But Maman grew more and more hostile when I brought anyone home regularly. Her welcome was frosty and my home soon acquired a reputation for being strict and not fun. If friends came for the afternoon, they were rarely invited to stay for dinner, never mind for a spontaneous sleepover. Those who were game enough to stay were subjected by my father to a lecture or a cross-examination on general knowledge and geopolitics that made me cringe with embarrassment.

When they left, my mother often sighed with relief, as if their presence had exhausted her. Her disapproval was often sufficient to kill a friendship with a single remark: 'She's a bit vulgar,' or 'She doesn't have very good table manners, does she?' was enough to make me consider companions in a new light and find them wanting. I was porous, malleable and easily manipulated.

Mostly, my parents rowed in private. I heard snatches of raised voices followed by door-slamming, but it seemed to me that my mother rarely gave as good as she got. Instead of matching my father's spiteful tirades of invective, she resorted to what we would now call passive aggression: stony silence was her weapon of choice. When my father's swearing reached tantrum pitch, she walked away with an exaggerated sigh of exasperation, her features hardened into death-mask-like rigidity as if all her bones had become more angled or her flesh sunken from combat.

Sometimes she rolled her eyes and covered her mouth with her hand, pretending to stifle a mocking laugh of contempt.

The violence was mainly verbal, though I do remember an occasion when my father pulled one of the heavy wooden drawers out of his wardrobe and hurled it down the stairs. My mother and I were out of range as his balled fine-denier socks bounced down each step like skimming stones.

Both my parents were champion sulkers and could go for days without speaking, even at mealtimes. I learned from the best of them and was able to sit across from my father at the dinner table for up to three weeks without us exchanging a word. Even in the car on the way to school—a ride that lasted up to forty minutes—I could endure the entire trip without saying anything.

Building up inside me was a geyser of contempt and hatred. I wanted my father dead, nothing less. His presence changed the very nature of the air we breathed. When he was in one of his furies, the atmosphere in the house became thick and leaden or else it fizzed with static electricity, as if the oxygen might combust at any minute.

Occasionally, my mother matched fire with fire. When the pressure in the house rose to intolerable levels, she took refuge in the garden, where she created her own controlled inferno, hefting piles of raked leaves and twigs to build an enormous bonfire. This pyre was her distress beacon, a flare sent high into the sky fuelled by incandescent rage. The leaping tongues of flame alarmed neighbours, who called the fire brigade. Once it was clear there was no danger, they disappeared, little realising where the real threat lay. When my mother came inside, her face was often smudged with soot and her clothes reeked of the bitter smoke of burned chestnut. It was acrid but not entirely unpleasant: hugging her, I rubbed my face in the corduroy of her gardening jacket, inhaling the reek of defiance.

How she continued to dish up exquisite meals throughout this period baffles me; I thought she should sprinkle ground glass in my father's food. Even when they were not on speaking terms, he ate wolfishly.

Listening to my parents' barbed exchanges, I absorbed the tactics of both sides. I had inherited my father's short fuse and explosive temper, my mother's harsh judgement and dripping sarcasm. As a thin-skinned adolescent, quick to take offence, I interpreted every comment as an insult, every remark as a jibe. As angry as a scorpion, I grew bratty and insolent, picking fights. Occasionally, when I went too far, my exasperated mother would threaten me with a slap. I kicked, I bit, I swore, mostly in French, borrowing my mother's expressions and turning them back on her: '*Fiche moi la paix*', *espèce d'enquiquineuse*', ('leave me alone, you bloody nuisance'). We sparred vigorously, she swatting me away with a spatula or spoon like a nuisance fly. At my most aggressive, I lunged, ducking her brandished wooden implements, pinching her hard on the upper arm. I don't remember her landing blows, but she must have, because these scenes usually ended in tears, with her locking me out of the kitchen. I was foul.

On holidays the pressure increased, like the tropical build-up before a monsoon. Special occasions that should have been the focus of heightened anticipation were sabotaged by the pressure of expectation anxiety. At Disneyland my parents had some kind of major meltdown in the car park before we even reached the turnstiles, prompting my mother to lead me away in one direction. Together we worked our way through the rides joylessly while my father sat at the entrance, chain-smoking furiously for three hours. Something similar occurred at the Sistine Chapel: a sudden unprovoked explosion of rage from my father meant that we filed into the hallowed space too shocked and cowed to raise our heads to the celestial glories above us. Only at the last moment did I lift my gaze from the patterned mosaics on the floor to catch a glimpse of heaven, but I was looking up from hell.

By the time I was fifteen I had been out and about enough to know that my parents were unusually severe. When I challenged their ways, my father's explanation was always the same: 'They don't love their children like we love you.' I would have traded some of that love for freedom like a shot.

Never more so than when my Russian teacher announced that she would be taking our class to Leningrad (as it then was) for an intensive two-week language laboratory course. I was, by common consent, the class's star pupil, and expected to do extremely well at exams the following year. The intensive immersion program would give me a boost in achieving top marks. It would also be my first experience of travelling with friends rather than family. I was bursting with excitement at the prospect.

I had allowed myself to be persuaded into studying Russian by my mother's passionate Slavophilia. My preference was to choose the easier and more seductive Spanish, like my closest friends. But biddable again, I let the decision be made for me. I knew the words (if not their meaning) to simple Russian folk songs like 'Kalinka' from hearing them sung in the recordings by the Red Army Ensemble my parents often listened to at weekends. The sonorous bass voices stirred something in me, resonating in my chest like big deep bells. Maman sang along, having taught herself rudimentary Russian as a teenager in Paris as the result of an intense friendship with Natasha Babel, the daughter of Soviet dissident and writer Isaac Babel, who was sent to a gulag by Stalin.

Eager to please her, I embraced Russian after initial resistance, and soon found that I had a gift for it. Our teacher, Madame Manoras, insisted that we all choose Russian names at the start of the first year, to immerse ourselves more fully in the culture. My mother encouraged me to choose Natasha. The name suited my unformed longings, while the language fuelled my tendency towards melancholy. I became fascinated by the last Romanov archduchesses and their fate at Ekaterinburg, dwelling on the fact that when they were shot, the bullets ricocheted off the diamonds sewn into their corsets. I steeped myself in the tragic poetry of Anna Akhmatova and the yearnings of Chekhov's women trapped on their estates in the provinces. I watched slow languid films full of birch trees and snowy landscapes, and recognised my spiritual home. I fantasised about being a Russian princess, wearing sable and riding in a *troika*, like Tolstoy's Natasha Rostova. The very sounds of the language, with its whispering

SHs and SHTCHS, and its caressing AYAs and OUYOUs, called out to my overheated teenage romantic nature.

In class, I made friends with a shy girl with real Slavic heritage carved into her high cheekbones. When she took me home to meet her histrionic family of White Russian émigrés, I felt instantly at home in the clove- and sandalwood-scented ambience of incense, amber beads, fringed shawls, glinting icons and nostalgic tales of treasures left behind. The name of Fabergé was whispered in asides of gentle regret. Candles were lit for elaborate meals at Easter. I had found my very own Romanovs, living in converted stables in Chelsea. Elated by their authenticity, I watched my mother fall under the spell of their bohemian charm. She felt welcomed as she did not in English homes and I relaxed to see her enjoying the chaotic meals we shared there—so different from our own.

My Russian receptivity forged a new connection between Maman and me. She sat with me while I did my homework, learning new words and grammar by my side, rekindling her own long-dormant linguistic talent. Little did we suspect where this ability would lead.

When my parents refused to let me go on the class trip to Russia, it came as a bolt out of the blue. For months, I had been imagining myself walking down Nevsky Prospect and coming face to face with the astonishing green façade of the Winter Palace, catching sight perhaps of a last few melting ice floes on the Neva. All my diligence and success were rewarded with privation, which made no sense either to me, or to my teacher, who came to our house personally to plead with my parents to reconsider. I wept, I begged, I promised all manner of things, but they were unmoved. I was too young to travel without them, no matter how much Madame Manoras reassured them of constant supervision and care. 'We will take you there,' they said, failing to grasp that I ached to go with my classmates.

In an act of pure masochism and melodrama, wallowing in the misery of being denied, I insisted on going to farewell my comrades at Victoria Station. My father drove me there. I stewed in silence until I reached the platform. Then, as the train pulled out of the station, I made a shameless scene, sobbing and wailing while my friends Sasha, Dimitri, Varvara and Yelena waved goodbye. My face swollen and my throat raw from sustained crying, I was most probably hysterical.

When I was allowed to go on the class trip the following year, my former classmates had abandoned the language and the cohort I travelled with was less close-knit and less talented, making the experience a disappointment. By the time I learned that I had scored the country's top marks in my final-year exams, I wanted nothing more to do with Russia. But Russia, as it turned out, had other plans.

# CHAPTER 11

# *Vogue*-ish

After the epiphany of seeing my first poem published I wrote incessantly, obsessively, compulsively. Like a child who has just discovered masturbation, I simply could not leave it alone. I stole sheets of copy paper from my father's study and hand-wrote stories in which I punched holes and tied together with hair ribbons to make into books. Sitting in Sasha's bed by the kitchen radiator, I read these aloud to my mother, always an appreciative audience while her hands were in a mixing bowl or she was sewing or ironing.

Basking in the praise of having my essays read out in class by encouraging English teachers, by the time I was fourteen, I knew I wanted to be a writer. No one disputed the aspiration as folly. On the contrary, I was taken seriously. By way of encouragement, my father gave me an Olivetti typewriter to make my work look more professional. I loved trying to match the high speed of his typing through the wall between his study and my playroom, and the way the little bell rang when the carriage needed to be returned by pulling on a winged metal handle. Precocious in my ambition, I looked for opportunities to be published.

When I spotted an ad in *Vogue* magazine (a publication I scanned regularly at the library) for a writing competition, I entered without even bothering to read what the first prize was beyond publication in a future issue. All I craved was seeing my name in print again.

To my amazement, I was shortlisted and invited to lunch at Vogue House in Hanover Square for the final hurdle. My mother helped me choose a new outfit for the occasion—a beautifully cut French printed blouse and matching skirt with just enough of a contemporary edge to disguise my schoolgirl status with more sophistication than I possessed. It allowed me to walk into a roomful of strangers with a semblance of poise.

At sixteen, I was by far the youngest of the candidates. Some were outrageously attired, in outfits that looked more like fancy-dress costumes, including a monocled fellow from the Royal College of Art who had a waxed moustache and wore a frock coat with a large spotted orchid in his buttonhole to great effect. I felt distinctly underdressed.

The final round of the contest was social. First, we were to help ourselves to food from an elaborate buffet, demonstrating our ability to coordinate cutlery and conversation smoothly. I approached the spread with confidence. Brought up on hotel smorgasbords, I knew how to balance a plate and pile it not too high. But I soon recognised that this was no ordinary buffet: it was booby-trapped. All the food was slippery and chosen to test our dexterity. Textures were soft, gelatinous, silken, semi-liquid or hard to grasp. It was not a question of helping yourself to a simple slice of ham or a spoonful of well-bound chicken salad; unfamiliar rogue ingredients wriggled and skittered across vast platters or fell apart as you tried to lift them to your plate. I opted for an elaborate fish-shaped salmon mousse covered in scales of cucumber: it looked safer than oysters, which I had never eaten.

Sitting randomly on gilded chairs in pairs at tables of four, with two of the magazine's editors, we attempted to make ourselves sound interesting, talented and original. Disconcertingly, at any given moment, without waiting for us to finish our sentences, the editors rose and circulated to other tables, until every editor had sat with every finalist, in an elaborately choreographed quadrille that lasted several hours.

I disgraced myself at once. Talking too enthusiastically, I dropped a large dollop of mousse in my lap. Scooping it back up onto my plate without missing a beat, I thought, *Well, that's that. Might as well relax and enjoy lunch.* At one point, knowing all was lost, I even spoke with my mouth full while regaling my table with an account of my recent school trip to Russia.

After lunch, we were given a guided tours of *Vogue*'s editorial premises and a sneak preview of the next season's colours, of which my only memory is eggplant. We were promised an audience with David Bailey upstairs in the photographic studio where he was shooting with Marie Helvin, but when we got there, the door was locked. The editorial assistant who was our navigator knocked, was briefly admitted, sworn at, and pulled the door smartly behind her, murmuring, 'Perhaps not today,' as her cheeks flushed with embarrassment. I later learned that she was Princess Diana's sister, Jane, prone to blushing fiercely and frequently.

We were told we would be summoned to the boardroom in an hour. But the hour passed, and no decision had been reached, so we were all sent home. I travelled on the tube and found my mother waiting at the station, where she handed me my first-ever telegram: I had won.

It was as simple as that. My destiny was decided then and there: journalism. The prize, it turned out, was a year working for the magazine, which I planned to take up as my gap year before going to university. This gave me tremendous kudos at school: paid employment at the world's most glamorous magazine conferred instant status. Teachers shook my hand in the corridor. Even the stern unsmiling headmistress offered muted congratulations.

Six months later, I turned up for work at *Vogue* having made a surprising discovery: back in 1951, the most illustrious predecessor as a winner of the US version of the same contest was none other than Jackie Kennedy. We were connected at last, if not by family, then by employer.

⌒

Day one threw me in at the deep end.

'You speak Russian, don't you?' asked the beauty editor, remembering our exchange at the finalists' lunch. 'Tony's shooting some Russian ballet dancers upstairs and they don't speak a word of English. Could you go up there and interpret for him?' Her clipped tone suggested it was not a request.

Up in the studio were Valery and Galina Panov, two defectors who had been under house arrest prior to their escape to Israel, where they were starting a new life as guest stars on tour to Britain for the first time. Tony turned out to be Lord Snowdon, perched on a ladder while the dancers went through a series of poses and arabesques. Without acknowledging me, he barked various instructions for them to turn this way and that, angle their head more up or down, twist their arms more to the right or left. I translated falteringly.

Later that day I was given a desk in the features department, facing that of Joan Juliet Buck and in the same space as writers Georgina Howell, Lucy Hughes-Hallett, Polly Devlin and the towering Titian-haired beauty that was Candia McWilliam. My duties were not defined but I was to answer the phone, take messages, compile a diary of upcoming premieres and other cultural events for the magazine, and try my hand at a few captions.

At the time, Joan was conducting an affair with someone who called frequently from his suite at Claridge's. I had been brought up by my father to take detailed phone messages and to always ask for a caller's surname, so when this man announced himself as just 'Donald', I insisted. He declined, but must have mentioned my persistence to Joan.

'It's Sutherland,' she laughed, amused at my pedantry.

I had only just seen the actor buck-naked in the terrifyingly adult *Don't Look Now*. The explicit sex scene in it, rumoured to be for real, was not easily forgotten. Joan would return from her afternoons with him seemingly unaware that her mascara was running halfway down her face. Were there no mirrors at the hotel? Could she not look in a powder compact on the way back to the office in the taxi? The smudged bad-girl look (perfected as *très* rock'n'roll by French *Vogue* editor Carine Roitfeld many years later) was unnerving: evidence of just how sweaty things must have got on that side of Mayfair.

Fashion was turning towards the New Romantics. Candia adopted this look with *élan*, wearing vintage, bias-cut, satin nightdresses garnished with cascades of lace. Inevitably the elaborate full sleeves caught in the carriage of her typewriter, resulting in desperately contorted attempts to wrench herself free without tearing the delicate antique fabric or staining it with ink. As she leaned into the typewriter to salvage her sleeve, she would catch some of her opulent curls in the machinery, compounding her distress and the similarities with a stylish game of Twister. I took messages from her beau, too, a Rothschild with whom she spent grand weekends at country houses that sounded like locations from the television adaptation of *Brideshead Revisited*, by which the entire nation was gripped every Sunday evening.

The editorial team were opinionated, eloquent, funny and sharp. They wore bohemian and vintage clothes trimmed with velvet, satin petticoats showing deliberately beneath their hemlines, their feet in embroidered Turkish *babouches* or green wellies depending on the season, paying no lip service to the dictates of fashion that the magazine expected readers to follow slavishly. I inhaled the office chat of daily reviews of films, plays, books and exhibitions as if it was super-charged oxygen. I rarely ventured into the world on the other side of the corridor, peopled by creatures as exotic as birds of paradise or coral-reef fish and ruled over by Grace Coddington. She strode past like a haughty empress with a mane of crimped pre-Raphaelite flame-coloured hair. No one entered her kingdom without an invitation. Sometimes models looking for her would hover at my desk and I would redirect them, while trying not to stare at their poreless perfection and chiselled bone structure.

At lunchtime I window-shopped up and down Bond Street or ate a sandwich from a brown paper bag on a bench in Berkeley Square, reminding myself of my good fortune. But the truth was that despite the glamour of the masthead and the prestige of my win, my day-to-day job grew increasingly dull once the gloss of novelty wore off. It was formulaic drudge work and there was no mentoring or apprenticeship to feed my appetite to learn and be stretched.

Possessed of formidable cheek, within a matter of just a couple of months I made an appointment to see the editor-in-chief, Beatrix Miller, known to all as Miss Miller. Queen of the pussy-bow blouse, she rivalled Mrs Thatcher when it came to the permed helmet coiffure. Stern of visage, she had a voice that crackled like desiccated autumn leaves thanks to her smoking habit. She wore a seemingly inexhaustible wardrobe of Chanel tweed suits whose gold buttons gleamed like polished medals, turning her outfits into the chic version of a forbidding military uniform and leaving no one in any doubt: she was the top brass.

I announced to an incredulous Miss Miller that I was bored and contemplating leaving before my time was up: I simply had nothing substantial to get my teeth into and was not prepared to settle for captions. Momentarily stunned, she mulled for a moment, puffing on her cigarette holder, then barked into the phone and told me to report to Polly Devlin on a new book project, a history of the magazine's fashion photography. Our exchange lasted less than five minutes.

My work experience was recharged on the spot. Given enormous responsibility by Polly as her researcher, within days I was on a plane to Paris to interview Helmut Newton. I had never heard of him, but together with his wife June, he received me with mild-mannered hospitality at his apartment in the Marais, wearing a slightly effeminate puffy-sleeved Liberty floral-print shirt. I was plunged into a world of hunting down negatives and prints, scouring archives and libraries, talking to curators and learning what made an image iconic. It was a crash course in visual language, sexual politics, art, pop culture, fashion and design.

Thanks to *Vogue* I got to know the work of the world's greatest fashion photographers. Soon I could tell a Richard Avedon shot from an Irving Penn, a Sarah Moon from a Deborah Turbeville at a glance. My eyes got sharper, taking in the layers of nuance suggested by how an image was composed, lit and cropped; how a location, a model and a dress could tell a story, express an emotion and sell a product. Long before anyone described glossy magazines as 'aspirational', I learned to assess whether an image was exploitative, degrading or empowering, and whether the fantasies *Vogue* conjured gave women more or less freedom (for decades my answer to this flip-flopped before coming down squarely in the negative once I was more secure in my feminism). I discovered how to read a photograph and decode its sensationalism, seduction, aggression and shock value. I understood that women and their bodies were commodities, that their beauty was made and unmade like a bed. It was like being presented with a hyper-world painted in a fresh palette of brighter pigments or lit in neon.

But despite the job giving me legitimacy and focus, I remained very much a junior outsider. I was still mostly wearing clothes my mother had made me. Neither urban punk nor cashmere-and-pearls Sloane, I did not belong to any of the tribes that made up the *Vogue* nation. I was too young to make long-term friends with my sophisticated colleagues. It was time to go to university.

# CHAPTER 12

# Oxford

Although we argued about most things, on one thing my father and I were in total agreement: I would go to university. And not just any university. From the time I knew what such a place was, only one name was mentioned: Oxford. In my overheated imagination, it came to symbolise every kind of freedom, a place where you could try out identities until you found one that fitted perfectly. A place that polished you until you shone, turning you from a pebble into a jewel.

I had seen Oxford on television many times, most gloriously and glowingly in *Brideshead Revisited*. Collecting the names of illustrious women with brilliant careers who had emerged from its colleges—Tina Brown, Benazir Bhutto, Margaret Thatcher—I recited them to myself like an incantation or prayer. Zuleika Dobson, the fictional undergraduate femme fatale of Judas

College, who conquered every heart with a lethal combination of looks and brains, became my patron saint. I spent hours daydreaming about riding a bicycle (however shakily) along cobbled streets to the Bodleian Library and charged encounters with a suite of sighing suitors. This was where Life would begin in earnest.

Entry, I knew, was fiercely competitive, but my teachers encouraged me, talking up my chances with confident expectation. I staked my entire happiness on admission. Nothing in my seventeen years had ever mattered more. The application process itself was intensely satisfying: acknowledged as part of the A team, working in a small coterie with a common purpose, supervised and encouraged by adults who spoke in a subtly changed accent of respect. It was thrilling to discover that my point of view might have equal validity to my teachers' opinions.

Today I understand the ferocity and intensity of my ambition in ways I could never have articulated then. I was desperate to shine for my parents: I saw what pride in my achievements meant to them, how it swelled their chests with satisfaction, validating their unhappy union. I knew, in some deep, instinctive, unspoken way, that they were still outsiders—foreigners, migrants—and that for me to get into Oxford would confirm our right to a place in British society.

I had not been subjected to overt racism. It was just the cumulative mispronunciation of our surname that reinforced a sense of otherness, of not quite fitting in. 'How do you spell that then?' was the first question in any new encounter, asked sometimes with curiosity and sometimes with a mild undertone of hostility. At school I had regularly endured the teasing that came with distorting my name to Bum or Bomb. Only once had I come face to face with explicit prejudice, when my mother inadvertently stole a parking spot, reversing into it unaware of another driver about to manoeuvre nose-first into the same space. Outraged, the woman knocked forcefully on my mother's window. Once it was lowered, she stuck her face in, bristling with aggression. Before my mother could apologise, she narrowed her eyes and hissed 'Bloody Pakis!' We laughed off her mistake, but the episode was unnerving. I registered that we could be judged by our complexions as Not Belonging. That hostility could surface at the slightest provocation. That acceptance was conditional on fulfilling unspoken norms.

Having absorbed my father's regard for such pillars of the Establishment as Oxbridge and the BBC by osmosis, I wanted desperately to join one of these exclusive clubs to make our status somehow more legitimate, as if I could weave us into the very fabric of Britain. Little did I know that when my father was my exact age, he'd had an identical aspiration.

A day visit as preparation for the entrance exam confirmed all my hopes and dreams; the place was achingly beautiful, reeking of scholarship and admission to the elite. This was where I would flourish and find kindred souls. Everything hinged on Oxford.

With the self-contained independence typical of an only child, I undertook the complex selection procedure on my own, without consulting my teachers or seeking advice about strategic course choices. Cocky with overconfidence and proud to boot, I insisted on applying for the course to which it was hardest to gain admission—Philosophy, Politics and Economics—at the most popular and exclusive women's college, Somerville.

A more canny and informed strategy would have been to choose a less high-profile college and a less demanding course, more within my academic grasp. In languages, I had achieved near-perfect grades, among the best in the country, I was told. But I despised these, as they came too easily, and refused to apply to study either French or Russian at Oxford. It was a fateful mistake.

Handicapped by ignorance, I did not share my correspondence with the university with anyone who might have steered me on a different path. In those days, we had no careers advice. Without such counsel, I rejected not one but two highly desirable and prestigious scholarships from colleges that were not my first choice, little knowing that the key to the whole process was simply to get in: one could always switch later. I never compared notes with fellow students as no one else I knew was aiming for the same objective. Unschooled in the whole process, my parents trusted that my grades would win me the place of my choosing. For once they did not interfere.

The last of three letters from the university arrived on Christmas Eve, 1976. It was brief and to the point. It said that since I had refused the scholarships offered, there were no further options available and my application to Oxford was now declined.

Clutching the letter, which I read and reread, I threw myself on my father's bed, howling like a mortally wounded animal until I thought I would vomit. My throat was so raw from crying I felt sure it would bleed. Eventually I became hoarse and lost my voice from sustained wailing. This was my first experience of failure and disappointment, and it gripped me like a convulsive fever. I had no plan B and nowhere else to go.

I have no memory of my mother's reaction to the news. She was downstairs in the kitchen when I opened the letter. She probably thought my reaction was melodramatic and that Oxford did not matter that much. I don't want to give the impression she was any less cerebral or cultured than my father—quite the contrary. Her intelligence was very different from his, but just as sharp. As an autodidact, she made up for her lack of formal education with voracious inquiry and wide reading. She did not, however, set the same store by status and prestigious academies. She did not believe that fulfilment hinged on admission to an august institution.

My father read the three lines on the crested sheet of note-paper and lay on the bed beside me and wept with me, his hopes as withered as mine. His daughter, who had never wanted for anything nor ever wanted anything so much, was being denied and he was powerless to help. For once he did not reproach me, or blame me for the stubborn pride that had caused my fall. He was all empathy. Our crying fell into step like a rhythmic chant of loss and regret. Keening, the Irish would call it. He, who had lost so much, knew and recognised the sound I was making as primal sorrow. I will never forget the kinship between us in that moment.

Christmas was dire. I wandered around in a stupor of bereavement, adrift and with no sense of purpose or direction. Elated friends who had been successful in their bids for other courses at other colleges were stunned at my news and could not think what to say by way of consolation: we had assumed we would all 'go up' together.

My head teacher, learning the news on the grapevine, rang to express disbelief and sympathy. It was some time before I understood that my own unbending determination had cost me what I cherished most, which only made the reality harder to live with.

For the next twenty-five years, I could not visit Oxford. If it appeared on television I looked away, as if crossing to avoid an old lover in the street after a bitter break-up. I was invited there for parties and weekends and always refused. Once I had to go past it in the car and on glimpsing the gleaming spires I got down on the floor of the back seat and hid.

Regret is like envy. It gnaws and corrodes the wiring of the soul. It is a futile and impotent emotion some are blessed never to experience. But regret is hardwired into my DNA, inherited from a father whose burden of *if onlys* was too heavy for one lifetime. He never told me how his own Oxford dream had been thwarted by a lack of funds. I only discovered his private disappointment when I read Mary Hughes's diary, decades later. He must have felt my hurt keenly as a repeat of his own. Now he could afford anything, but could not buy me the one thing I wanted more than any other.

Humbled and chastened, I decided I would not apply to Oxford again but would accept one of the offers from other universities. I selected York, a modern university that was the antithesis of everything Oxford symbolised. My father was delighted. At the time, he told me almost nothing about his association with the city, never mentioning that he had an adoptive family there that I could have met or taking me to his favourite haunts. He was not yet ready to uncover the past.

# CHAPTER 13

# An assignment

By the time I graduated, I had secured a sought-after job at the BBC as a researcher for Michael Parkinson. The prestige of the position helped heal the Oxford wound. At last, I had the respect I craved from my parents and my first real taste of independence and professional responsibility. I was living away from home, earning good money and embarked on the career of my dreams, dealing in the currency of celebrity my parents prized so highly.

At barely twenty-one, I was the baby on the team, younger than all the rest by about five years, with a lot to prove. The pressure was particularly intense because in the year I joined the show, we went from making one program a week to two, which stretched us in terms of sourcing guests. Even in London, some weeks talent was thin and we scrounged around for old hoofers or repeat visitors on whom Mike could count for a new store of anecdotes. The deadlines were relentless.

Unlike the seasoned researchers who had speciality areas—such as sports stars, actors or politicians—I had no time to carve out a niche as a specialist and was a free-ranging trouble-shooter, often called on to do the jobs no one else wanted or to fill in for someone who was on another assignment while I developed my chops. This was how I came to score big names like Lee Marvin, my first interviewee, whom I met in his suite at the Berkeley Hotel. He was dressed in an impeccable navy pinstripe suit, looking for all the world like a wealthy banker instead of the Hollywood hell-raiser he was supposed to be. I was mildly disappointed that he was gracious, polite and sober. Not what I expected at all.

My second interviewee was Ingrid Bergman. She had just written her memoirs, and was dying of cancer, though we did not know it at the time. She was one of Mike's favourite guests, one of the leading ladies of his heart—he simply melted in front of her. At her Knightsbridge home, she was formal, chilly and reserved, sitting erect on the edge of the sofa. When she came to the studio she was different. She sent the make-up artist away, allowing only me to stay in the dressing room while she prepared herself.

I knew that when she came to Hollywood she had refused to have her teeth fixed or the shape of her brows altered. Her down-to-earth Scandinavian nature would not tolerate anything artificial. But she had, over the years, learned the tricks of the trade; now I had the privilege of watching her apply foundation,

powder, eyeliner and lipstick with total concentration and professional skill. She knew that she could not disguise the puffiness
due to the drugs she was taking, nor could she stop one eye from
weeping erratically, but the lines and the textures she applied
helped her draw on a mask that would enable her to get through
what must have been an ordeal, designed purely to promote her
book. Perhaps she needed the money, as did many stars at the end
of long careers. It was an honour to watch the transformation.

On set, the magic happened. A light came into her eyes,
the soft Swedish lilt of her voice gained warmth from Mike's
adoring gaze, and we were all entranced. Afterwards, she was
relaxed enough to linger in the green room for drinks, despite
her shyness, because she liked the other guests. I still have a
photograph of the occasion. When she left, she gave me the
bouquet of flowers that had been in her dressing room.

It sounds petty but the tiny telling details you remember about
these encounters are who offered you a cup of tea in their home
and who did not. Who touched you a little too much. Who had
no books on their shelves. Who displayed their award statuettes
prominently. Who had a flashy car in the driveway. Whose fur
coat was the most sumptuous. In those days, whether you liked
it or not (I did not), you got to hold a lot of fur coats. On a
scale of one to ten, Kiri Te Kanawa's was an eleven.

Despite careful preparation, things did not always go to plan.
I had a nightmarish time with Royal Ballet star, prima ballerina
Lynn Seymour. She was struggling with a drinking problem that
I was way out of my depth to handle. Capable of unparalleled
dramatic and sexual intensity on stage in tragic roles such as

the lead in *Mayerling*, she regularly left audiences emotionally wrung out. But that kind of talent takes its toll, and she was destroying herself while reaching for greatness; it was public and painful to watch.

When she came to the studio, she was intoxicated by at least one substance, slurring her words and dressed in what looked like a torn fishing net. The make-up people had to find invisible tape to hold her clothes together and cover up several gaping holes in awkward places. Behind the scenes, faced with her dangerously unpredictable behaviour, we wondered whether to send her home and just ask the other guests to talk for longer. But in the end we decided to risk it and she held herself together—just, and only thanks to some real safety pins in judicious places.

The audience sensed that this was someone fragile and on the edge, and were riveted, but the anxiety backstage was palpable and Mike was not amused. When a guest took him out of his comfort zone, he blamed the researcher. It was not his best trait, and he too was having a problem with drink, as he later admitted, but it was a reality we all danced around.

⌒

Within a few months, I realised that Mike had not warmed to me. As a result, I felt the need to prove myself, week in week out, whereas other, more senior members of the team with an established rapport and track record got a lot more leeway. Having earned their stripes, they could rest on their laurels a little and josh him out of a bad mood with shared war stories of tricky guests and near disaster averted.

When I gave him my brief after a thrilling afternoon with the Royal Shakespeare Company director Trevor Nunn, he threw the document back in my face, furious, and told me to start again. It was too highbrow. He did not want a bloke delivering a lecture about Shakespeare and Dickens (Nunn was just about to stage his landmark eight-hour production of *Nicholas Nickleby*). He wanted anecdotes, jokes, behind-the-scenes gossip. What we would now call the Luvvie Stuff. I got what he asked for, but he bore me a grudge for weeks and I felt I had lost the little trust I had earned.

Anxious and insecure, one weekend I watched a rerun on television of the film *Serpico*. The story of the whistleblower cop, played with dazzling commitment by Al Pacino, was a welcome break from celebrity caprices.

At the Monday morning editorial meeting when we threw names around, I piped up 'Did anyone watch *Serpico* over the weekend? I wonder what happened to him?'

His face like granite, Mike turned his attention to me.

'Find him,' he said, walking out of the room and leaving the challenge hanging in the air.

The team looked at me with undisguised pity.

After being shot at point-blank range through the face following his revelations of corruption in the NYPD, Serpico had gone into hiding. Where to start? I had no idea. But I did remember the film was based on a book by Peter Maas. I tracked Maas down through his agent. Did he know where Serpico was? Could Maas contact him for me? A kind man who could probably hear the desperation in my voice, he said he would get back to me. Hours later, he called. 'He's willing to talk to you.'

He was, Maas reported, living at a commune just over the Welsh border. He gave me a number. When I called, a softly nasal voice agreed on a date and offered to pick me up at the station. Elated to have got this far, I consulted train timetables and told no one about the progress I was making. I wanted it to be a big surprise, my way back into Mike's good books with a flourish.

In those days, there were no mobile phones. Also, in those days, any duty of care that producers or editors had towards their staff was never made explicit. We acted as independent adults and the issue of liability in doing our job was never discussed. There were no guidelines about personal safety. We came and went from the office, usually only casually mentioning to a colleague that we were going to be out for a few hours or a day and that was it. I had never heard any stories of researchers having problems beyond the odd unwelcome pass or flirtation or the guest who turned up slightly the worse for wear.

I was going quite a distance but could make it in one day if I caught particular trains, allowing for a couple of hours to assess Serpico as suitable talent. Of course in my mind I could not help but expect Al Pacino. When I got there, the station was a tiny isolated stop in the middle of nowhere. A man with curly hair and a pick-up truck was waiting in the car park. It could only be him.

Frank Serpico was no Al Pacino, but he had a noticeable scar on his face from where the bullet had hit him and explained that he was deaf in one ear, from where the bullet had exited.

'I thought I would take you to the village pub for lunch. They do a nice local trout,' he said. When we got there, he came around to my side of the truck to open the door. How gallant, I thought, but the next minute, in the main street of the village, he pushed me against the wall of the pub, arms and legs splayed, and frisked me. It felt like being tickled just a little too hard. Embarrassed, I laughed and asked what was going on, as if the whole thing were a joke.

'Just had to check you're not wearing a wire,' he said, as if this were completely normal. Without any further comment, we went into the pub.

After lunch we drove to a remote commune. I took in vegetable gardens, stone dwellings, a barn, and felt the loneliness of the place. A good place to hide, heal, recover from physical and psychological wounds, perhaps. Frank introduced me to his large sheepdog companion and took me to his room. There was only one chair and he took it. I perched on the end of the bed with my notebook.

By now I knew he was not right for the show. Too damaged, too self-absorbed in his paranoia. I was being polite, biding my time until I could go home. I admired him for what he had been, but felt sorry for what he had become and was puzzled by his willingness to come out of the shadows and talk; he must have craved the attention for complex reasons that I did not fully understand. I felt it would be unfair to expose his vulnerability and replace the heroic image people had of him with this far frailer thing. Better to leave him where he was to try to remake his life.

Before I knew it, he was on me. I wriggled under him and he drew back, pointing a gun at me. To this day, I could not tell you whether it was a Colt .45 or a water pistol. All I managed to do was to say, very lamely, that my parents were expecting me for dinner and could he please take me back to the station. He switched back to sensible mode, pulled himself together and drove me to the station. As the train was pulling in, he kissed me on the mouth. I replayed that kiss, the final shaming punctuation mark in the whole episode, all the way home.

The next day I went to work. At the editorial meeting I told the team in the sketchiest of terms that I had found Serpico, met with him and that he was not for us. There was a brief flurry of curiosity and amazement. To get him on the show would be a coup, Mike persisted. Was I really sure he was not up to it? I had to insist on Serpico's mental instability. I told no one about what had happened between us. And that should have been the end of the story.

A few months later my friend Yvette rang to tell me she had scored a prized apartment in the heart of Kensington that was too good to miss. She could not afford the rent on her own and asked if I wanted to share. The decision had to be made very quickly as the owner was going overseas suddenly and was in a hurry to get the matter settled.

As soon as I saw the flat I knew we had to have it, even though it meant the disruption of moving within a week. Everything happened very fast, and within days Yvette and I were carting boxes up two flights of stairs to our high-ceilinged expansive space. We had hardly had time to give out our new phone number to family. We'd let friends know once we'd unpacked.

When the phone rang, I assumed it was for the owner and prepared to take a message. I heard pips that told me the caller was in a phone box.

'It's Frank,' said the caller.

'Frank who?' I asked, not recognising the voice.

'Frank Serpico. I'm at Heathrow, I'm just calling to say goodbye. The commune collapsed. Lost all my money. I'm going back to the States.'

'But how did you get this number?' I asked, dumbfounded.

There was a pause. Then he said slowly: 'I've known where you were all the time. Bye.'

To this day I still don't understand what that call was about or how he got my number. He did not speak to my parents. No one at work had taken a call for me.

⁓

Yvette was a well-connected ambitious young American who had come to London to study drama. She reminded me of a modern-day Henry James character, eager with unformed ambition and naïve confidence that her charm would open any door. Somehow, she had become the protégée of Hollywood veteran Douglas Fairbanks Jr, who took an avuncular interest in her career progress and invited her to the theatre whenever he was in town. When the phone rang a second time, it was him. He'd got the number from Yvette's parents, was staying at the Dorchester and wondered if he might take us out for dinner. We accepted as happily as only two young women keen to escape unpacking boxes would.

He was as suave and charming as his name suggested. So much so that I mentioned him at our next editorial meeting; he appeared on the show that week, a feather in my cap at last, even if not the one I had intended.

Trialling independence with tentative steps, I never told my parents about the Serpico episode because they were so overprotective. I feared they would try to impose restrictive conditions on my working life and embarrass me with my employers.

Something else prevented me: the acute, persistent awareness that children raised in an atmosphere heavy with silence have, a kind of sixth sense for unspoken trauma. They guess at it, even if they don't know its size, shape and exact colour. My narrow escape from a predator happened several years before my mother told me of her own. I was the same age my mother had pretended to be when she was raped. And unlike her at the same age, I was sexually active, a fact with which she found difficult to come to terms. The only comment she made on learning that I had lost my virginity was, 'I always found sex very messy.' The implications of that remark were too sad to contemplate.

We were not given to easy confidences, like some mothers and daughters I know. A friend told me her mother once came into her room when she was a teenager and said without a shred of embarrassment, 'Now look, I know you've stolen my vibrator.' Sensing that my mother's prudish reserve hid a deeper pain, I kept my brush with danger to myself.

Even though the Serpico episode had shown me fame unhinged, that did not deter me. Even if they were damaged and flawed, or perhaps because of these handicaps, the famous continued to exert an irresistible force over me. An edge of fear in the presence of these types only added to the thrill. Fear was an emotion with which I was all too familiar, even though I would have been unable to recognise the adrenalin rush it provoked as my flight-or-fight syndrome kicked in.

But this charge attracted me to work for men who resembled my father—after Parky, with his irascible hard-to-please nature, I foolishly signed on as a cookery book researcher for *Time Life*; on paper the job looked safe enough, but in the kitchen I was faced with a venerated gastronome who also turned out to be an A-grade tyrant and bully before such egos were fed by television ratings. On days when I was responsible for coordinating a food photo shoot, I would first lock myself in the toilet and repeat to myself that I would not cry or vomit (as others did when faced with our prima donna's rages, brought on by something as trivial as finding a stock cube in the pantry). From here I transitioned to the most complex version of the same impossible-to-satisfy version of the same character in Melvyn Bragg.

Recognising his demanding, exacting personality, I thought I knew the territory: a charismatic perfectionist and fault-finder prone to a quickly flaring temper, but also capable of generosity and lavish praise.

The interview for a position on his prestigious television arts documentary team was unlike anything I have ever experienced: there were five people in the room, four producers and Melvyn himself, which was intimidating enough. Without preamble, Melvyn launched into an idea for a hypothetical documentary about Rudolf Nureyev and how to make a film that was different from all the previous ones. I offered some thoughts but no matter what I said, he came back at me arguing every point, rejecting every suggestion I made to see if I would stick up for myself. It was just like being at home. We ended up having the most knock-down argument I have ever had with a complete stranger. It was gladiatorial combat, verbal jousting. Voices raised, gloves off. It was curiously enjoyable. Intoxicating, because it was about ideas. I knew what I thought and did not back down. It was him and me, *mano a mano*. No one else in the room said a word.

Afterwards I staggered to the elevator, winded, and burst into tears. I wanted that job more than I had ever wanted anything since Oxford. I had been too vehement, too heated. As I waited for the elevator, Melvyn came out, smiled fleetingly and said, 'Nice work.' The next day I was offered the job. Of the two thousand who had applied, two were picked. No pressure then.

Our relationship over the next two years was an uneasy dance of one step forward, two back. We never quite found our rhythm. I put in a poor piece of work on my first film and he withdrew his trust. Grudgingly, he gave me a second chance and I redeemed myself, but was never secure—ours was only ever a truce, not a lasting peace treaty. Working this way was nerve-racking, like trying to build foundations on quicksand. Meanwhile, the tectonic plates at home were also shifting.

# CHAPTER 14

# The Cold War

Usually the first thing I do when I get to my parents' home in London, after making the obligatory pot of tea, is look in the fridge. It delivers me an instant update, a state-of-the-nation report, like an electrically powered oracle. Tell me, oh great Westinghouse double-door fridge–freezer with ice-maker, how are things round here? Will I get through this visit without tantrums and tears? I should, of course, just pay attention to its constant, thermostat-controlled existentialist message: CHILL.

I'm not sure what prompts me to open the door, beyond relentless insatiable gluttony. It is a completely unconscious reflex action. But it's not a behaviour unique to me. Often, in Hollywood movies, you see people get up in the middle of the night and open the fridge. There, in the darkness of the kitchen, light pours out like a beam of wisdom while they lean in to find a bottle of milk. Sometimes they don't even bother to retrieve anything: just contemplating the contents seems to help the players in any overheated domestic drama cool down a little.

What I am looking for is reassurance and love. Because of all the places to find love, it is more likely to have survived in this frosty universe than in the rest of my parents' stuffy hothouse, where rows eventually occur because I am opening too many windows and complaining that I can't breathe or sleep and my face is swollen and puffy from near suffocation.

My parents store love in the fridge, where it will not perish as rapidly: in jars, bottles, packets and opaque Tupperware containers. The ingredients refrigerating there are the most unconditional expression of affection possible between my mother and father. And between them and me. So when I look in the fridge, they are proud that it is full to overflowing, as if it were proof not only of boundless prosperity—particularly for two survivors of World War II who know about hunger, shortages and rationing—it is also incontestable proof of their capacity to share this plenty with me.

But while my mother is always happy for me to look in the fridge, to admire its contents as if I were looking into a cabinet of curiosities, sometimes she doesn't want me to touch. She is saving some things to eat on certain occasions, and does not want me to pre-empt those plans with my random foragings. She gets apprehensive if I start rummaging or help myself, as if she would prefer it if the fridge came with a PIN number to which only she had access.

On an ordinary day, this is what I might find in the fridge if I went on an archaeological dig to the very back of the shelves:

A tin of goose fat from Fauchon in Paris
A tin of foie gras
A jar of *rillettes de porc*
Eighteen—yes, really—different kinds of mustard and chutney
Imported Scandinavian herrings in dill and mustard sauce
Several cheeses: a bitey aged cheddar in its red wax coat, a Coulommiers on a bed of straw in a wooden round box, *demi-sel* cream cheese in little silver foil squares, *fromage blanc*, Cantal, Leyden, Emmental
A pair of *weisswurst*
A *saucisson à l'ail*
A vacuum-sealed *cotechino* sausage
A jar of sauerkraut
A bunch of long small radishes, brought back from a French market
A corn-fed chicken with giblets in the body cavity.

This small sample of ingredients represents the United Nations kind of food we ate at home for the eighteen or so years that I was fed on a more or less daily basis by my mother. Between them, my parents speak English, French, German, Russian, a little Italian and some Spanish. But my mother's library of more than 2000 cookbooks includes many in languages she does not speak but can cook in. When she developed a crush on meatballs and wanted to make authentic *frikadeller*, she simply bought a Scandinavian cookbook on the subject and translated the recipes.

Each night my mother served up a three-course meal cooked from scratch. For many years it was a matter of pride that her repertoire was so varied that she did not repeat herself unless by popular request. The food was gobbled down by her appreciative audience in a matter of minutes; while my mother ate at a dignified French pace, my father, having learned to eat at speed in the English public-school system, passed on the urgency to me in the form of contests to see who could finish first and secure a second helping, his greedy shovelling mouthfuls punctuated with carnal grunts of appreciation. Then, when the plates were clean, dishes were discussed and critiqued with the same seriousness as a concert or play.

So imagine the chaos, the confusion, and the sense of threat when one day in 1980 I came home from university, opened the fridge and was faced with an entirely unfamiliar set of ingredients: stacked glass dishes of herrings, fermented red cabbage, beetroot soup. Things smelled yeasty, sweet but sour: slightly farty.

That was how I learned that Vitya Borovsky, my mother's Russian teacher, had moved in with us for an unspecified period of time that was to stretch to nearly a decade.

My mother had taken it upon herself to rescue him from woeful rented digs after hearing his sob story of how, when he first arrived in Britain, he lived on a park bench. He was now ensconced in a cheerless bedsit where he could not play the cherished record collection he had acquired with his earnings to remind him of his glorious musical heritage. When she took me to meet him after class one day, our first exchange was baffling.

Me: So, Vitya, what did you do before you came to the university?

Him: I was a postal order.

Me: Sorry? (stifling urge to giggle)

Him: (firmly and more slowly) I was a postal order.

(I dare not look to my mother for clarification as I can see from the corner of my eye that she has her hand over her mouth, smothering her urge to laugh, which only makes mine worse.)

Me: A postal order? But that's a piece of paper.

Him: A postal loader, is that how you say? Yes, a postal loader.

(By now my mother and I are convulsed with laughter. Vitya looks on, delighted to have entertained us with such a humble job description of delivering mail bags.)

Once Vitya was installed, my mother found herself feeding an assortment of Russian dissidents who dropped in on their former compatriot whenever they were let out of their country on brief cultural visits: dancers, film-makers, conductors, theatre directors and designers. The fridge was stocked in a state of hypervigilance, ready for half the Red Army, should it choose to defect, to eat at our place.

After a few vodkas, bowls of my mother's authentic *borschtsch* or *shchi* prompted high-profile dissidents to suddenly announce that they either would not or could not go home. Our house was invaded as swiftly as Czechoslovakia, except without the tanks. All the rules changed. Meals were eaten at irregular hours. The phone rang very late at night. People we hardly knew came to eat and to stay. The only thing that remained the same was that copious amounts of tea were drunk, though Russians like to drink it from a tall glass and suck it through a sugar cube.

At first, I paid little attention to the guests at the kitchen table beyond taking the opportunity to revive my lapsed Russian vocabulary. I was too absorbed in my shaky career and serving the cultural tsars who were my bosses. But gradually, our visitors became more stellar than anyone I was meeting at work. One day I came home to find Mikhail Baryshnikov wrapped in one of my father's bathrobes watching *Dynasty*, his tousled hair still damp from a shower.

Speechless in front of someone I'd had a major crush on since the age of sixteen, I stumbled into the kitchen.

'What's HE doing here?' I stammered.

'He shared a flat with Vitya in Leningrad,' said my mother casually, savouring the impact of her superstar visitor. He had, she added, arrived bearing a tin of the very best caviar and she was now preparing blini for dinner, as if this were an everyday occurrence.

'Mischa', as he was known, was shooting a film called *White Nights* and on his days off, he would visit our home to relax, sometimes singing plaintive Russian songs or repeating jokes told to him by his best friend, the poet Joseph Brodsky.

On several occasions he brought his co-star Isabella Rossellini with him. Shy, scrubbed free of make-up, quick to blush, and without any of an actor's customary vanity, she carried a tube of truffle paste in her handbag and squeezed it liberally onto whatever food was put in front of her. She also insisted on doing the washing up.

For my father, to whom ballet was a total bore, Mischa was no one special (he referred to him as 'that nice boy') but he almost swooned listening to Isabella talk. Closing his eyes, he could conjure up her mother, Ingrid Bergman, one of his screen goddess pin-ups. Having met Bergman, I could hear how mother and daughter shared the same intonation, accent and cadences to an uncanny degree. In Isabella's presence, my father wore a foolish, lopsided smile I rarely saw. As for myself, I could hardly look at Mischa, I was so churned up with puppyish devotion.

His visits were social rather than political—he had defected much earlier and remade his life brilliantly in America. But others who came to visit were in a much more precarious situation. Gradually, without us even noticing, our home, once a solemn fortress to which strangers were never admitted, was turned into a safe house for those who needed a discreet sanctuary in which to seek counsel and refuge. Sometimes for a night, sometimes for weeks. Having had very few of my friends stay the night as a child, I was somewhat put out to discover my mother was having wild sleepovers that involved group singsongs, rowdy jokes and cheeky impersonations of world leaders. She blossomed in this company: became more beautiful and more animated, emboldened by her rapidly improving Russian and the new audience's appreciation for her skills and cuisine. She laughed more than I had ever seen, which made her seem girlish and suddenly younger.

My father raised no objections to the changed rhythms and habits of the house. In the past, whenever I have thought about this time, I have always seen this as my mother's story: it was she who invited Vitya into our lives, she who came to converse fluently with him and his friends, fed them, translated documents, made calls, drove them to meetings, acted as intermediary and messenger in endless to-ings and fro-ings. Vitya made her vital.

But while language was a barrier to my father, excluding him from much of the soul-searching that went on deep into the night, he provided a kind of still centre in all the emotional chaos of the Slavic soul agonising over questions of leaving behind homeland, and in some cases family, that took place over countless dinners around the kitchen table. My father offered counsel in these endless conversations about strategy, conducted in an atmosphere of conspiratorial intensity.

He may only have ever learned to say 'pass the salt' in Russian, but Papa commanded the respect of men who had faced real tyranny. He also did not hesitate to lecture them about their own culture: one night he delivered a sermon-like address to Mischa on the importance of reading Tolstoy, who listened graciously and without interrupting.

When the high-profile theatre director Yuri Liubimov came to London to present his critically acclaimed production of *Crime and Punishment*, we suddenly and unwittingly found ourselves caught up in a real political maelstrom.

A canny operator who had triumphed over censorship for many decades at his progressive Taganka Theatre company, Yuri decided to defect during his visit, and sought asylum in our home with his wife, the daughter of a Hungarian government minister. He was leaving behind a remarkable career and all the privileges that his status at the helm of a major company brought. It was a major embarrassment to the Soviet Union, which considered him its most high-profile defector since the cellist Mstislav Rostropovich.

Yuri gave a defiant interview to *The Times* in our sitting room, where he was photographed proudly wearing a crucifix around his neck and declaring his religious faith in protest at the Soviet regime's official policy of atheism.

Then he calmly asked my father if he could borrow his study to make a private phone call, oblivious to the fact that my father did not let anyone use that room, ever. When he came downstairs, he told us with solemnly that he had just spoken with Yuri Andropov, the ageing leader of the Soviet Union, at the Kremlin, telling him that he was resigning his citizenship. After that, it was on for a cat-and-mouse game at the highest level.

Fearing that his rental apartment was bugged by the Soviets, Yuri decamped in secret to a safe house provided by a network of supporters, which caused me significant headaches at work.

As a result of his novels selling well in the Soviet Union, Melvyn had become interested in all things Russian. When Yuri brought his Dostoyevsky adaptation to Britain, Melvyn decided to make a documentary about the production. I was assigned as the researcher on the film because of my Russian language skills. But I was unprepared for the tricky conflict-of-interest loyalties the situation produced.

One morning shortly before his defection had become public, Yuri did not turn up to film an interview with Melvyn. I knew where he was hiding. But sworn to secrecy as to his whereabouts and situation, I could not tell Melvyn why he had been stood up. When I was eventually given permission to do so, my boss was visibly annoyed that I had the inside story.

Mrs Thatcher offered Yuri her personal protection. Whenever Yuri visited my parents, MI5 parked a car outside their home, matched on the other side of the street by a car belonging to the KGB. Meanwhile, to add to the general cloak-and-dagger atmosphere, a young Latvian conductor, Mariss Jansons, then a rising star, turned up at our house one evening with a device he had bought on tour in Germany that was meant to identify bugging devices. Sure enough, our phone, which had been making constant clicking sounds during conversations, was tapped. A few days later, the drama ramped up another notch: after Yuri left his secret address under escort to attend rehearsals of his production, he was threatened by Soviet thugs in a botched kidnapping attempt at the theatre.

Saturnine by nature, Yuri began to feel hemmed in by captivity after three weeks of lying low. A message came to us via one of many defector networks that Rostropovich was offering him the use of his house at Aldeburgh, a small fishing town on the east coast where his great friend the composer Benjamin Britten had founded an annual music festival. My mother drove there with Yuri and his wife, accompanied by an unmarked police car. I followed a few days later. When Maman and her top-secret cargo reached the house, they were unnerved by the police requiring them to pose for photographs so they could be identified in the event of kidnapping. Temporary panic buttons were installed in case they needed to raise the alarm. Things were starting to feel a little surreal.

The stakes were very high not only for Yuri but for his production designer David (Dodik) Borovsky, who happened to be Vitya's cousin. After the play opened, Dodik decided to return to the Soviet Union, knowing that once there he would face punishment for allowing his high-profile comrade to slip his leash. We knew it meant he would probably not be able to work and would lose his position at the Taganka, but might it mean more? How severe would his interrogation be? And the recriminations? Could he be sent to a gulag or banished to Siberia? None of us knew, but we feared the worst. Dodik did not waver. He had a wife and children at home, spoke no European languages and had no desire to remain in Europe.

With the heaviest of hearts, Vitya, my mother and I took Dodik to Victoria Station, pushing trolleys of electrical goods that he was taking home as gifts. We tried to remain cheerful and optimistic, hugging and kissing till the very last moment, but once the train pulled out our masks fell. On the very same platform where I had sobbed my heart out farewelling my friends leaving for Moscow seven years earlier, I now clung to Vitya, both of us undone.

We did not hear from Dodik for years and feared the worst.

There was furious rivalry, mistrust and paranoia among defectors and dissidents as to how genuine their status was: some believed others made up their credentials and claims to political oppression and censorship, and denounced them as opportunists. They competed to see who was the most authentically Russian and who was the most significant loss to their nation's pride.

Film director Andrei Tarkovsky thought Yuri's religious gesture of wearing a cross was pure showmanship and posturing. Introverted and shy, Andrei came to our home many times, always intense, oblique and elliptical in his pronouncements. When he decided to defect, he left a young son behind, causing great misery and personal sacrifice. Only once he developed terminal cancer did the hardline Soviet authorities relent, allowing his son to visit for a final goodbye.

Andrei loved nature and being outside, so my mother took him to Richmond Park, where he shot a whole lot of photographs of her with his wife Larissa, only to discover when they got home that he had forgotten to put any film in the camera. On set, someone else always took care of that kind of thing.

Unlike Yuri, who was a master at playing the political game and relished every move, Andrei had no interest in politics, brinksmanship and strategy, despite being a keen chess player. He just wanted to be left alone to make his films, and found the Western film media's adulation tedious and puzzling. Scholars pored over his every utterance as if he were some priestly poet of higher truth, but in person, away from public scrutiny, he was modest and simple in his needs. My father had never seen any of his films and had only the dimmest awareness of who he was. Andrei was impressed by my father's grasp of history, his socialist convictions and musical literacy.

Throughout this entire period my father never complained that the situation was putting his family at risk or at any inconvenience. Nor did he ever ask any of our long-term guests when they might be leaving, even when Yuri had to all intents and purposes commandeered our house as the nerve centre for his risky and constantly changing plans. He teased and taunted the Kremlin, issuing terms and conditions under which he might be prepared to go home.

Despite the tension and melodrama, there were moments of humour. At dinner, Yuri regaled us with brilliant impersonations of the many leaders he had weathered; his bushy eyebrows, bulging eyes and broad girth made his irreverent impressions of bloated Soviet leaders like Leonid Brezhnev and Yuri Andropov particularly convincing. He and my father forged a mutual respect for each other, despite having no shared language, which culminated in a perverse compliment when Yuri joked with me one day: 'You know, I met Stalin, but I think your father is more terrifying.'

If I ask myself now what was going through my father's mind in those years, I suspect that his motives for putting up with all this were mixed. The snob in him was probably flattered to have such distinguished and eminent houseguests, even if he was only dimly aware of who they were. He was probably also relieved to see my mother so animated.

The Russian invasion diverted my mother's attention from the loneliness of the empty-nest syndrome, which had probably caused her to take Vitya in as a surrogate child upon whom she could lavish endless care. He was as needy and demanding as a baby bird, and my father was probably grateful to him. His antics included eating with his mouth open, displaying a poor example of Soviet dentistry in a prominent row of uneven gold teeth, holding his cutlery like spears. As a child, Vitya had survived the terrible famine of the siege of Leningrad by licking the potato starch in wallpaper glue—and perhaps far worse. So when he ate, he lowered his head to the plate, shovelling fuel into the furnace of his body like a Stakhanovite worker. He was prone to singing vast quantities of opera by heart (including soprano roles), and performed a daily circuit of Soviet Army calisthenics in the garden every morning; by then my bootcamp gymnastic circuit had been pulled down in our backyard, otherwise he would have made ample use of the rings and trapeze.

'Baby, punch me in the stomach, ppp-leeze, punch me,' he would urge after these exertions. When I obliged, my fist met abs like concrete, which bruised my knuckles.

As well as a repertoire of filthy Russian swearwords which he deployed liberally, Vitya stuttered to great effect, using his inability to spit out more than one syllable as an expression of exaggerated disapproval—especially if the word started with NO as in 'He is a NN-NN-NOBODY,' or 'There is NO-NO-NOTHING he can do'. He harboured absurd prejudices, such as believing that 'only homosexuals wear slip-on shoes' (a common Soviet opinion). These attitudes and his various neuroses had great novelty and comic value. Vitya willingly became our resident exotic and clown. Invited into grand houses by philanthropists and pillars of the establishment, he was happy to play to the gallery, a Russian dancing bear who entertained his starchy hosts with fiercely accurate mimicry of the opera stars he coached, backstage gossip and his pseudo-peasant table manners.

Over ten years my mother befriended him, virtually adopted him, fell in love with him, fought with him and eventually in utter exasperation, threw him out. He was, in every sense, our family's Rasputin: charismatic, manipulative, devious, duplicitous, intellectually brilliant, melodramatic, an unapologetic serial seducer (despite being self-consciously unattractive) and chauvinist. He was as unpredictable and volatile as spring weather, frequently taciturn to the point of rudeness at meals for no apparent reason, petulant and sometimes puerile. One day when he was feeling particularly exuberant, he picked my mother up and wedged her in the kitchen sink where she giggled helplessly, stuck.

The two of them collaborated closely on Vitya's scholarly biography of Fyodor Chaliapin, the great Russian bass; with no formal training, my mother proved herself a first-rate researcher and translator, which gave her a tremendous sense of personal achievement and satisfaction. By the time the 600-page volume was complete, her Russian was so fluent and her accent so flawless that she passed for a native speaker and embarked confidently on reading the complete works of Chekhov and Gogol in the original.

Vitya and I rubbed along more or less well: at first I was grateful that he pulled focus from me, like a substitute sibling, though I was less than impressed when my mother moved him from the spare room into mine without asking me.

Hardly the most patient or tolerant of men, my father indulged and even spoiled Vitya. When Papa took us on an extravagant family pilgrimage to the Bayreuth Festival, Vitya came too. He bought Vitya Hermès ties and introduced him to the merits of Marks and Spencer menswear, tried to explain British socialism to him, managed his finances, gave him professional advice about how to negotiate fees and contracts, and helped him secure a mortgage.

In return, Vitya introduced my parents to his friends and colleagues—they dined with endless divas and maestros, patrons and impresarios—including them in the exclusive embrace of the musical world he inhabited. On the phone to me, my mother name-dropped her latest encounters—'Domingo called today', 'We had dinner with Abbado'—boasting of her new social cachet and using it as a lure to draw me home more often.

My father was probably grateful to Vitya for diverting my mother's affection while he was most likely playing away from home himself. In a moment of girlish infatuation, my mother confessed to me that she wanted to leave my father and start a new life with Vitya. Although I wanted her happiness and felt she should have left my father years before, I was sceptical about this plan but said nothing.

There were scenes of high melodrama when my mother turned back at Heathrow from a planned weekend in Paris with my father on hearing that Vitya had become unwell. Often in tears, she confided in me like a bashful teenager. I was embarrassed by her gushing and the awkward role reversal but said I would support any decision she made.

Eventually, she recovered her sanity and the crush passed, averting what would have been a disaster. Fortunately, her feelings for Vitya were not reciprocated. He may have exploited my mother in other ways, but he did not take advantage of her physically. She was not his type; he preferred wispy, fey creatures. Later, my mother became a confidante to several of his hapless and short-lived girlfriends, giving quiet thanks that she was not one of them. By all accounts, he treated his lovers appallingly.

When the Soviet Union collapsed, Vitya returned to Saint Petersburg several times but was unwilling to settle there permanently, recognising that the scars to the national psyche would take longer than the rest of his lifetime to heal, and that corruption would remain embedded in the great cultural institutions. By the time he died of painful stomach cancer, the rift between him and my mother was ravine-deep and unreconciled. Although he owed her everything, he left her nothing. Once again, she was disappointed.

And what of the dazzling comrades whom Vitya brought into our lives for that tumultuous period? Like Vitya, Yuri Liubimov also returned to his former country. He was reunited with his friend and colleague Dodik Borovsky, who later returned to visit us after the collapse of communism. Following a period of being blackballed, Dodik resumed a distinguished career in Russian theatre until his early death from illness. Today, his creative workshop in Moscow is the only museum in the entire country devoted to the work of a set designer. We never heard from

Yuri again, though he continued to work internationally well into his eighties. Though shy and often aloof in public, Mischa stayed in touch. He and I had dinner together when we found ourselves in the same city. Once, backstage, he introduced me to a renowned choreographer, saying that my mother was the best cook in the world.

When the Russians invaded our lives, tea consumption soared. We really should have installed a samovar. Once they departed, the fridge returned to normal: the herrings and cabbage rolls disappeared, the contents reverted to their original cultural palate. It was as if the Cold War had never taken place.

# CHAPTER 15

# My father's daughter

Never one for spontaneity, my father was a planner. He made no distinction between professional travel clients and his wife and daughter. Holiday itineraries were typed and issued to concerned parties as a *fait accompli*. I don't remember him ever consulting my mother about destinations. Alone in his study, in a vapour of cigarette smoke, bent over the fine print of his reference library, he scrutinised maps, timetables and guide books, whether he was designing a tour for five hundred students, two hundred senior executives, fifty dermatologists or his family.

He was an acknowledged pioneer and leader in the tourism industry, admired for his uncompromising standards in recruiting staff, finely tuned budgets and elegantly choreographed itineraries. His secret weapon, apart from the surgical precision with which he planned every minute of a trip, leaving nothing to chance, was the calibre and charm of the couriers he trained to escort his groups. Often suave and good-looking, these exclusively male Oxbridge graduates were under strict instructions to 'keep their hands off the merchandise', as my father put it, referring to the impressionable American women who made up the bulk of his earliest groups. Couriers stuck to the script of a Bible-like manual my father wrote once every two years, providing them with heavily editorialised historical background and cultural context for their trips. Over four decades, he mentored people who went on to become competitors, applying his exacting standards of excellence to their own version of his concept of tailored travel.

I inherited my father's restlessness and, unlike my mother who was a fearful passenger, loved planes. As a child, if I was very, very good, the stewardess would invite me to pass the basket of boiled sweets around to passengers. I might be allowed into the cockpit to meet the pilot and given an enamelled wings badge as I disembarked.

When it came to inspecting hotels, which all of our holidays involved, by the time I was ten, I was an eager patron of room service, confident at ordering my favourite club sandwich and a bowl of French fries, waiting with anticipation for that discreet knock at the door and the magical entrance of the trolley with its concealed heated cabinet. Like a trophy hunter, I was always looking for souvenirs to add to my stockpile of miniature soaps and shampoos, rivalled only by my impressive collection of miniature airline salt and pepper shakers. By puberty I had been on so many so-called site inspections that I knew at a glance what rating a room or suite deserved.

Accommodation was booked well in advance, and always at the upper end of the scale. If not the newest, splurgiest, most luxurious hotel, then the one with the finest historical pedigree—for my parents there was no greater accolade a place could earn than to boast that Mozart, Napoleon, Churchill or de Gaulle had slept there. Preferably all of the above. Travel time was scheduled to the minute (long before GPS existed). Nothing was left to chance.

My father did it all by the book. One book, to be precise: the *Michelin Guide*. The green edition for historical and cultural sightseeing; the red for accommodation and eating. He never trusted anyone else. When his sources became outdated, he remained steadfast. We never played it by ear, or adapted to circumstances, or made do with a pit stop or had picnics. Weeks before departure, my father booked ahead, reserving tables, calibrating the trip to the gastronomic equivalent of an orchestral crescendo. First, the mild overture of a pleasant one-star bistro, then the swelling expectations of a more formal two-star *relais*, and finally, the symphonic climax of a three-star temple of gastronomy. By the time I was fifteen I had eaten in half a dozen of the finest restaurants in the world and tasted turbot, truffles and palm hearts. When it came to sauces, I knew my *romesco* from my *gribiche*.

I learned to be a planner by osmosis. Logistics became a fascinating kind of puzzle, a satisfying game of strategy. Could you design a neat sequence in which you could connect a flight to a train without too much delay or criss-crossing a city? Get from A to B the most efficient or scenic way possible? Avoid traffic bottlenecks by a cunning detour? Find your way to inaccessible places?

To celebrate my father's sixtieth birthday, I wanted to demonstrate that I had learned everything he had taught me. But how? By plotting and deploying all his signature tactics, I devised an elaborate plan to turn up in London on the day as a surprise. But that was not enough: I wanted to bring him something special that would involve a challenge and degree of difficulty that proved mastery of his own skills.

I roped my mother in as co-conspirator, but being a bad liar, she was nervous about giving the game away. I would not, she told my father, be able to celebrate in person on the date, but would fly back for Christmas instead. She resisted his suggestions they go out for lunch, saying she would prefer to make him one of his favourite meals at home. Thus tempted, he offered no resistance.

What could I bring him that he cherished? Chocolate was too banal and he already made regular trips to Paris to stock up on cheese and charcuterie. Suddenly I had it: wild strawberries. I'd seen him almost swoon while sniffing punnets of them in markets across southern France, rhapsodising on the delicacy of their scent. Despite his natural greed, he resisted his usual tendency to gulp them down, savouring each miniature bliss bomb with uncharacteristic restraint while rolling his eyes heavenward. They were his ambrosia.

But in October, when his birthday fell, they were also out of season. So I would go for the next best thing: wild strawberry ice cream from his favourite Parisian *glacier*, Berthillon. He had introduced me to its legendary repertoire years before and, despite the fact that I did not like chilled food or drinks, I had to admit that the intensity of the flavours had a magical effect. Although cold usually lessens the impact of flavour, somehow by freezing their syrups and fruit purées, Berthillon enhanced the original taste. Its green apple sorbet was a miracle of tartness that made you shiver with pleasure. Yes, I would arrive in London with *glace au parfum fraise des bois.*

I loved the degree of difficulty this challenge set and immediately sprang into action. First, I called Berthillon to make sure the flavour would be available as some were strictly seasonal.

'*Oui, madame,*' the voice on the phone responded with plangent serenity.

I explained that I needed to take it with me on the plane to London (this was in pre-Eurostar days).

'*Aucun souci, madame, nous pouvons vous préparer un petit coffret congélateur.*' Perfect: they would provide a chill box to keep the ice cream from melting for a limited amount of time.

I arranged to fly to London, change planes there, fly on to Paris for a couple of days to get over jet lag so that I would be fully alert once I reached my parents' home.

On the second day, bristling with the purpose of a secret mission, I walked to the Ile Saint-Louis, joined the eternal queue at the Berthillon Tea Rooms in the Rue Saint-Louis en L'Ile with scores of tourists—mostly American—and placed my order. It all went without a hitch. Soon I was speeding to the airport with my cooler packed with ice. When I boarded the plane, I handed the box to a flight attendant and asked her if she could store it for me in one of the galley fridges. She obliged without raising an eyebrow or asking to see the contents. Imagine that happening today.

At Heathrow, my mother met me with an insulated food bag, having snuck out of the house on a pretext. Although she was a mess of nerves, both of us revelled in our collusion and hoodwinkery.

'You ring the bell. I'll wait in the car,' she said when we reached home.

When my father opened the door, his face was neutral, prepared to say a polite but firm 'No thank you, not today' to someone offering to wash his car or asking him to donate to charity. When he saw me, he did a violent double-take: his head swung back in a whiplash jolt. His whole body followed in a jerky lurch. He stumbled backwards, as if edging away from a vision in horror. I was his Banquo's ghost, come to spoil his imminent feast. It was as if his brain could not trust the evidence of his eyes. It lasted about a second, but it shocked me into realising I might be causing a heart attack. I had not thought this through. I had not calculated the impact of such a surprise. I had not factored in health and age considerations. I might kill my father there and then.

My mother watched from behind me, horrified. She, too, thought my father was about to die. In which case, she would be complicit, an accessory. Guilt froze her face into a frown of concern.

By the time all this had registered, the cogs in my father's brain had aligned and begun whirring smoothly enough for him to fall forward on to me, in a heavy embrace. I carried the weight of him, wondering if my knees would buckle and we would both fall to the floor. Somehow, we made it inside, my father's eyes watering with emotion. I took the chill box from my mother.

'I brought you something,' I said, suddenly awkward and embarrassed at how vulnerable the moment had made my father.

'I'll just get lunch ready,' said my mother, happy to escape the charged atmosphere by fleeing into the kitchen, her customary refuge.

My father opened the chill box and read the lid of the ice cream container. He looked up in disbelief.

'You mean you . . . ?'

He could not even finish the sentence.

I nodded.

Bewildered, he shook his head, lifted the lid of the tub, dipped a finger into the rose pink mixture flecked with tiny seeds. My heart swelled with pride. My father began to sob, his shoulders heaving. We stood there, laughing, crying, too bashfully shy of the tidal wave of emotion surging between us to look at each other.

'Come on, you two, lunch will be ruined,' said my mother, briskly ushering us into the dining room where she had cleared away all her sewing paraphernalia and set the table with the best bone china, crystal and silver.

Over a champagne lunch, Papa made me tell him every minute detail of my plot, as if replaying a favourite film sequence in slow motion to catch every frame: exactly how I had made the arrangements, deceived him, enlisted the help of my mother to distract him.

'Of course I will pay your airfare,' he said, with the customary munificence he always used to smother anyone's attempt at generosity. I shook my head vehemently. No. Not this time. For once, he did not insist.

We ate the ice cream as if we were slightly tipsy, merry with elation and infectious congeniality. Old wounds and grievances set aside or forgotten, we licked our spoons in sync, sugar flooding our veins and tricking our minds into an insulin-spiked state of benign bliss. Every mouthful or so, my father would look up at me in disbelief, as if he needed to check I was not going to disappear as suddenly as I had appeared.

Of course this loved-up truce did not last. It held longer than it took for the sweetness to stabilise in our bloodstreams, but within days we were back to our cloudier, tetchier selves. Even so, nothing could dull the inescapable fact that whether I liked it or not, I was very much my father's daughter. From then on, he consulted me about itineraries, sending through drafts of proposed trips for my approval. I would send them back annotated with comments like a teacher correcting homework, mostly insisting that his plans were too rushed, or that he was overlooking a place of interest. He would also defer to me when I had local knowledge, or had been somewhere he had not. I became, in effect, his co-pilot. I had earned my planning stripes.

But on most of our trips my father's need for control was stifling. Once, though, for my mother's birthday, she and I went ahead on our own for a few days to Paris, where my father would join us for a celebratory dinner somewhere swish. Left to our own rhythms, we wandered like true *flâneurs*, got lost, sat at terraces for endless coffees, chose where to eat on the look of a place and its clientele, without any recommendations, reservations or guide books. Unleashed, we were as carefree and abandoned as two girls who had escaped boarding school. We ate at unusual hours, went to the cinema and sat through two films because we felt like it, and took cheeses and patisseries back to our room for in-between meal snacks. By the time my father arrived, genteel anarchy was well and truly in place and we resented his attempts to shape our days.

Having mastered the fine art of passive aggression singly and jointly, my mother and I simply ignored him. As we wandered the streets aimlessly browsing, my father followed, asking with mounting frustration where we were going and what our destination was. My mother giggled girlishly that we had none.

Bewildered, outnumbered and outgunned, my father had no choice but to follow along narrow pavements in single file, baffled as we stared into the dark windows of galleries, antique shops and boutiques.

'Shall we go in here?' he ventured, always up for a bit of purchasing power to bolster his self-esteem.

'No, we're just looking,' we always replied, trying to get him to understand the pleasures of *lèche-vitrines*—literally licking windows. Deflated, he followed with hangdog meekness, as if being subjected to a form of torture.

In his element when trips revolved around an event or spectacle, Papa was never better than when he was in charge of us as a small platoon under his command, going to a festival such as Bayreuth or Salzburg, for which he prepared as if about to engage in battle.

There, he spoke the language, understood the rules, and had all the on-the-ground intel from years of experience: he knew where to stay so that you could walk to the theatre and save yourself the bother of parking hassles, had deals for discounts in all the best places, and often got upgraded suites because of his regular custom. He appreciated the complex unstated codes and protocols of these elaborately formal occasions: where the best seats were, how to pre-order drinks for the interval to avoid the scrum, where was the best place to stand and watch the *passeggiata* of patrons wearing their heirloom finery, where to eat quickly before or after the show. Calibrated by decades, if not centuries of ritual, there was something pleasing in the seamless efficiency of their execution. 'If you stand here, you will see the trumpeters come out on to the balcony to summon the audience in for the performance,' said my father outside the Bayreuth Festspielhaus, bursting with pride that he could afford to bring his family to such an exclusive occasion in style. And he was right: we were in exactly the right spot to see the brass gleam in the afternoon light, fanfaring us into Wagner's Valhalla.

Thanks to him I developed a love of pomp and pageantry. He thought nothing of standing for three hours to watch a parade or of sitting on uncomfortable bleachers for a march, fly-past or *son et lumière* show. He believed in bearing witness to history, celebrating victories, honouring heroes, paying his respects; with so few family anniversaries, instead we marked the births and deaths of Joan of Arc, Oliver Cromwell, Horatio Nelson, Napoleon Bonaparte and Winston Churchill as if they were the flamboyant overachievers in our small tribe. At the age of eighty, he stood for hours among the crowds in the sun outside Westminster to catch a glimpse of Nelson Mandela on his first visit to London.

The apotheosis of all my father's organisational acumen was a trip to Paris in July 1989 for the bicentennial of the French Revolution. The occasion had been years in the planning. Feeling expansive, my father booked us into the most extravagantly *luxe* hotel in town, reserving a suite at the Crillon. The historic establishment overlooks the Place de la Concorde, site of the guillotine, where an evening parade would culminate in a rousing rendition of the national anthem with fireworks. It was a lavish, over-the-top gesture, even by my father's own standards, costing an eye-watering sum. But occasions like this only come once in a lifetime, he reasoned. So he was livid when, just months before the big day, the Crillon wrote to him with barely a semblance of courtesy, informing him that the entire hotel had been commandeered by the government to host its international heads of state. Unceremoniously bumped, his booking was nullified. He wrote to the Elysée Palace to complain, but the president's office was impervious to his appeal to *Liberté, Égalité, Fraternité.* Short of becoming a world leader, he could not have his suite.

Undeterred, he found another hotel, further from the Champs-Elysées, where the much vaunted *défilé* would pass on its way to the Place de la Concorde. He finagled an invitation from colleagues with an office in a prime position to stand on a strategically located balcony. So far, so good. But there was one unforeseen obstacle. We were staying on one side of the Champs and our viewing point was on the other. Security barricades along the avenue prevented pedestrians from crossing. The crowds were already banked up ten deep when we realised our problem. The underground walkways were blocked off for security reasons. Paris was cut in half and we were in the wrong half.

What to do faced with this unexpected setback? For the first time, my father looked worried. To be unable to reach our destination, which we could see, would entail a severe loss of face and huge disappointment.

'Let me see what I can do,' I ventured, emboldened. Perhaps being Australian conferred special status. Surely no one in this vast crowd could have come further than I?

Gripping our invitation to the exclusive address on the other side as if it were a *laisser-passer* of the most official kind, I bowled up to a gendarme. Speaking as deferentially as possible, I told him that we were from Australia and had come all this way specially for the celebrations. My parents looked humbly at the ground while he studied the card closely. Fortunately, it was stiff and embossed with a crest, giving it an almost heraldic look. Miracle of miracles, he pushed his way to the front of the crowd with a brisk '*Suivez moi*' and, to the great displeasure of the people at the front of the nearest barrier, pushed it open to allow us through. For a brief heady instant, we were the only people standing on Paris's grandest avenue, able to look up and down its entire length at the hundreds of thousands gathered there, waving their *tricolores* towards the Arc de Triomphe, where a giant version of the flag swayed gently in the summer night air.

The French cannot abide unfair advantage: spectators grudgingly let us through on the other side of the road, wondering aloud why we had been accorded this special privilege. My father looked relieved. All his planning had hung in the balance, hingeing on one unforeseen hurdle that could have scuppered everything. And I had come through, playing Australia as my trump card.

Many hours later, we walked back to our hotel elated by the sheer scale and fantasy of the parade, humming 'La Marseillaise' while the city's nocturnal street-washing carts rinsed away all traces of revolutionary fervour.

# CHAPTER 16

# Couch potato

As he drifted into his sixties, my mother and I taunted my father regularly with the question of what he would do when he retired, pointing to his workaholic personality and lack of hobbies. He was never going to take up golf or become a volunteer guide at a museum. My mother dreaded having him under her feet all day.

When retirement came, my father was marooned. For the first time in his life, he did not have a plan. He shuffled about, sorting papers, claiming to have embarked on a major clear-out. But nothing was ever thrown away and his desk was increasingly colonised by towering piles and files. He remained on boards, spoke at conferences, attended a few public lectures, but his vaguely stated intentions of writing a book never materialised. He was undeniably reduced by stepping down as company director.

The offers he expected did not eventuate. Disappointed, disillusioned, he spent his days in futile but caustic correspondence as an ardent consumer/complainer, arguing with the council, borough, City of London and beyond about all the aspects of British life that infuriated him. The rest of the time he sat back in his recliner watching daytime re-runs of *Friends*. It was a pathetic sight, and I teased him about it with cruel insensitivity. 'I like that pretty girl's smile,' he said lamely, referring to Jennifer Aniston without even knowing her name.

My father was not one for made-up words but one day he surprised us by describing his current state of mind as *houdry voudry*. The word was made up, he told us almost apologetically, as if he were embarrassed by its non-dictionary illegitimacy. A childhood nonsense expression invented by one of his Hungarian cousins to convey a sort of *comme çi comme ça* melancholy. He had never used it before; now, out it popped from some deep recess, summoned perhaps by this new unfamiliar feeling of uncertainty. Maman and I both loved the word and adopted it instantly. It was as close as my father ever got to admitting that he might be depressed.

Now that he was home all day, he squabbled with my mother more pettily than ever, and they scratched at each other's frustrations like peevish chickens. He subjected her to a near-constant barrage of demands and needs, mistaking her for a member of staff. Like a maharajah to a chai wallah, he shouted 'TEA!' almost hourly from his top-floor eyrie, only to find his request ignored.

In 2000, the near collapse of the Equitable Life Assurance Society affected my parents' financial security, along with that of thousands of others. Their nest egg shrank. Incapable of frugality, they tightened their belts by taking shorter holidays and eating at less fancy establishments. The shopping sprees ended. My father hid his worry as best he could, but we were not fooled.

Desperate for new sources of income, my father came up with his least sensible scheme to date. *Rösti* (pronounced rerr-shti) is a Swiss dish of coarsely grated raw or boiled waxy potato, shaped into patties and fried in butter. Once considered the traditional breakfast of farmers in the Bern canton, it soon became a popular national dish, resilient and versatile enough to withstand adulteration with the addition of interloper ingredients such as cheese, bacon and onion. The border between Switzerland and France and Switzerland and Germany is known as the Rösti Ditch.

My father adored *rösti*. As a historian with a firm grasp of genealogy, he liked to enhance its appeal in terms of its gastronomic lineage. Adopting pompously pontificating language to ennoble its humble provenance, he explained that it was 'related on the mother's side' (one of his favourite expressions) to the Jewish *latke* and 'on the father's side' to hash browns.

This distinguished family tree did nothing to disguise the real appeal of *rösti*: it is an ambrosial conjunction of carbohydrate and fat, differing only in texture from chips. For unfathomable reasons in a country that loves potatoes—and fat—it had never taken off in Britain.

My father was never one to ask for advice. Instead, he dispensed it freely, on all manner of subjects. As a child, I was infuriated when he offered unsolicited coaching on how to play tennis and how to ski, though he did neither. Now he embarked on a second career in food wholesale without any expertise. A wiser head than his would have pointed out that very little Swiss food was known in the UK and that introducing some would involve a massive public education and promotional campaign.

Apart from chocolate and cheese, it would be hard to think of a single Swiss dish that Brits could identify. If they were health-food consumers, they would be aware of Bircher muesli; if they had been on a skiing holiday they might recognise French-inspired cheese fondue and *raclette*; but it was doubtful they would have heard of *bündner nusstorte*, *zürcher geschnetzeltes*, *spätzli*, *cervelat* or *zopf*, to name a few of the country's tongue-twister gastronomic highlights. The Swiss may have been eager to promote their watches and discreetly proud of their banks but they had done precious little to proclaim their cuisine.

Undeterred by my mother pleading with him not to embark on such a folly, my father decided that he would become the Colonel Sanders of *rösti*. Desperate for a get-rich-quick scheme to replace lost funds and give purpose to his floundering retirement, undaunted by his lack of experience in the food importation and wholesale business, he made contact with a reputable Swiss supplier, Hero, well known for its high-quality jams and condiments, of which my father was a connoisseur and loyal customer. They sent samples of their various products, which my parents trialled over several dinners. The purist original version (without the new-fangled additions of either cheese or bacon) won the day comfortably. Boasting a forty-year-old recipe, Hero was only too happy to oblige and filled an order for hundreds of vacuum-sealed foil packets of which my father took delivery in numerous cartons.

He had no business plan that we were aware of. There was no budget or campaign to launch the food on unsuspecting British households, to suggest how to cook or serve it, and no game plan for countering prejudices against it being a tasty combination of the two food groups many consumers were trying hard to avoid. My father did not consider advertising, had no leads or introductions to how key outlets like upmarket supermarket chains and prestige gourmet stores might be targeted as premium customers. It was, to use one of my father's favourite expressions, a hare-brained scheme.

At first my father filled a few small orders from Jewish delicatessens with a loyal but dwindling clientele of older generation Europeans. But several months later, boxes of *rösti* cluttered his study, their expiry date drawing ever closer. There is only so much *rösti* two people can eat. My mother made valiant efforts to add interest with fried egg, grated apple, ham and other flavourings, but the appeal soon waned. Potatoes were not going to make my father rich. Instead, they may have contributed to his demise, depending on where you stand on the factors that contribute to clogged arteries.

# CHAPTER 17

# Estranged

In my late forties I did something that might have been more appropriate in my teens: I became estranged from my parents. After twenty years of living in Australia, I walked out on them in London following a turbulent visit and simply did not see them for three years. Emotionally a late developer, this was a long overdue act of assertion and self-preservation for me. I had never done anything so extreme.

During my late teens and twenties, I witnessed my peers rebelling, but lacked the stomach for it. I looked on as girlfriends trashed themselves, stumbled incoherently through hangovers in class, failed exams, wept over abortions, pierced themselves in the first wave of punk. No matter how provoked I was by a sense of raging unfairness, my nerve always failed me. I was too conventional for revolution, and its anthems sounded jarring to my ear, raised as it was on classical music.

Perceptive friends suggested that my decision to go to Australia was in fact my late revolt—choosing to go as far away from my parents as I possibly could to escape their clutches. But I denied the theory emphatically. Love had brought me here, then work and a new love had caused me to stay.

When I did finally rebel, I did it out of sync, when everyone else was calming down, finding understanding and forgiveness for their parents' failings as they navigated the turbulence of parenting themselves. Childless, I experienced no such charity or serenity. Each encounter with my parents left me roiling with fury and frustration. Eventually I felt I had no choice but to turn my back and walk away.

I had come to London to celebrate my mother's birthday—a significant one. Always optimistic that this time would be better, that I would not fall into old habits of childishness, I felt confident that I could maintain the equanimity that was a sign of maturity.

Things got off to a bad start. Much as Native Americans would sit down and smoke a peace pipe together to establish cordial relations with a visiting tribe, we always began a visit home with a cup of tea. On this occasion, wanting to demonstrate good intentions, I offered to make a pot—a role that was traditionally my mother's. My parents had only recently downsized to a new riverside apartment, and I was keen to show my appreciation of their fixtures and fittings. But the gesture did not go to plan. Within fifteen minutes of arriving, I had almost managed to set fire to their home. I had put the kettle on the stove and lit the gas. For as long as I can remember, my mother has had a kettle that sits on the stove and whistles when it has boiled. Now, in my absence, she had bought an electric model.

The first indication that something was amiss was a ribbon of black smoke coming from the kitchen, accompanied by an acrid smell of burning plastic. Running to the crime scene, I processed the evidence: I had burned the base of the kettle, rendering it inoperative.

My mother shrieked as if mortally wounded. I apologised, promising to replace it within twenty-four hours.

'That's not the point,' she shrugged.

'It's my favourite kettle,' she said, as if talking about a beloved pet or heirloom antique. I was not aware that people had favourite kettles because I assume people only have one.

'I doubt you'll get that model again, it was from one of my mail-order catalogues,' she said, as if that made it a limited edition collector's item.

But the real damage was not to the kettle, it was to our already tense and precarious relationship. I was no longer a reasonably competent middle-aged woman, I was hurled back, as if by a powerful gravitational force, to being an irresponsible child, who, left alone, could imperil my parents' domestic safety. How? My mother was very quick to list the possibilities: I could leave taps running and flood the place. Or fail to switch off the computer until somehow it overheated and cables started to fry, or do the same with the mobile-phone charger, which had caused a fire in a friend's apartment. So many dangers.

In the past, she had insisted that all electric appliances be turned off at the socket every night, long before doing so was considered environmentally responsible. No machine was to be left on pause or sleep, as she had read that there were risks involved. The fax machine had to be turned off overnight, too, which was the only time it was going to receive messages from people in different time zones, thereby completely defeating its purpose. She really believed the whole place was waiting to combust.

A few days after the kettle incident, our celebratory trip to Paris unravelled with spectacular speed. The mask of civility between us fell swiftly. Conversations became barbed. My parents' opinions and prejudices, trivial dislikes and discords, impatience with traffic and swearing over navigation caused an escalation in tension followed by protracted sulking. The atmosphere stewed like sour plums.

One day, I had a panic attack in the car, leapt out in traffic in a sweat and ran back to the hotel, my guts churning. The cramps sharpened with a sudden flashback to infancy: we are on a skiing holiday in Switzerland. My bowels churning on the back seat of the Jaguar. I squirm on the back seat, clenching my buttocks to hold in everything that is feeling increasingly liquid and swishing around in my insides like slops in a bucket on the deck of a listing ship. In the end I can't help it and detonate a terrible mess of *caca* that spreads like hot lava across the red leather, streaking it with runny ochre. As I emit a plaintive howl of distress, my father swerves abruptly, pulling over into a snowy bank. My mother yanks me out, furious, strips me roughly out of my cumbersome layers of ski clothes, catching my skin on a hastily tugged zipper, complaining bitterly as she rubs me and the seat down with handfuls of snow. I can feel her disgust in every brisk wipe. My skin burns from contact with frozen water while I am aflame with shame. Shit and shame. Shit and shame. Bawling, indignant, humiliated, betrayed by my body, I am, I understand in that moment, utterly unlovable. The car has a sweet faecal reek for days.

Decades after this incident, I made it to the hotel in Paris just in time to reach the bathroom but was too sick to join my parents for dinner. My mother was resentful at having no one to dilute my father's morose company or to distract them from their mutual boredom. At breakfast the next morning, she handed back the birthday presents I had chosen so carefully for her, including an album I had compiled of favourite photos of us together around the world. We drove back from France in silence leaden with hostility.

All the way I mulled over the dynamics of the couple sitting in front of me: he the bullying tyrant, she the compliantly passive victim. As we crossed the Channel I worked myself into a bitter stew of contempt, my nausea exacerbated by the aroma of market-bought cheeses ripening in the car's warm fug. As the Vacherin and Reblochon released their sulphurous vapours, I stifled mine.

Within hours of reaching my parents' apartment, the already suffocatingly overheated air from the cranked-up central heating became even more stale with tension and resentment. My eyeballs felt dry and I was constantly thirsty. My skin flaked and my hair crackled with static. Meals were eaten without a word being exchanged. No one asked me what I was doing or where I was going. No one said good morning or goodnight. My parents' faces hardened into blank masks.

In bed at night, the mattress beneath me felt like a hot plate, burning with fury and frustration. I was incandescent: radiant heat spread under my body for hour after hour. I threw off bedclothes and surreptitiously opened windows and turned off radiators. But the inferno must've been inside me, because it never cooled down, no matter what I did.

I lay there and smouldered, thinking about the toxic way my parents spoke to each other, the nagging and wheedling, the sarcasm as corrosive as battery acid and infantile tit-for-tatting. A bitter banter of disappointment now had a shared focus for their regret: they were united in the complicity of disapproval against their Bad Daughter. One night a news item on television announced legislation allowing children to prosecute their parents for physical abuse.

'So, are you going to report us?' they sneered in joint provocation. That dare hit harder than a fresh blow.

As a circuit-breaker, I moved out for a few days, pretending a friend had asked me to house sit. But when I got back, my absence had done nothing to clear the air. I was met with stony faces.

At my wits end, I changed my ticket, booking an earlier flight home. No one kissed me goodbye when I left. It was the first time I had ever gone to the airport on my own.

Within weeks back in Australia, I felt a real sense of release. Sorrow visited me specifically as a sharp pang of regret when

I walked my local beach on glorious days—it felt like being poked in the ribs with a splinter of glass to think that my mother might never see the beautiful place where I lived. I longed to share it with her, to renew the ritual of my childhood when we had gone beachcombing for seashells together. That did trouble me.

But I was free from the constant carping, negativity, incessant criticism and relentless judgement, implicit and explicit, and, above all, the endless triangulating, in which my parents played me off against each other. I felt detoxed, as if I had come out of rehab. I thought of myself less as a daughter, unmoored myself from that rotten jetty and began to float free, drifting towards a different identity.

My mother recently told me that after my departure, my father said: 'We are just going to have to forget her.' Except he didn't. He persisted in writing me injured, reproachful and bitingly accusatory rants that made me feel like a combination of *King Lear*'s Goneril and Regan.

Ever since I had left home, my father had written me copious correspondence, mostly unsolicited advice about managing my finances or forthcoming trips. But instead of letters, they were always laid out like office memos:

*To: CB*
*From: HB*
*Re:*

This format made me feel like an employee, rather than a daughter. Each topic was numbered, sub-clauses indented with bullet points. The layout reinforced my feeling of being a minion to be bossed around. The tone was authoritarian. Often he wrote long meandering discursive essays to mark a significant historical date that he thought I should note (the Battle of Trafalgar was a favourite) or to express his frustration with government policy or some administrative malfunction to do with traffic or his *bête noire*, Heathrow Airport. Some of these lengthy despatches were sermons, essays or occasional raves about an opera or theatre production he wished I had seen or films he loathed. He also sent me copies of letters of which he was particularly proud. When they were addressed to MPs or the heads of statutory authorities, he deployed a formidable arsenal of scathing verbal flourishes and dripping sarcasm to illustrate his contempt for a policy or decision he condemned as 'cretinous' or 'asinine'. As a relentless consumer and ratepayer/complainer, his tone to bureaucrats and 'underlings' was withering. Nothing was too trivial a subject for his scorn: he wrote a detailed objection to the makers of his preferred imported menthol mouthwash, objecting, quite rightly, to the impractical shape of the bottle, which did not fit into his washbag.

I skimmed Papa's letters for essential information but am ashamed to say that I rarely went back to read them in detail. And yet, I kept them all. They are in two big fabric boxes near my desk. In a bushfire, I would grab them as readily as photographs. A friend who saw me riffling through them one day marvelled at their volume and said wistfully: 'Your father must really love you to write to you so much.' The thought had never occurred to me. But later, when I read them, I was shocked at how forcefully my father's personality jumped off the page. Reading his clever witticisms and word play, his polished phrases and well-shaped arguments, his diatribes and scathing critiques, I recognise the pride and pleasure he took in mastering so eloquently a language that was not his first. But it's also a different kind of revelation: I've cracked a genetic code and discovered that my father is the origin of my own desire to be a writer.

My mother rarely wrote to me. She said that doing so only made her feel worse about our separation, but when she did put pen to paper, she was droll, especially in her account of the intrigues and shenanigans of visiting Russians, which she recounted like episodes of French farce. Now, when the rupture of estrangement came, she accepted it as total in her all-or-nothing way. After being orphaned and let down every time she placed her trust in anyone, being abandoned had become her default setting—I was just the latest in a long string of betrayals.

When I first came to Australia, Maman went into a protracted and painful phase of deep mourning that may have been depression, but she never sought help for her condition. Each return visit I made seemed to sharpen the pain: in the days before my departure, the atmosphere would build up to unbearable levels of tension. Gradually, grudgingly, she got acclimatised to the separation. But now, this break was final. Stubborn and proud, she did not buckle.

Until I walked out, I had always been a harsh judge of those who cut off communication with their parents. I thought them heartless, selfish and lacking in compassion. But in those three years when we did not talk, I changed my mind.

Some relationships are just too poisoned to be fixed unless both sides are prepared to take responsibility, compromise or seek professional help. I knew I had failed to be a good daughter in their eyes and I recognised what a bitter disappointment that must be to two people who had invested everything in their only child, but it was a failure I chose to accept.

I did not know how long our separation would last. I did not rule out reconciliation. But I knew there was a risk that I might have to live with the guilt of that decision for the rest of my life, and I was prepared to take that chance. It allowed me to make some space in my head, without being tugged at and confused by conflicting values.

Slowly I felt myself taking shape. My blurred edges became sharper, as I made decisions free of the soundtrack of interference that had colonised my consciousness for years. It was a sad state of affairs, but with such a porous sense of my own borders, I felt I had no choice. I could not ignore that I had inherited many of the traits that had brought us to this point; I recognised that I too was impatient, with a tendency to flashes of anger and holding grudges. Knowing the origin of these flaws did not excuse them or make them easier to correct.

But gradually, with sustained distance from the source, I jettisoned tastes and values that I had adopted unquestioningly. It was heady not to have to pretend to enjoy classical music concerts. There was novelty in planning a less regimented holiday, discovering spontaneity and what could happen without a schedule, a map or a reservation. Gradually I let go of absolutism and definite opinions, cared less about money and material proof of success, rejected suspicion and anxiety as default settings. I avoided comparison with others as a yardstick of achievement and found the patina of things worn and used more appealing than the new. I made a conscious effort not to evaluate a person harshly and rush to judgement. I stopped striving relentlessly. It was like discovering extra lung capacity. I breathed deep.

Some shared enthusiasms remained, hardwired by positive experiences: food was one of them, though no longer at the fine-dining end of the scale. And comfortable travel: I never lost my love of room service or a fine thread count. I had no desire to reject every dish my parents had served me. But I chose to season and swallow them in different dosages.

Time blunts the sharp edge of resentment. You forget your grievances or their impact diminishes. You miss the opportunity to share a family joke. You wonder if they are watching the same television shows and how they are interpreting the news. If they too are feeling a little *houdry voudry* about the state of the world.

Three years later, it was France, the scene of our rupture, that provided the scene of our reconciliation. My mother's native country, beloved by my father since they had met there, emblematic of their initial optimism. When I came along, I was charmed by its language and beauty. Our regular holidays there made it feel like a second home.

In the past, France had always transformed us. On native ground, Maman became more assured. Switching into her mother tongue boosted her confidence: she peppered her conversation with quotes from French literature and puns that demonstrated a playfulness and agility that she rarely attempted in English. Meanwhile, my father basked in the glow of idol worship, retelling favourite anecdotes about his Gallic heroes as we made pilgrimages to their shrines: Domrémy, the village where Joan of Arc was born, the châteaux of the Loire, the Palace of Versailles, Malmaison, the cathedral at Chartres: we paid our respects at monuments to human achievement, exaltation and ambition, my father always leading the way, eyes moist with sentiment, his tone hushed with reverence. In France, communing with the past seemed to soothe his irritable soul.

An early adopter, Papa loved countries that forged ahead with new technology. 'Just look at these superb motorways,' he would say with unqualified admiration for progress as we sped south along the newly built Autoroute du Soleil, completed, my father marvelled, 'on time and on budget'. A confirmed believer in borderless Europe, when the Channel Tunnel was launched, he was one of the first to invest in it and drive through when it was completed. In France, my father swapped fault-finding for praise.

Childhood holidays there brought a rare spate of harmony to our trio, especially during the annual summer break in the south. Every summer on the beach at Cannes, my father shucked off formality, swapping his handmade suits and Hermès ties for casual shirts. Though he rarely swam, he took me out in a paddle boat, pedalling straight for the horizon when my own feet could not reach the treads, and became chief engineer and builder for lavish sandcastles, shovelling sand with purpose, urging me on as his labourer before the tide swept our bridges and forts away. Or the three of us immersed ourselves in our books, side by side under a fringed parasol on our blue-and-white striped mattresses, waiting for the ice-cream vendor to run across the burning sand shouting out flavours ('*Fraise! Vanille! Chocolat!*'), a cooler box slung across his tanned shoulders. My father, never able to keep to the shade of the parasol, would invariably burn, his extremities turning lobster red. Though he was supposed to be relaxing, even his reading was violent: he bent books till their spines cracked, his pace furious; he would start and finish a Harold Robbins, Mario Puzo or a Len Deighton in a day, biting his nails non-stop.

Our daily routines were insular and indolent: the rituals of *la plage, la terrasse, le marché, la promenade, la sieste, le restaurant.* In late afternoons the air shimmered from the oil of sappy cypress. Dark as olives, Maman and I sluiced our skin in the Mediterranean's clear azure brine. We ate unwieldly *pan bagnat* sandwiches of ripe tomatoes in bread soaked in olive oil. Peach and melon juice dribbled down our chins. In the evenings with Papa we dressed up and sat on the balmy terrace of the Carlton or the Majestic, bronzed and polished, stupefied by the sun, watching the world stroll by on the Croisette, ordering elaborate dishes from extravagantly oversize menus that looked like giant books of spells. Under my father's encouraging and approving gaze, I made bold choices. He beamed with pride at being able to afford the most expensive dishes and best wines, but for my mother the experience was slightly marred by his persistent habit of asking us to guess what the bill came to (in those days, and in those establishments, women were presented with a menu that omitted prices). She was content to be pampered, cosseted and kept in ignorance of what things cost whereas I enjoyed the game, though I was rarely accurate. Leaving a showily generous tip to demonstrate his largesse, my father signalled our departure. Fawned on by bowing waiters, we retired to our suite like potentates, glowing with privilege and satiated satisfaction.

Three years after the break with my parents, my husband David and I decided to spend three months in France. Ahead of our trip we made tentative contact by phone. The reception was frosty and wary but we persisted with solicitous questions. We mentioned that we would be passing through London and would like to see them. They made non-committal noises. Next, like an old-fashioned emissary sent from an enemy state, David visited them with peace offerings of flowers and chocolates. These were well received. He suggested lunch. They accepted.

We met on neutral ground at a gastro pub on the river in Bray. We were all nervous. The atmosphere was tense.

My father had more liver spots than I remembered, his face now dappled with splotches of pigmentation and moles. My mother looked haggard. Conversation was general, stilted and polite. We spent an inordinate amount of time praising the very good bottle of wine my father had brought and steered away from the personal, staying within the safer boundaries of current affairs.

When it was time to leave, my mother shrank from my embrace, but my father let me take his arm as we walked to our cars. Unable to restrain himself, he told me he did not like what I was wearing. I ignored the comment rather than rising to it.

Once settled in Nice, we called weekly. Anecdotes about daily life seemed to amuse them and begin a slow, gradual thaw. They laughed at our bafflement over extended lunchtime closing hours and our disgust at the quantities of dog shit on the pavements. Emboldened by the irresistible charm of our waterfront location, which we knew would meet with their exacting approval, we invited them for that ultimate peace-making festivity, Christmas.

It was a high-risk strategy. Christmas had never been a festive time in our household: being Jewish, my father would have preferred to ignore the date completely and only tolerated token elements of the occasion when I was a child. For most of December, he stewed in a state of bah humbug resentment, joined in surprising solidarity by my mother, who unleashed her Gallic vehemence against everything from street decorations to carols, mince pies, turkey and stuffing. We assured them that our Christmas would provide an escape from all of the excess they despised.

They accepted tentatively, with conditions. They would not stay with us, they would not stay very long. On the day of their arrival I left a bunch of violets, my mother's favourites, at their hotel with a note to say we would pick them up for dinner.

I can only describe what happened over the next five days as a magical alignment. A unique state of grace. Every small pleasure was shared, every delight mutual. We sat in easy conversation in squares bathed in winter sunshine, as if it had never been otherwise. They were keen to explore, enthusiastic about every suggestion, relaxed in surrendering all decision-making. Their amenable, easygoing disposition did not seem forced, as if they were on their best behaviour. Unrecognisably good company, they were like completely charming, urbane acquaintances one wanted to get to know better.

There was no mention of apology, no blame. No sub-text, no undertow or malaise, no hint of bitter recrimination that might rear up and break this fragile but miraculous truce. It was as if the constantly ticking bomb of our family had been defused.

We did all the shopping for Christmas lunch in less than an hour. No queues, no fuss. Minimal tinsel. My parents swapped their ritual refrain of complaint for the gentle hum of benign tolerance.

I cherish the memory of that Christmas as an enduring highlight of my adult life. All too soon, I would need to raid the currency of goodwill banked during those days of reconciliation, drawing urgently on what I would later realise was a life savings account.

# PART TWO

PART TWO

# CHAPTER 18

# A dutiful daughter

When I returned to Australia, my role as Good Daughter continued without significant incident or interruption: the French interlude had bought me an extended line of credit. Two years later, my father was diagnosed with bowel cancer and given a fairly optimistic diagnosis subject to an operation.

I took the news calmly. I soothed my mother's anxiety and worst fears, downplaying the crisis, making reassuring noises and telling her I would be there to support her.

We agreed that I would come just in time for the operation. In planning mode, I prepared a mental script for how this episode would play out. I would arrive early on the morning of the day my father was to have the operation to remove a tumour from his bowel, have a cup of tea with my mother and then go to the hospital with her to see my father before he went into surgery, to reassure him all would be well.

I intended to stay for two weeks, to make barely a dent in my work schedule, and to allow me, for the week leading up to the op, the long-planned treat of a holiday with David and friends at the Adelaide Festival.

I am, after all, my father's daughter and have taken responsibility for our group's logistics: I've arranged our accommodation, restaurant bookings and tickets to shows. I want to honour their trust and am already relishing the pleasure of how the components of the week fit into a seamless jigsaw.

I've also inherited my father's love of anticipation, the way it stretches an occasion's pleasure so that it begins weeks or even months earlier. Even though I try to live more in the present than in the future, there are times when having something to look forward to makes everything worthwhile. I love finessing the smallest details to make sure things go smoothly. I may have adapted his high-stress modus operandi over a more relaxed and flexible style, but it's still a responsibility I prefer not to delegate.

The Fleurieu Peninsula is a part of the world where I could imagine living. Its plentiful produce—almonds, olives, cherries—reminds me of Provence. Now I will get the chance to introduce friends to a part of the world they don't know and discover it again through their eyes. This way, I can have my cake and eat it too. Go to the festival and then leave for London. Win win.

But my plans do not go to plan. Three days before we are due to go to Adelaide, my mother calls to say that the hospital can take my father early: he's going to have surgery in two days' time. She is relieved because it saves her another week of anxiety, which has already dominated her life for two months since the diagnosis and because she'll get a better quality of nursing if they can avoid the Easter holiday period, when some permanent staff are bound to take leave and be replaced by agency personnel.

I am crestfallen. I can't fulfil my role as dutiful daughter. I won't be there when my father wakes up or to hold my mother's hand as she waits nervously for a call from the hospital to say everything is alright. When I give her the choice between me arriving for the op or when my father is home convalescing, where he will no doubt be a dreadful patient, she chooses the former, though friends tell me I might be of more use later. Damn.

She puts my father on the phone.

'Hello, Baby,' he says, sounding weary and frail. 'Can you come now?' he asks in a voice I do not recognise. Is that fear I am hearing? I don't recognise it. I hesitate. I make excuses about breaking work contracts, knowing this is something he understands and values. I play the professional card, which is how he likes me to sound. I am not lying: there is a day's work wedged into the Adelaide trip, but it is one I could pull out of, citing family circumstances, only I don't want to.

'Okay,' he says, caving without argument, 'just come when you can.' He is docile with acceptance. Normally he would apply pressure.

I am wrong-footed by his lack of insistence. He can be so manipulative, so scorchingly sarcastic if he wants to make me feel guilty for not jumping to his every command, but now he sounds as if he's surrendered to his fate. I agonise over my decision. Should I cancel the Adelaide trip? Heavy hearted, I decide to stick to the original plan.

In Adelaide, the temperature is over forty degrees for eight days straight, breaking a record. My eyeballs fry after ten minutes on the street, and the hot northerly wind aggravates the feeling of desert-like dehydration, sapping all energy. But the evenings are balmy and the company is stimulating, warm, funny, clever—the very best combination of people and ideas, all charged by being together and arguing with passion about what we like and don't like about what we see every day and night: *'Have you been to see the Aboriginal work at the Gallery?' 'I hate the way they've hung it.' 'Don't forget the museum collection.' 'The Jam Factory has a great multimedia show.' 'Let's go to the Persian Gardens tonight.' 'Guess who I bumped into from London?' 'Why can't all shows be an hour long?'*

We argue vehemently about Leonard Cohen and a controversial German production of *Cat on a Hot Tin Roof*—does the set overpower the acting? What is the live vulture for? And why are the actors so unsexy when the play is drenched in sex? Over an hour-long walk before the heat of the day sets in, powering by the River Torrens, before a communal breakfast where the opinions are fuelled by feast-like spreads, we never stop asking each other, challenging, interpreting, speculating. It's heady, intoxicating and fun, a real mental work-out based on trust, respect and relentless, avid curiosity. I feel energised by the group's enthusiasm.

One morning I step away from the pack as we are walking by the river to call my mother on my mobile. The operation went well, they seem to have got all of the tumour: 'The size of a tangerine,' she tells me, always one for a graphic medical detail. She sounds relieved and upbeat, perhaps charged with adrenalin, proud of having got through it on her own. She took a taxi from the hospital, something she hates to do as she often cannot understand drivers' accents and worries about not giving the correct tip. She likes the surgeon, the nurses, she remembers their names and feels my father is in capable hands. He's still very dopey. Now she can get some rest. She says the hospital is more cheerful than she expected, with lots of art on the walls, and that soon my father will have a phone by his bedside so I can call him.

Relieved, I catch up with the rest of the clan. The next few days are golden, burnished in my memory. In a matter of days, their recollection will help keep me sane: I will cling to snatches of remembered conversation as if my life depended on it.

For now, I am in a state of ignorance. I assume that it's possible to give my mother the support she needs at the end of the phone, like a general talking from a remote vantage point to the troops on the front line. Those few minutes first thing in the morning are neatly stowed away, the time difference adding to the convenience of being able to move on swiftly to more hedonistic plans without a guilty conscience. After all, the operation was a success, the worst is over, it is all for the best. My father has the constitution of an ox and a steely will. He is not ready to go and has come through.

⁓

When my mother starts to sound rattled by my father's post-op behaviour, I am not perturbed and try to downplay her concerns.

She tells me that he is ranting, and has become very agitated and abusive towards the nurses, has not slept all night, has wandered the ward disrupting the sleep of other patients. I reassure her that it is simply the after-effects of the anaesthetic, which we have been warned could take up to a week to wear off. She agrees that the nurses have ventured the same opinion, but she is the one who is getting calls in the middle of the night from my father insisting that she come and get him immediately, bringing lots of money, as he is about to be sold or killed by an unnamed enemy. A day later, she is not amused when he calls her by the name of a woman she knows has been his mistress. She says the nurses are pretty fed up with him, as he has kept the ward awake all night with his ravings. I tell her to just hang on, stay calm, not react and that I will be there soon. She sounds unconvinced.

I know the real ordeal for her will begin when he comes home and starts bossing us around, refusing to follow medical advice and unwilling to adopt new recommendations on diet, exercise or safeguarding his well-being. He has been a bitter, angry, disappointed man for a long, long time and that is not going to change. He has also shown a stubborn disregard for his physical self, as if he and his body were entirely disconnected. The cancer scare will have taught him nothing, the reprieve he has gained will not alter his perspective. I have suspected him of suffering from clinical depression for some time, and urged my mother to get him some help, but she has been more preoccupied with his physical symptoms of high blood pressure, general bad temper and forgetfulness to pay attention to a problem she does not fully recognise or understand.

All this is the backdrop to our conversations, during which I try to maintain the voice of a supportive, sympathetic but slightly detached counsellor in an attempt to calm my mother's rising alarm. Do I sound condescending? Bossy? Probably.

If I were there in person there is not much more I could do, I tell myself, but really, who am I kidding? The difference is she would not be walking into and out of the ward on her own with her emotions in tatters. She would not be coming home alone to an empty flat where there is no one to make her the all-consoling cup of tea and to help her debrief and unload, to cook her some dinner when she is too tired to make it for herself, and to chivvy her into watching something distracting on television. I am a bad daughter because I am not there, my heart hardened by my selfish priorities; any arguments I might offer to the contrary are self-serving.

Nagging at my innards is my biggest fear: what if I don't love him enough to take care of him? I know that I have limited patience at the best of times, but the history of conflict with my father is so complex and protracted and I have felt so little real love for him for some time that I think it might make me an unsuitable carer. I am afraid of that showing, afraid of the ugliness I feel it betrays in my soul, ashamed of feeling so little generosity in my heart.

I unburden myself to my friend Sean, who recently spent time by his father's side during his final weeks after a lifetime of virtual estrangement far more extreme than mine. In the end, he says, you forget about all that stuff, all the resentment, the grievances, the wrongs and hurts, and you just see a sick old man. You can't feel any anger towards someone who is as helpless as a child. Prophetic, wise words that I mull over on the flight to London, guilt-ridden for not going sooner to my mother's side.

# CHAPTER 19

# April

If irony is your thing, then I guess there is some irony in the fact that we took my father home on Good Friday. He was far from resurrected, though his wound had healed, the scar and neat stitching mending tidily.

When we came to the hospital to fetch him, he was asleep in a chair by his bed. A long drool of saliva was falling from his lips, which my mother wiped away briskly with a corner of a sheet. 'The medication makes him dribble,' she explained, quickly making an excuse for his loss of dignity.

I had never seen my father so dishevelled. It took quite some prodding to get him to wake from a very deep sleep—so much so that initially I thought he might be dead. I was just about to call for help when he eventually raised his head, still without opening his eyes, as if only semi-conscious. We assumed his dopiness must be due to the lingering after-effects of the anaesthetic.

No one at the hospital seemed concerned that it took more than an hour to get my father dressed. He raised his arms like an obedient child when told to, but did not participate in the process. Having been so eager, insistent and desperate to leave the ward in the preceding days, he was now apathetic, listless and passive, helpless when it came to putting on socks, shoes, shirt and sweater. My mother became more and more upset by his demeanour but eventually, with one of us supporting him on each side, he shuffled out of the ward to the lift, the foyer and into a taxi. In the taxi his eyes were dull, like those of a cooked fish, and he did not seem to recognise the streets through which we drove. When Felix the doorman welcomed him back, he said thank you without looking at who was addressing him, as if he were on automatic pilot, simply parroting a phrase he had been taught. He just kept shuffling forward, looking neither right nor left. Once inside the flat, he went straight to bed.

'Is he dying?' asked my mother.

'We all are, Mum,' I said in a flippant attempt to downplay her anxiety. But I, too, wondered whether this was the beginning of the end.

He got up for lunch a few hours later, and while he could shuffle to the table without stumbling and seemed steady on his feet, once seated he was strangely disorientated. He did not appear to be able to see the food right in front of him: he would ask for the salt and it would be within his grasp, but invisible to him. He said very little, never looked up or around him, never said that he was pleased to be home, or asked how long

I was staying. It was both as if I had always been there or was not there at all.

My mother sighed a lot and left the table as soon as possible, retreating to her room. Great.

After lunch I put on some of his favourite music, Mahler's 3rd Symphony. Within the first few bars, he recognised the recording.

'Abbado,' he said, 'and the Chicago Symphony Orchestra.'

My heart lifted; I felt he was returning gradually to the world. I congratulated myself on the inspired idea of playing him music, as if this were a direct conduit back into his consciousness and identity, as if I had instinctively plugged into the basics of music therapy. I persuaded myself that I was going to be good at this 'caring for a convalescent' business, that I had the magic touch.

He sat listening with his eyes closed, occasionally gesturing when the music swelled in a crescendo, but not, as was his habit in the past, conducting. He simply did not have the energy to wave his hands about.

He slept for the rest of the day, ate a little supper, and said he needed to go to the barber and intended to drive there the next day. He did not remember that the doctor had told him he would be unable to drive for six weeks.

At two in the morning I was woken by a shuffling sound, as if a large furry animal were snuffling around in the undergrowth. Disorientated, I thought of a ponderous wombat in the bush outside a tent, before I recognised the sound of my father's tread, then a jingling of keys, the zipping of a bag, the fumbling of chain and bolt, the turning of handle, the soft clunk of the front door closing.

Where on earth could my father be going at this hour? Having gone to bed naked, suffocated by my parents' central heating, I rummaged around urgently for a few clothes, found my non-slip socks with rubber soles, a woollen cardigan, and went to wake my mother to tell her my father had gone out. She was too sleepy to react, and just lay in bed moaning in alarm. I called the security guard downstairs and told him my father was on his way out and to stop him at the gates if possible, but the security guard told me my father had already left the building.

When I got outside it was snowing. The loose feathery kind of flakes that fall messily as if someone in the sky has burst a duvet. I could not see my father anywhere. The car was still parked in its bay, so he was on foot. I started down the road calling out 'HB, HB,' into a developing blizzard. Eventually I detected a shape ahead of me, the only person on the street at this hour. Running in my now wet socks, I came upon my father, dressed in his pyjamas, hair windswept, wearing my mother's dressing gown and his leather slippers, carrying his briefcase and leaning on a walking stick. My first thought: King Lear on the heath.

'HB, where are you going?' I asked, shivering.

'To the bank.'

'But it's two o'clock in the morning, HB. The bank is closed. Look at the sky—it's pitch dark and it's snowing. It's not safe to be out walking, you aren't dressed properly.'

My father looks up at the sky but does not seem to register the absence of light. Agitated, he is insistent and annoyed.

'I don't have time to stand here talking, I need to get to the bank.'

'Why don't we go back inside, get more warmly dressed, have a cup of tea and go in the car? I'll drive you there when it's light,' I say, reaching coaxingly for his arm.

He brushes me away, raising his cane against me, as if defending himself from an attacker. He has a wild look, like a horse when it shows too much white in its eyes and is about to kick.

'I have to get to the bank, NOW!' he shouts. 'I need to see Steve Powell.'

Steve Powell is his bank manager.

'If you want to see Steve, we can go when it has stopped snowing.'

My feet are soaking and my toes have gone numb. He does not seem to feel the cold.

'Come on, HB,' I beg him, taking him by the arm and turning him towards our building. He takes a few steps with me, yielding briefly before turning back to where he was headed before. I realise he still has a fair amount of strength.

It takes me forty minutes to persuade him to come back inside with me. I am exhausted and chilled to the core. Once inside, my father slumps, defeated, into a chair and asks for a cup of tea. I make tea for both of us and lead him, all forlorn docility, by the hand back to his bed, tuck him in, turn out the light, lock and bolt the front door and hide all the keys. I go back to bed, wondering if this is typical behaviour for someone recovering from an anaesthetic.

In the morning, it is as if this episode has never happened. My father gets up for breakfast, seems more alert and lucid, scans the newspaper and announces that he will go to the barber. I remind him that he can't drive himself and that I will take him, and he goes off to get dressed.

When he is ready to go, he says, 'I don't want you to drive, it would be better if I drove.'

I repeat the explanations with unusual patience. 'You know what the doctor said, no driving for six weeks. This is not negotiable. I know it's very frustrating, but you're not well enough yet and it would put pressure on your scar, which needs more time to heal. You know I'm a good driver, my name is registered for the car, I'm happy to drive.'

'You may be happy to drive, but I'm not happy to be driven.'

When we reach the car, the argument begins again.

'I can't let you drive,' he says and starts walking away.

Half an hour later, my father agrees to get in the car as a passenger. He gives me precise, clear directions as to how to reach the barber and where to park, and walks with clear intent. His spatial cognition seems much improved and he is in good spirits. He even praises my driving. He does not mention a desire to go to the bank, even when we walk past a branch. Suddenly he ducks into a health-food shop, somewhere he would normally avoid.

'Where are you going?' I ask, surprised.

'I need the loo,' he says. With the confidence of someone who has clearly cased the joint before, he crosses the shop floor and heads down a staircase marked 'staff only'. An angry woman tries to stop him but he brushes past her.

'Excuse me, Sir, you can't go down there, those are not facilities for customers,' she calls after him.

'Bugger off,' replies my father quietly and locks himself in the bathroom.

Mortified, I apologise and explain that he is unwell but the woman is not mollified. She is more furious than the incident warrants and instructs a male member of staff to knock on the door and tell my father he has to leave. I try to find her compassionate side, but she is obdurate and officious. My father ignores the man outside the toilet door, shuffles back up the stairs, says 'Thank you very much' briskly to the irate store manager and continues on his way.

I feel flushed with panic and embarrassment at the prospect of him being caught short further on, but we reach the barber without incident. My father's sense of direction has not let him down and he seems at home in familiar surroundings. They seat him in the chair and proceed to lather his face.

I sit behind him, watching in the mirror as the ritual proceeds. The barber, a young Lebanese man in his thirties, treats my father with courtly deference, the way I imagine his culture shows consideration to the elderly. He is respectful without being patronising. The only woman present, I am in an entirely masculine world of grooming. Other wives, sisters, mothers, daughters and girlfriends may be doing the shopping or having a coffee next door. But I don't feel I can leave my father unattended for a moment, and I quite like the atmosphere of testosterone. Generations come in to be trimmed and clipped, most of them regulars known by name, from little boys of six or seven, to men like my father. He seems to be enjoying the old-fashioned shave with a blade. It must feel clean to have the bristles he grew in hospital disappear, to have hot towels applied, to feel the caress of the shaving brush and the precision of the razor expertly handled. This is an intimate moment I have never shared with a man before. I savour its ritual and the sense of community that comes from the constant bustle and traffic of male comings and goings, greeting each other as familiar, chatting and popping back in with a coffee. When it is over, the barber helps my father on with his coat and is obsequiously grateful for his generous tip.

'Let's go next door, I want to show you their meringues,' says my freshly groomed father. The shave has restored his dignity and fastidious care about his appearance. He has new vigour, a sprightly step, a shinier eye. He seems to be able to take in more of his surroundings with every hour that passes, and I can sense that his condition and well-being are improving, like mist lifting from the landscape.

The meringues are like giant clouds piled high in the window. Their allure is irresistible. 'Your mother doesn't like it here.' He is clearly pleased that he can introduce me to somewhere I don't know, relishing the fact that we can do so without my mother's objections.

'Let's go in,' I say, playing up to his complicity in this uncharacteristically impromptu foray.

The place is buzzing with young families out being European in the backstreets of Hammersmith, having strong coffees over the weekend papers. An atmosphere of homely warmth envelops us. I would like to sit down but worry that lingering might tire my father, so we buy some Florentines the size of small pizzas and make our way back to the car.

The outing has been a success. My mother is so delighted she opens a bottle of champagne and we all toast my father's recovery, he with a sip, and us with the rest. He eats well at lunch, and for the first time in days my mother laughs. We seem to be on the right road, and the hiccup of the night is negated by the progress of the day. When I put my father to bed for a nap, he has an endearing crooked smile on his face that makes him look like a child.

But during the night I am woken again. First the soft shuffling steps, then the rattling of the chain on the front door. Instantly alert and filling with dread at how my father will react when he realises the keys are nowhere to be found, I brace myself; my ears become suddenly sharper but also thud with the sound of blood pumping as my adrenalin surges and my heartbeat quickens. I lie still and wait.

First there is some whispered swearing and cursing, next the sound of pacing up and down, of zipping and unzipping—my father's briefcase, perhaps as he searches for keys he thinks he has mislaid, then an unfamiliar scratching sound. I creep downstairs to spy on my father from over the banister. He is attempting to open the door with a credit card, the way a thief might in a crime thriller on television. The sight of him standing there in his pyjamas, sawing away futilely, is pathetic but I am not sure whether to leave him be or interrupt him. I am so tired from being disturbed again, and I don't fancy reasoning with him or making more tea and trying to get him back to bed without waking my mother. I wonder if he will go into the kitchen and try to find a sharper instrument, a knife perhaps, in which case perhaps he is a danger and a threat to our safety. Perhaps I should have thought to hide all the kitchen knives before now. I steal back up to bed and lie there, alert, wondering why this urge to go to the bank comes upon him at night. I doze, but am woken again by louder swearing and cursing, then banging. Looking over the banister again I see my father pounding his fists against the front door, a prisoner in his own home. He has woken my mother, who comes out in her nightie and looks at him, appalled.

'What do you think you're doing, Harry? It's three o'clock in the morning,' she says, as stern as a schoolmistress. I know this tone will only antagonise him and wince inwardly.

'Open the door or leave me alone,' says my father, peremptory and barely suppressing fury.

'I am not opening the door in the middle of the night. You are not well and need to go back to bed,' says my mother before turning on her heel and returning to her room.

My father continues to pound the door. I worry he will wake the neighbours.

'Hello, HB,' I say as softly and neutrally as I can. 'Is there anything I can do to help you?'

'You can open this bloody door NOW so I can go to the bank.'

'HB, it's the weekend and the bank isn't going to be open now. We'll go when it is.'

'Okay,' says my father, just like that, as if he has snapped out of a trance. He sounds just like Dustin Hoffman in *Rainman*. I take him by the hand and lead him into the living room and put the kettle on. It is another hour before I can persuade him to go back to bed.

In the morning, it is snowing. The sky is heavy with flakes that fall like kapok, swirling in gusts of wind, dancing but not settling. The view is a white-out and seals the city in a cloak of soft silence. I look out at it and feel mixture of wonder and despair. It's impossible to go out for a walk, to escape the feeling of being trapped with a stranger and his unpredictable behaviour. It feels like I'm in a Bergman or Tarkovsky movie: nothing much happens but people look out at weather and landscape, their silence pregnant with meaning.

My father appears by my side.

'It's the first time I've seen snow in London for twenty years,' I say with forced jollity as if this were a special treat or an occasion for celebration.

His eyes are dull again, with that cooked egg look that seems to veil them. 'Can you show me?' he asks, and my heart aches at the humility and innocence of the question. I point to the flakes the size of goose down tumbling and melting on our balcony, but he does not appear to register them.

'What can you see?' I ask, as neutrally as possible.

'A train,' he says dully, correctly identifying one travelling on the opposite side of the river.

'Anything else?' I hate myself for sounding so patronising.

'No,' he says. Does that mean he cannot see the Thames flowing directly in front of us? I ask him where he is and he replies with his formal address, like a child repeating important information he has learned by heart. 'Peterborough Road.'

'And where is that?'

'London SW6,' he says, again using that mechanical flat *Rainman* tone that imparts facts without emotion. He does not say, 'Home,' or, 'For God's sake, stop treating me like an idiot.'

He starts to rummage around, looking for his briefcase. When he finds it, he unzips every pocket, searching for documents. He gets out his bus pass, his passport, chequebook and some bank notes, counts them, and then puts everything back in the case.

He rubs at his leg and says matter-of-factly, 'My left foot is falling off.'

My mother and I stare at each other, equally baffled and bewildered and trying not to laugh. 'Show me,' I say, but he doesn't.

'I am surrounded by dirt,' he says, curling his mouth into a twisted expression of disgust.

*What is this?* I ask myself. Paranoia? Is he hallucinating? I call the hospital but none of the team that cared for my father are on duty. Several have gone on holiday over the Easter break. The voice at the end of the phone tells me that I will have to wait until Tuesday or else call an after-hours doctor. She gives me a number and they promise to send someone round within twelve hours.

In the meantime, I decide to pursue my music therapy method and put on some Mozart. This is no time for the brooding darkness of Mahler. I choose a jaunty, sparkling sonata but within a few bars my father says, 'What is that noise?'

'What do you mean, HB?' I assume he is joking. 'That's not noise, that's Mozart.'

'I don't care what it is. Turn it off.'

'But you love this music!'

'Turn it off. It's hurting my brain,' he says, rising to leave the room.

'Would you prefer to listen to something else?'

'No, I just want SILENCE!' he bellows.

More than any other moment now or later, this is when I realise I have lost my father. Whether the loss is permanent or temporary at this stage I don't know, but the shock is profound, devastating and goes to the core of who my father is and what he represents to me. Mozart was hardwired into his brain from the earliest days of his Viennese childhood, so that even if at some stage he failed to recognise me, I was sure he would always recognise the music with which he grew up, the holy trinity completed by Bach and Beethoven. My mother, witnessing the scene, is speechless. Music has been the one constant in my father's life, the one love he has remained faithful to no matter what, the consolation for all the disappointment he has experienced, the escape route that has offered everything from solace to pleasure. I know now that we are in serious trouble. If my father has lost the ability to enjoy music, he has lost the will to live.

CHAPTER 20

# Damaged goods

Two things compound my increasing sense of apocalypse: the snow becomes heavier and starts to settle. It will eventually go on record as Britain's heaviest in two decades, causing nationwide chaos and shutdowns. When Eurostar is forced to cancel trains, the company spokesman quoted in *The Times* blames the French for 'the wrong kind of snow'.

The white-out muffles the senses and blankets us in deadening silence. If I venture out, the ground is slippery, a perfect illustration of the uncertainty of the situation. Staying home feels stifling, but this is not weather to venture out in for anything other than necessity. As if this feeling of confinement were not bad enough, my mother and I huddle together to watch television, hoping its glow might provide the same comfort as a fire, only to hear news full of dire headlines about a financial collapse sweeping the world. I am grateful that my father is not sufficiently conscious to take in the predictions of a crash, which would provoke more alarm and anguish. On high alert for catastrophe, Maman adds the crisis to her list of woes and feelings of impending doom. For her, it's all personal.

Seeking reassurance about my father, I call my doctor friend Niki in Australia. But she does not set my mind at rest. 'Sounds like you've been sold damaged goods. You need to take him back,' she says as if referring to a faulty toaster.

I rely on her characteristic bluntness when I need the unadulterated truth. Even so I am a bit taken aback. I want her to tell me that his aberrant behaviour is quite normal for elderly people recovering from an anaesthetic, but she doesn't.

I ring the hospital again and ask them what my options are.

'You could bring him into emergency but we're pretty busy, it being Easter,' they tell me, and I wonder how on earth we could persuade my father to go back there. 'Or you could call an ambulance, but the waiting time is long,' says the hospital. I decide that's too dramatic and to wait for the out-of-hours doctor.

My weariness from sleep deprivation, combined with the stress of being permanently hypervigilant, begins to make me feel lightheaded and dizzy. My mother is so on edge she can't sit still, but she finds the sight of my father so upsetting she leaves the room whenever he appears.

It is as if all the years of resentment have eroded her capacity for simple tenderness. When my father wanders into her room to lie down on her bed instead of his own, she becomes agitated and asks him to leave. I think it would be kinder to let him lie there and fall asleep but she's having none of it, and insists on preserving her boundaries of privacy. When my father reappears later wearing her dressing gown, she overreacts instead of dismissing his mistake with a joke. She tells him sharply to take it off and give it back. Forlorn, like a bewildered child who does not understand what he has done wrong, he slumps on to her bed and says, 'I am being murdered with misery.' Exasperated, she walks out of the room. When she returns, there is a wet patch staining the carpet. She wonders aloud, indignantly, accusingly, whether it is urine and makes clucking sounds I associate with a hen. I am utterly exasperated. Who the hell cares? I don't want to investigate the nature of the damp dark patch so I just dab at it with a moistened cloth and dry it off with a hairdryer.

I am too on edge to concentrate on a book so I spend the time flicking through food magazines, fantasising about normality and cooking for friends back home. Daily calls from David only reinforce how far apart we are. I am homesick and hungry for any details that remind me of the life I have twelve thousand miles away.

A couple of hours pass peacefully while my father sleeps, and then he reappears, this time shaking with rage and stuttering incoherently.

'Jac, Jac, Jacqueline . . . come here immediately . . . listen to me, stop what you are doing and OBEY!' he screams and it looks as if he is going to fall to the floor in an epileptic seizure.

'Harry,' she says, assuming a falsely calm tone guaranteed to infuriate my father and provoke further aggression. I can hear years of baiting in her voice.

'Where, where, where is the key, the hotel room key, key, key, key, key to the car, car, car . . . ? he stammers, his hands trembling with distress and fury.

'My keys are in my handbag, your keys have been put away to keep them safe until you are well enough to go out,' says my mother sounding like the matron in a British black-and-white film set in a boarding school.

'If you like, HB, I can take you out now,' I intervene, attempting to be the peacemaker.

'Yes, I need to go out IMMEDIATELY. I will catch the bus,' he announces, making for the front door.

Here we go again.

'It doesn't run on Sundays,' says my mother, a triumphant edge to her voice.

'Don't argue with me!' yells my father. 'I will call a taxi.'

'I'll come down with you and call one for you from the front desk.' I pretend to go along with his hotel delusion and give my mother a meaningful glance that I hope will shut her up.

'And where do you think you're going?' asks my mother, all sarcasm.

'Peterborough Road,' replies my father in that mechanical *Rainman* voice again.

'But this is Peterborough Road,' says my mother, baffled.

'YOUR MOTHER IS NOT RIGHT IN THE HEAD!' screams my father, turning to me.

'You're a fine one to talk. You don't even know where you are,' my mother retorts.

'I know perfectly well we are in Paris and we have to leave NOW, NOW. NOW, you IMBECILE. Out of my way!' yells my father.

As a child, I feared my father, even when he was in a good mood. His hugs were too tight and nearly suffocated me. His pale pork-sausage fingers crushed mine when he held my hand to cross the road. His footsteps shook the landing of our home, his snores rattled its doors. It was like sharing the house with a giant. On Sundays he played recordings of classical music at deafening volume, conducting with my mother's knitting needles, bending them out of shape with the force of his strokes.

Some of his tantrums were so spectacular they became known by their location—Méribel, Vouliagmeni—like significant historical battles. After these hurricanes, he rarely apologised but might come home two or three nights later with long-stemmed roses the colour of fresh blood for my mother and plant a conciliatory kiss on her cheek.

Now I steer him out of the front door, dressed for the cold weather, and guide him to the lift. I have no idea what we are going to do when we get downstairs, but I know I have to get him out of the apartment and play along. I will just have to improvise and rely on the front-desk staff to cooperate with whatever scheme I can come up with. At least my father regards me as some kind of ally instead of the enemy, which is clearly how he views my mother.

We get down to the front desk, where my father politely asks the security man on duty to call him a taxi. I am standing behind my father and signal to the man to ignore my father's request. He knows about the previous night's escapade, and cottons on to the fact that something is not quite right. Pretending to cooperate, he appears to dial a number and request a cab, and reports back to my father that because it's Easter Sunday and snowing, there's a delay. I shoot him a covertly grateful look and follow my father towards the gates into the street, where he intends to hail a taxi. Does he still think he's in a Paris hotel, even though everyone speaks English and cars are driving on the left?

A car pulls in just as we are leaving and my father goes up to the driver, a resident in our building, and asks her if she's a taxi. I apologise and tell her quietly that my father is not well. Frustrated at every turn, he retreats to the warmth of the foyer to consider his next move. He looks beaten and close to tears.

It takes me twenty minutes, but with some gentle kisses on the cheek I persuade him to come back upstairs and wait for a taxi there. He takes my hand, suddenly biddable, and lets me lead him home, sad and confused. It's the shuffling of his feet that floods me with pity. It is such an old man sound.

Fortunately, a few moments after we get inside, the doorbell rings and the out-of-hours doctor introduces himself. He is German, which is unexpected and slightly troubling: given my father's history, could his nationality trigger a hostile outburst? It's a risk we will have to take.

Wrong-footing my apprehension, my father could not be more pleasant. The moment I introduce the doctor and he hears his slight accent, my father switches to speaking to him in his native tongue. He asks where he studied as if he were conducting a job interview, and seems lucid and rational. My mother and I exchange glances of exasperated disbelief. We need the doctor to see the ranting lunatic we've been living with for the past two days, not the sober convalescent gentleman now before us. How can my father be cunning enough to put on an act when only moments before he was totally delusional and raving? The whole thing is so spooky it makes me doubt my own sanity.

'Can you tell me where we are now, Sir?' asks the doctor.

'In Munich,' replies my father in German.

Aha.

'And what are you doing in Munich, Sir?'

'Attending a conference.'

'And where are you staying in Munich?'

'At the Four Seasons Hotel.'

'Are you travelling with anyone, Sir?'

'Yes, my wife and my daughter from Australia,' says my father, acknowledging our presence with a regally condescending tilt of the head.

'And where do you live when you are not in Munich?'

'In Paris.'

'What is your address in Paris?'

'65 Peterborough Road.'

My mother sighs heavily and rolls her eyes, shaking her head at this nonsense.

The doctor nods as if these answers make perfect sense. He takes my father's temperature and blood pressure and asks him for a urine sample. My father refuses. 'Can I go now?' he asks us testily, reverting to English. Shaking the doctor's hand, he thanks him for coming as if this were a perfectly pleasant waste of time, and leaves the room.

The doctor tells us that my father may well have an infection that is causing him to behave erratically. When we describe the violent outbursts and night-time attempts to escape, he prescribes a sedative that he says will give us some respite, but he urges us to take my father back to the hospital as soon as his team is back on board. He apologises for not being more definite or helpful.

Braving the treacherous black ice on the street, I go out to get the drugs that will calm my father's anxiety while nothing will calm my own. We have to get through another twenty-four hours before we can call my father's specialist gerontologist and ask him what the hell is going on.

Mercifully, the tranquillisers do the job. My father sleeps through the night and so do we. He's pretty dopey for the rest of the next day, which gives us some breathing space and lowers the tension in the flat, as we are not forced to be permanently vigilant. My mother and I take it in turns to go out. It's a relief to escape the state of siege, however briefly. Even a quick sortie to the supermarket provides respite for Maman, who finds cruising the aisles relaxing and goes there every day instead of doing a weekly bulk shop. It's the French way, a habit of going to your favourite local shops daily and engaging in conversations about produce, seasonality and flavour; even though that is not the London way of life, she maintains the habit as an act of cultural defiance as a true *Parisienne*.

We decide not to administer the sedative on Monday night so that the hospital can see my father in the state we've endured for the past few days. We go to bed anticipating a disruption and, sure enough, my mother is woken in the middle of the night by my father, again dressed in mismatched garments that belong to her, clawing with his bare hands at the door chain and bolt, which he has managed to unscrew from the wall. She is furious and remonstrates with him, which only escalates the tension. Meanwhile I discreetly slip into the kitchen, grab hold of all the sharp knives and hide them. Then, for the umpteenth time, I put the kettle on. What would this hellish scenario be like without the comfort of tea?

I can hear my parents rowing in the hallway and decide not to intervene. My mother walks off in a huff, leaving my father at the door like a wild animal scratching at its cage. I go out to him.

'Come on, HB, I'm really, really sorry about all this but it's night-time and we just don't think it's safe for you to go out in the cold right now. Let's wait until morning and we can sort this out,' I say as soothingly as possible. Once again, I take his hand, and kiss his cheek. Touchingly, when I do so, he makes kissing sounds in response. We drink our tea together, and I lead him back to bed, meek and compliant.

It seems like only minutes later I am being summoned to his room.

'CAROLINE!' he calls out in a tone that warns me there's trouble brewing.

'Coming!' I shout as I run down the stairs.

'You need to pack our bags; we are leaving for Paris IMMEDIATELY. Make sure you pack all my toiletries and my shoes,' he says in a voice that brooks no contradiction.

'Certainly, HB. I'll do it straightaway. Are we catching the Eurostar? Shall I order a taxi to take us to the station?'

'Yes.'

I run to my mother, who has barricaded herself into her room and is determined to avoid contact with my father, and brief her on my proposed scenario: I will pretend to pack some bags which we will have to take with us. I will order a taxi to Chelsea Hospital under the pretext that we are going to St Pancras. She shrugs a typically Gallic shrug that could mean either yes or no, but agrees to go along with the scheme. I pull together some lightweight canvas luggage and throw a few things at random into the bags. But my father is not easily fooled.

'You have not packed my mouthwash or my aftershave,' he barks.

I do so, and tell him everything is ready. He packs and repacks his briefcase, obsessively checking and rechecking that he has his documents. The taxi arrives. As my father steps into the cab, I whisper 'Chelsea Hospital' to the driver and pray we get there without incident.

When we turn onto the Fulham Road my father says 'CUNT!' loudly. I've never heard him say this word before. He's noticed that we are not on the route to St Pancras. His ability to recognise his surroundings, including his own home, has been so poor in the past few days that I had not expected him to take in this kind of detail. But this morning he does.

'It's alright. We're taking a diversion because of roadworks, HB,' I say, ashamed of my ability to lie so smoothly.

We reach the hospital, where I tell him we have to pop in and get a document signed to allow him to go overseas so soon after an operation. He offers no resistance to sitting in Emergency while I surreptitiously attempt to get him admitted. This takes longer than expected and my father becomes restless and impatient. I warn the staff that he may abscond and has an explosive temper. Every muscle in my body aches with tension. Eventually we are taken into the ward to wait for a doctor to examine him. My father protests, but only mildly.

After a seven-hour wait, my father grows increasingly restless, refuses to lie down and paces the ward threatening to leave. Our anxiety levels are so high we can barely speak. Other patients shoot hostile looks at my father, apprehensive that his abusive tone and disruptive behaviour will disturb their fragile state. I feel embarrassed and offer them furtive apologies.

Eventually, a tall handsome Indian called Dr Sharma strides into the ward and introduces himself with a firm handshake as the registrar. He has the most impeccably ironed blue-and-white striped shirt on, and looks ridiculously dashing in this dull setting. I imagine the nurses are all in love with him. He radiates confidence and purpose, and is extremely well spoken. My father, snob that he is, takes an instant shine to him when Dr Sharma says he studied at Cambridge. He asks my father a few questions. Exasperatingly, for the first time in days, my father appears to know where he is. As he did with the German doctor, he becomes polite and lucid. Dr Sharma then asks him to follow his finger as he moves it above and across my father's face.

He pulls the green plastic curtain around my father's bed and asks my mother and I to step outside it.

'We did a brain scan this afternoon and I am afraid the news is bad. Mr Baum has vascular dementia. I'm terribly sorry.'

My mother stiffens. I can see her whole body going rigid with dread as if she has been turned to stone.

'What does that mean exactly?' she says, suddenly sounding particularly French.

'It means that at some point he has experienced some small strokes, probably when he was undergoing his operation; these are like small explosions that have gone off in his brain and affected his cognition.'

'Is there a cure?' asks my mother.

'I'm afraid not,' says Dr Sharma. 'However, his condition may improve and we would like to keep him under observation so we can rule out infection, of which there is currently no sign, but just in case, we'll need to keep him in order to determine what the best care for him will be.'

'And how long will that take?' My mother's voice quivers with distress.

The doctor explains that it will take several days to assess my father and, with a small smile of condolence, excuses himself to attend to other patients. He pops his head around the curtain to speak to my father: 'Mr Baum, we are going to need to keep you here overnight, I'm afraid, but you'll be in very good hands and I'll visit tomorrow to see how you're doing.'

My father nods without protest. I know I need to get my mother home quickly before the shock sets in, or she will crumble in front of my father. We bid him a hasty farewell and take the bus home, barely speaking, each of us caught up in trying to make sense of what we have just heard. Damaged goods indeed.

# CHAPTER 21

# Cars

'Of course we'll have to sell the car.'

We are riding home on the bus from one of our daily visits to the hospital. Faced with the enormity of my father's diagnosis and its implications, my mother is struggling to gain purchase on priorities and practicalities. Her whole landscape has been reconfigured and she can't find a place to start navigating it.

The top deck of a London bus is a good vantage point for perspective. Looking down on the gridlocked traffic ahead, my mother wonders aloud: was that an early warning a few years ago when we found ourselves facing the wrong way on a motorway at night, headlights approaching at high speed, flashing their rapidly blinking alarm, my father seemingly oblivious to the disorientation, his split-second reflexes dulled, his famous sense of direction lost? Just in time, he snapped to and reversed away from the oncoming cars without apology or explanation. The incident was never discussed. Was it what is known as a silent stroke?

The car is the least of my mother's worries. But perhaps it symbolises everything that is over. Mastery and control, gone. My father's wheels have come off. He will never pull too forcefully on the handbrake again. He has crashed.

The Jag, as my father called it, was virtually a member of our family. Always upgraded with the release of each new model, and yet always replaced in the classic colour scheme of a navy-blue exterior with a walnut and maroon leather interior, conferring continuity. The Jag (which my father always referred to as a 'she') was incontestable proof of his self-made success, and he was as proud of it as he would have been of a champion racehorse. While he complained of its excessive gas guzzling, absurdly temperamental engine and expensive maintenance, he loved the fact that he could afford such an indulgence even if it made him look like a Tory when he was a dyed-in-the-wool socialist, albeit of the champagne variety.

When I was five or six years old he sat me on his lap in the driver's seat, put my hands on the ridged steering wheel, and led me in wide zigzags along the cypress-lined roads of Provence in dappled sunlight. It was as if the car were dancing, as we followed the shimmering, looping cadences of Schubert's 'Trout' Quintet recorded on an eight-track stereo cassette (the latest innovation in sound technology). I laughed at his silliness from my raised vantage point while my mother cautioned my father to stay on his side of the road with a mildly reproachful 'Harry!'

These were carefree, gilded days. My parents radiated a quiet glow of contentment and success. Papa was at his most relaxed, never more light-hearted, never more playful and at ease with me. When my hands were strong enough, he let me change gear for him, cueing me when to push the stick shift into position as he applied the pedal. Forty years later I learned from a passing remark in Mary Hughes's diary that her husband John had allowed my father to do the very same thing for him. Always eager for signs that I was worthy, I basked in the responsibility and trust this role suggested, fancying myself a co-pilot. In the car, as nowhere else, we were a team.

On Sunday mornings, my father would come to the door of the playroom and ask: 'Baby, would you like to come to the car wash?' It was rare for him to issue an invitation rather than an instruction, and I always welcomed the interruption to my homework, thinking we might stop on the way home at a local sweetshop where my father liked to bulk-buy Crunchies and Kit-Kats.

In the London of my childhood, an automated car wash was still a novelty. Papa was an enthusiast for any labour-saving device, buying the newest from American mail-order catalogue Hammacher Schlemmer, a company specialising in quirky products that solved problems you did not know you had. My favourites: a spoon with a kink in its handle so you could rest it on the lip of a jam jar; a miniature silver golf-club-shaped utensil that cooled your tea, perfect for an impatient man always in a hurry.

Other families might go to church, but we communed at the car wash: cleansed physically if not spiritually, soothed into a more serene state by the gentle rhythmic vibrations of the machines as we progressed along tracks through various stages—rinsing, sudsing, polishing. I laughed without fail when the car was pummelled, rocked slightly from side to side by the initial bursts from the water jets. I liked to watch the long fringes of fabric licking at the windscreen and feel the hum through the car door as the hard bristles whirred, buffing the duco. It was like a fairground ride without the fear.

I don't remember us talking during the four or five minutes it took to get through the wash, so perhaps my father was savouring the same sensations. I pretended the noises the machines made were a terrible storm from which we were safely protected. We emerged back into daylight, buffed by chamois cloths to a shellac shine, as if we had undergone a ritual of purification, all the tensions that encrusted the chassis of our family washed away. When the car was clean, it was possible to believe we could start again.

～

For twelve years, every weekday morning, Papa drove me to school on his way to work. The Jag fogged up with the haze of his chain smoking (Benson & Hedges Gold filter, my job to push the lighter in for him then—oh horror—deliberately inhaling that delicious first hit of burning tobacco, which blended perfectly with the slight manure smell of the car's leather upholstery). There he'd treat me more like an adult, discussing world affairs, explaining territorial disputes in the Middle East or old enmities between European nations, his grasp of history dazzling in his ability to quote from speeches, string together dates into chains of events across centuries, to draw maps of changing and disputed borders in the air, while displaying his natural aggression as a driver, a split-second reflex overtaker, tailgater and lane changer, intimidating and antagonising other drivers with showy manoeuvres.

His driving made me feel ashamed. On the passenger side I often met the irritated or more openly angry gaze of drivers he had cut in on. Sometimes I could see their lips move as they swore at him. At times I would adopt a sorrowful pleading expression as if I were his captive begging to be rescued, but no one volunteered.

Once my father had driven colleagues, they refused to get in his car ever again. Friends emerged from the back seat pale and shaken. But my mother was his most anxious passenger, sucking in her breath loudly when he almost grazed other vehicles, making small sounds like a wounded kitten. I refused to react, feigning indifference, though my *sang-froid* was merely for show.

When he needed to park in the centre of London, we would pull in to the forecourt of a hotel where he knew the concierge and I would see him hand over a fiver and say, 'Look after that for me, will you?' before we walked through Knightsbridge, Soho or Piccadilly on some retail errand. My mother found this method embarrassingly arrogant, but I liked the efficient and lordly way he could dispose of the car without having to endure the endless circling back to a meter that would run out before we had achieved our objective.

One way to humour Papa was by feigning interest in other cars, pointing out unfamiliar models and asking him to identify them, which he did with the accuracy of a birdwatcher or train-spotter. One day when I was about ten I pointed to a low-slung coupé. The unique concave curve of the roof had caught my eye.

'Papa,' I asked, 'what's that car with the bashed-in roof?'

My father laughed heartily at the description. Later, he loved to remind me of my expensive tastes by quoting that innocent question back at me. 'That, Baby, is a Mercedes 280 SL. Also available as a convertible,' he said in the caressing tone he reserved for the highest approbation.

'When I grow up I'm going to buy one of those,' I announced, demonstrating the kind of aspirational confidence my father favoured.

'Over my dead body,' my father retorted.

'Why?'

'Because it's German.'

'So?'

I knew the answer already but liked to bait my father, enjoying the ensuing argument like sport.

It always boiled down to the war. That was why my mother did not have any German equipment in the kitchen. And yet: my father was a committed Wagnerian, attending numerous performances of that most Germanic and Hitler-approved cultural Olympiad, the Ring Cycle.

This double-standard provided me with easy ammunition to taunt my father throughout my adolescence. But he always shrugged off the inconsistencies: he earned the money, he made the rules.

'But when I am older I can do what I like,' I needled.

'You can,' acknowledged my father, nodding with equable reason before delivering his ultimatum, 'but if you do that, I will disinherit you.'

He uttered the punchline threat with a satisfied smile, implying that he had amassed enough wealth for that to be a significant countermove.

⌒

By the time I was seventeen, my parents' marriage had hit an all-time low. Doors slammed regularly; weekends were punctuated by my father's shouting and my mother's tears. To escape the fighting, I enrolled in a journalism summer school in the US. Too preoccupied with their battles to exert their normal control and pleased at my ambitious initiative, they let me leave their war zone.

When term was over, my father came to meet me at the end of a business trip. He drove us from Pennsylvania to New York, finding a comfortable ease in the rhythms of Route 209 until we were stopped by a police motorcyclist and my father was fined on the spot for speeding.

'Don't tell your mother,' he said, the first time he had recruited me to such complicity. Many more instances were to follow. I never betrayed him, even going so far once as to sign a statutory declaration that I was in the driver's seat when the car was caught by a speed camera. Soon, I would be losing points on my own licence, having inherited his lead foot.

⌒

When I told my parents I was moving to Australia, my father's despair was showy and bottomless: he mourned as if his only child had been struck by a terminal illness. He begged, he cried, he pleaded, wallowing in bathos. He had escaped the Holocaust. Survived a fraudulent theft that left his business on the verge of ruin and rebuilt it. But this decision broke him.

'Baby, if you stay, I'll buy you a Mercedes 280 SL.'

I blush with shame to think how desperate he was. Enough to sacrifice a lifelong principle.

⌒

The bus nears our stop as my mother weighs up her options. She does not want to keep my father's car, though it is barely six weeks old: a sedate Prius, bought at my suggestion when Papa could no longer afford or justify the extravagance of a Jaguar and that, surprisingly, he had grudgingly come to like. She thinks it will be too hard for her to learn its silent, electric ways, and prefers to stick to her tried and true smaller, more compact Toyota Yaris.

Paralysed by the shock of my father's diagnosis, I drift around the apartment, unable to settle to any task. For distraction, I thumb through the latest edition of my father's mail-order Innovation catalogue, noticing that he has circled an invention preventing speed cameras from photographing your numberplate. Incorrigible still, at eighty.

There are other people my mother could call first, to share the news of my father's diagnosis. Only a handful, but still. Instead she calls Nomi, the unusually tall Japanese dealer who has sold my father all his cars. He has a French wife, she says, they have exchanged Christmas cards, as if this makes them close. I hear her tell him the situation in a voice shock has robbed of its normal slightly singsong intonation, as if she were on automatic pilot. He agrees to take the Prius back. Having achieved that much, she goes to bed before it is even lunchtime.

For the next few days, she remains there, her face turned to the wall, barely rising to wash or eat, never getting dressed. Like a car with a flat battery, she refuses to start. My mother has stalled. My father was her power steering.

A few days later, two psychiatrists interview my father to assess the severity of his condition and determine where he should be placed. We are invited to attend. Asked where he lives and about his interests, my father delivers an uninterrupted monologue about the build-up of traffic in the neighbourhood, detailing his frustrations with lights that have no right turn and cause crossroads to clog up.

Beyond work, history, music, theatre and food, critiquing and avoiding road congestion was one of my father's few abiding interests. It was not so much a hobby as an obsession. Nifty shortcuts without consulting maps were a source of pride in the days before sat navs. Too impatient to wait in a jam, he watched with mounting horror as London became progressively choked.

He reserved special scorn for the so-called orbital ring road M25 motorway and the proliferation of cones that marked out extensive, seemingly endless roadworks along verges. He detested bus lanes, ignored them and refused to pay the congestion tax. He made U-turns where they were forbidden and once or twice drove on pavements when he thought it necessary, adopting the methods of Parisian drivers, parking bumper to bumper into the tightest spaces, while pedestrians looked on in disbelief.

These flamboyant manoeuvres were accompanied by a near-constant correspondence with transport authorities about bottlenecks and other impediments. In one memorable letter dripping with sarcasm, he complained to the local council about their fixation with putting roundabouts in the long street where we lived, suggesting that if it were to become a truly Olympic equestrian course, it might benefit from the additional hurdle of a water-jump.

Cars, too many cars, filled his consciousness, together with battles over parking restrictions, one-way streets, speed bumps and the absence of zebra crossings. Now he responded to all questions as someone literally driven round the bend.

I delayed taking the car back to Nomi, dreading the burial-like finality of it. I told myself it was just another chore on a 'To do' checklist that never seemed to get any shorter, no matter how many items I ticked off. When it could be put off no longer, I emptied the car of the last evidence of my father's ownership and disconnected the sat nav he argued with so vehemently, shouting at the synthetic syllables of its implacably calm female voice when he disregarded her instructions. Unplugging that cable felt like switching off life support.

I drove to the showroom taking back roads, lingering behind the wheel, switching on the heated seat for that cosy electric-blanket feeling of comfort. But nothing could stop me shivering as I approached my destination. I asked for Nomi at reception. Before I knew it, a slim elegantly suited man stood behind me, all stillness and solemnity. He bowed lightly with the upper half of his long torso. There was an awkward moment while I wondered how to respond, before stretching out my hand for him to shake. He took it with his head still lowered.

'Mercedes 280 SL, still your favourite car, yes?' he asked, attempting to lighten the mood. Getting no response, he tried again. 'Prius your idea, yes?'

Choked for words, I could only nod.

'Perhaps Mr Baum will make good recovery?'

I shook my head.

'I am very sorry,' he said, presenting me with papers to sign.

I could not see them clearly. My eyes swam with tears, spilling down on to forms about vehicle registration.

I rested my forehead on the cool clean glass surface of the desk.

'Perhaps some tea?' suggested Nomi.

Brushing the tears away, I wrote my name, left the car keys and exited wordlessly, stumbling between new models on display to the bus stop. I got on the first bus that came, knowing it was the wrong one, not caring, just wanting to be taken away from that place as quickly as possible.

Such a mundane chore. It was one of the saddest days of my life.

# CHAPTER 22

# The Os and Qs

The social worker assigned to my father's case has multiple piercings. I try not to let this distract or unsettle me but I find myself wondering about what it is meant to signal, since it is such a public, prominent decoration.

I always thought that social workers were for other people. People who were poor, uneducated, lost in a system whose codes they did not understand. I never expected, as a middle-class educated professional woman, that the fate of my father would hinge on an assessment made by a badly paid public servant. I thought social workers were for single mothers, heroin addicts, the unemployed, the mentally ill and the disenfranchised. In other words, I was pig-ignorant and a snob to boot. We were used to paying our way and paying for the best, thank you very much. We were not dependent on welfare, even if ideologically, we supported the existence of the welfare state. But I am about to become totally dependent on how one man interprets my father's situation.

It is getting urgent. My father is marooned in a ward in which he does not belong, where his behaviour is disruptive and distressing to patients and staff alike. He is giving nurses Chinese rope burns, touching them inappropriately, spouting obscenities, throwing food around, slipping into other people's beds, stealing their medication and causing chaos in the middle of the night, screaming that he is being chased and kicked by gangs that want to kill him. Sometimes he grabs the phone at the nurses' station and wakes my mother in the middle of the night, sobbing that he is being tortured. 'Bring money, bring my keys and my passport,' he begs. One night he calls and tells her to steal a car. When I visit him the following afternoon he is sitting on the edge of his bed chewing the bedsheets. Another time he asks my mother to remove his leg. When she pretends to oblige on the left, he says, 'No, the other one.' When she repeats her attempt on the right, he points to empty space, to a third limb that is not there, but that he wants gone.

A few days later, a nurse calls us at home, sounding sheepish. 'We have lost Mr Baum.'

'What do you mean, lost?' my mother asks sharply.

It seems he managed to leave the ward with a group of visitors and that his absence was not noticed for several hours. The police have been called and are searching the area. It is cold and dark. He is inadequately dressed, having left his jacket and footwear behind.

Six hours later, dishevelled, disoriented and shivering, he is returned to the hospital's front desk by a kind stranger who has found him wandering the side streets.

At the suggestion of his medical team, we try to have him sectioned, but his psychosis does not match the admission criteria. For the second time in his life, my father is a refugee.

⌒

After reviewing my father's case notes, the social worker suggested that I go and have a look at a few nursing homes funded by the state, where he would be entitled to admission if the National Health Service (NHS) decided to offer him what they called continuing care.

Continuing care is a British scheme that pays for the total funding of an individual's needs in a nursing home. It is only available to a small percentage of the most extreme cases. As one nursing home administrator put it to me bluntly: 'You have to be half-dead to be eligible.' The alternative, if one does not fulfil the criteria, is self-funded care—which is very costly. The average private nursing home in the UK charges around one thousand pounds a week for its services at a basic level. It goes up substantially for residents who require more personalised attention.

Assessment for continuing care is determined by a panel of psychologists who rate key factors such as poor cognition, lack of ability to feed oneself and incontinence. In order to be entitled to the scheme, you have to score highly in at least two of these categories. Then there has to be room for you at the appropriate facility in your area—not based on where you live, necessarily, but the area under the jurisdiction of the hospital by which you have been referred. There is a complex network of health trusts to navigate as part of this process, and it is almost impossible to understand how it all works. Suffice to say that it is a procedure as frustrating and as byzantine as trying to get your child into the right school if they have special needs.

My father would be assessed in the coming few days, and in the meantime we could visit some of the available nursing homes. The social worker advised me that some places would automatically rule themselves out as they could not provide the level of security necessary to deal with a client who wandered and showed a tendency to attempt to abscond. I thought immediately of the distinction between maximum and low-security prisons.

We agreed right away that proximity to home was an important factor. The facility needed to be somewhere my mother could either drive to easily or get to by public transport with minimal fuss. We shortlisted three places and steeled ourselves to visit them. Phone calls determined that there was no availability at one of them, where the waiting list was already long. That left two. We decided to knock them off in one go to get it over with.

Both of the places we visited were staffed by women from the Philippines, often recruited together from villages so that, at least, when they come to an unfamiliar new country, they are with their friends. The nursing homes were almost identical. Contrary to what we expected, neither place smelled particularly bad—no lingering cooking smells or the choking vapours of disinfectant masking bodily functions. Dining rooms looked cheerful, staff smiled greetings at us in corridors, there were flowers, both fresh and artificial, on windowsills, pictures on walls. But the lounges were dismal.

This was where residents were parked while their rooms were cleaned, or waiting for family and friends to visit, abandoned to the mercies of daytime television. Most were asleep or semi-awake, dribbling, coughing or nodding off. 'We call them the Os and Qs,' said a friend who has long-term experience of visiting such places. 'The Os have their mouths open, the Qs have their tongues hanging out.'

Hacking or rasping provided a constant background noise of throat-clearing punctuated by the occasional snore, grunt or moan.

So this, I thought, is Purgatory.

My mother and I scrutinised noticeboards to get an idea of the in-house activities organised to keep residents stimulated. In one, there was a pat-dog scheme, in which a trained, licensed dog comes in to be stroked on a weekly basis; in the other, cake decoration and flower arrangement were the only two programs. We could not see my father engaging in either.

On the way home, my mother tried to persuade herself, and me, that either of these places would be tolerable. I knew they were not and that my father would wither and die if he were left there. Defeated, we went to bed early.

Once it became clear that Papa would never be coming home, I had moved into his room, where the bed was more comfortable than the futon in the spare room. Now, as I lay on my side, listening through the thin walls to my mother tossing and turning, the mattress gave way with an audible sigh, almost toppling me off the edge. Could anything be more symbolic than its sagging springs collapsing?

It was as if the bed sensed that its rightful owner had been usurped and was rejecting me. Or maybe it was sympathetic and merely expressing the state I was close to. Rolling to the other side, which had not caved in, I listened to honking geese flying over the Thames, racking my brains as to how we could convince the authorities that there had to be a better alternative than the places we had seen.

In the morning, I remembered that Carolyn, a friend from my earliest schooldays had a grandmother in a nearby nursing home. Knowing that her family were successful Jewish businesspeople who enjoyed high standards, I could not imagine they had chosen anywhere that was less than five star. I gave her a call.

'Look no further than Nightingale House,' Carolyn said. Her certainty made me feel immediately reassured. She explained that her family had 'researched exhaustively, believe me, and would have preferred somewhere near their home in St John's Wood, but were prepared to schlep to Wandsworth on the other side of the city. Because it's worth it.'

Wandsworth—right on my mother's doorstep. It seemed too good to be true, but this was the kind of endorsement I could trust from a discerning source. Her father, Carolyn added, happened to be on the board of Nightingale House, and could fast-track us if there was any problem. Within minutes, she rang back to say the CEO was expecting my call and looking forward to welcoming me and my mother to inspect the premises.

We were there half an hour later, a bit surprised by the grandeur of the façade, which looked like that of a stately home. Nightingale House, a plaque by the entry told us, was formerly the home of a lord mayor of London until it was donated to a Jewish charity.

We were greeted at the door by the director, who took us into the sunny café and asked about our situation. He nodded sympathetically, putting our minds at ease straightaway that there were places available immediately for either short- or long-term respite care or permanent residence, and that individuals could come to Nightingale either on a private self-funding basis or under the auspices of the NHS. There was special unit for high-risk dementia patients, and he suggested we take a walk around it. My mother, visibly tense, relaxed a little when it emerged that the director had a French wife and sent his children to my school. Tribalism and its little details can be very reassuring at such times.

We noticed that rooms were slightly smaller than in the other two facilities we had inspected, and were told that this was because residents were encouraged to spend as little time as possible in them, with a range of activities that were meant to keep them interested and active. These included a music appreciation and film society, French conversation classes and a reading group run by former Tory MP Edwina Currie, whose membership included several vigorous centenarians. We were shown an art studio where residents learned pottery and ceramics; a fully equipped physio and fitness centre; a theatre with a raised stage and cinema projection; extensive gardens with benches, gazebos and fountains;

small lounges for private family gatherings; and larger rooms for watching television. The place felt busy and dynamic, as if everyone was occupied rather than in God's waiting room. Every resident's door featured a photograph of them, and the date was clearly displayed on each floor. The staircases between levels were secured with gates, and there was a security man at the front door to make sure that no one could wander off and get lost. The menu for the week was posted on every floor and varied weekly. It was, of course, strictly kosher. We declined a visit to the synagogue.

'Actually, our religious counsellor is away with some of our residents this week,' the director mentioned. We nodded polite interest. 'He's taken a group of them to Paris for a few days.' We struggled to imagine the logistical challenges of such an outing, but were too shy to ask. 'They went on Eurostar,' he added, registering our curiosity. Suddenly, old age and infirmity were not looking quite so bad.

The very existence of Nightingale House lifted our spirits. It became the benchmark against which we measured the other options and we realised there was no choice. But would they accept him as an NHS patient and would he pass the relevant assessment? My mother was adamant that she could not afford the fees. As far as I was concerned, nothing less would do. I could not have my father's well-being on my conscience. But would the NHS pay for what was clearly a much more costly facility than the ones it had suggested to us? Nightingale was the Ritz by comparison with the cheap motels they had nominated.

The burden of the responsibility for doing the right thing was so oppressive that it made it impossible to think of anything else. I felt more alone than at any other point in my adult life. As in childhood moments of desperation, I reverted to my childhood habit of asking myself what my favourite fictional heroines would do: except now, instead of Scarlett O'Hara or Jo March, I turned to the always level-headed and crisis-cool C.J. Cregg in *The West Wing*. I watched a couple of episodes to try to boost my morale, but this was no political scandal or policy conflict.

That's when I realised: the thing no one tells you about being an only child is that it really hits home when you are an adult. None of the attention lavished on a singleton can help or prepare you for the level of responsibility when your parents need you. Suddenly I understood, in the starkest possible terms, that there was no one to share that burden and sense of duty with. My husband was far away and unfamiliar with the care landscape I was trying to navigate. Apart from Carolyn, friends were at a loss: none of them had yet faced a similar situation.

I wanted to do the right thing by my father. One of his favourite mottos was 'Nothing but the best'. He had always tried to give me that and now it was my turn to do the same for him. But it seemed perverse to hope that when it came to the assessment, my father would behave as badly as possible and be seen as an extreme and therefore deserving case.

At about 3 a.m., the classic hour of despair, it came to me, lying on the uneven lumpy mattress, almost in a blinding flash, except that I was too weary and strung-out for anything so energising. I began to sweat. Of course. How could I have been so stupid? I had forgotten to tell the social worker the one crucial piece of information that could determine where my father was cared for. It had determined his fate once before. Now, it just might again.

I could not wait for it to become light, for me to be able to get on the phone, to start preparing my case. I knew what I had to do. I lay in bed, plotting and strategising. Then I went to the computer and wrote a three-page report about my father's childhood.

As soon as I could, I rang the social worker.

'I need to come and talk to you,' I said.

He agreed to meet me at the hospital in half an hour.

When we found each other in the coffee shop, he was with a slight young woman in faded denim jeans. He introduced her as the colleague to whom my father's case had been assigned. It was her job to find the suitable placement for him, and she would be making a recommendation to the panel after seeing my father, talking to me, and hearing what the specialist psychiatrists had to say. I realised that this young woman, who looked barely out of her teens, wielded tremendous power over our case. I knew that my appeal to her had to strike an emotional chord. I needed to make her care. Perhaps those hours watching C.J. were not wasted after all. What I needed was to channel her skills and lobby eloquently and persuasively for my father.

Almost immediately, the ice was broken when she revealed that she had studied in Melbourne. The fact that she had been to Australia created a bond of kinship as we joked about how obsessed Australians are with good coffee, and how dreadful the coffee in England is. She turned out to be Swedish and I stored that fact away, knowing I could use it when my time came.

While we made small talk, I was preparing a performance. I keyed myself up for what I knew were the most decisive and crucial minutes of my life. Every bit of skill I have in communicating, in creating a quick and warm rapport, in reading body language from years of interviewing people, came into play. I tried to access the adrenalin that always energises me at live events, when it seems to sharpen my brain and make my responses smarter.

I am not an actor. Despite years of work as a television presenter, I'm self-conscious. I cannot improvise or speak off the cuff, and get paralysed by nerves before any public event. I have never understood how some actors can cry on demand. But I knew I would have to cry now; in the heightened state I was in, sleep-deprived, psyched up, frayed with emotion and anxiety, it was not that hard.

'I need to tell you something important about my father,' I said, and almost immediately the tears started to fall. 'I have written it down for you in more detail but the simple main point is that he had his identity stolen from him once and I am not prepared to let that happen to him again.'

It was easy to cry now, choked by the significance of the moment. Though I was in a public place I did not care who saw or heard me, or how I looked, or that my voice quavered and wobbled and suddenly shot up an octave like a pubescent boy whose vocal chords are still working out which register to speak in. I knew I had their attention. I did not want to overwhelm them with too much information, and knew I had to keep it short, to maximise the impact of my story.

'My father is Jewish,' I said. 'He was taken from his parents in Vienna when he was ten as part of a refugee rescue operation for children in Europe in 1938. He lost his father in the Holocaust and was adopted into a family here in England after several traumatic episodes. He made a life here but never really recovered. He needs to be looked after somewhere he can hear Jewish words and prayers and eat Jewish food.'

The two social workers hardly nodded, and said nothing, but I knew there had been a subtle shift, like a mild change in the weather. The moment was intense, the silence pregnant. I looked straight into their eyes, trying not to blink from the constant wash of tears.

I wasn't lying, exactly. But I was, as my father would have said, being economical with the truth. He had never gone to a synagogue, never chosen to belong to a Jewish community or eaten kosher food, although he had a fondness for traditional Yiddish dishes such as potato *latkes* and herrings in dill sauce. Once, when we visited Jerusalem, we had a chance to take part in the traditional Friday-night seder (sabbath) dinner at the King David Hotel, but my father opted for the coffee shop instead. I think he did not want to be embarrassed at not knowing the ritual or the prayers that would be said. But the fact of the matter is that he was born into the Jewish faith. Now was not the time to argue over the semantics of Semitism. Now was a time to convince these two people, and any others I needed to persuade, that this was the single most important fact about my father's sense of self.

I turned to the young Swedish woman.

'After the war, my father worked to set up the travel arm of the National Union of Students, and at that time he became friends with your countryman Olof Palme,' I said, knowing this would impress her. Palme had gone on to become the distinguished and much-loved socialist prime minister of his country, until he was murdered by an assassin's bullet. My father mourned him as one of his fallen heroes. C.J. would have approved of my calculated comment.

The case manager nodded almost imperceptibly. I handed her a copy of my three-page report on my father. She immediately started to read, her colleague craning to do so too. I let the stillness of the moment resonate, as if we were not in a busy place with strangers milling all around us. We had created an oasis, just the three of us, and I did not want to hurry and break the spell. I knew the longer they spent with me now in this state, the more invested they would be in representing my father's interests.

The young woman looked up. Perhaps there were tears in her eyes, I couldn't be sure, because they were already such limpid pools.

'I promise you that I will be the best advocate for your father. I will make sure we get him the care he deserves,' she said. Her colleague smiled encouragingly. I felt a surge of relief in my body, like warmth flooding my veins. Human connection is so mysterious. When it is genuine and sincere, you just know. I felt sure I could trust them.

'Thank you, thank you,' I said, the tears flowing hot and free as we stood and shook hands. 'I am counting on you. I have to go home to Australia in a few days. I cannot leave my mother to cope ... breakdown ... no other family ...' I said, my sentences getting more incoherent and shorter as my distress increased. 'I'm an only child,' I finished, worn out.

'We will do our best to see if we can speed things up because of the circumstances,' said the young woman. 'We'll be in touch. Try not to worry. You've done the very best you can in helping your father. Now I'll go upstairs and meet him.'

I prayed that he would be on his worst behaviour and then felt like a traitor for the thought.

'Tell him you're Swedish,' I urged. 'He'll like that. If only this country were as compassionate as yours in the way it looks after the elderly,' I said, shaking my head. 'You should be very proud of your country.'

'Thank you,' replied the young woman, with a big open smile. 'I am.'

I cried all the way home, when it no longer mattered, staring out of the window of the bus. I cried with gratitude at finding people who seemed to care, who radiated integrity and kindness. I cried because C.J. had come to my rescue. And because my father would never know what I had done.

# CHAPTER 23

# Scammers

When my father was a boy and fear was spreading through Vienna's Jewish community, con artists preyed on families, promising schemes to secure their most precious possessions. One claimed to have arranged a special shipment of bicycles to Australia, filling their inner tubes with small valuables and jewellery. My father's trusting family handed over whatever modest treasures they possessed.

After I told my father that I was going to live in Australia, he said that perhaps I could investigate the fate of those bicycles. Some part of him still believed they really had made the journey across the world, their tyres filled with gemstones and precious metals. Perhaps some unsuspecting child or postman was cycling along a dirt road or a suburban street, crunching on diamonds and rubies.

He never had much luck with jewellery: in the lead-up to my twenty-first birthday, relations between us were at a new low, so I was surprised when Papa called a temporary ceasefire with a showy box of red leather tooled with gold, which I immediately recognised as the livery of Cartier.

When I opened it, my heart sank. Inside was what could only be described as a manacle: a single wide band of yellow gold, fixed with two impossibly fiddly screws. A little leaflet explained that this was 'A Love Bracelet' and the symbolic act of bolting it on expressed eternal devotion. Looking at the small gold screwdriver nestling in the satin lining of the box, I could only think of a handcuff or fetter symbolising bondage and servitude. I loathed it. My father evidently attributed no such sinister meaning to this showy status piece.

Anxious by nature, my mother found a new reason to worry; she fretted about a trend she had heard of on television: hit-and-run motorcycle thieves. If they found that their simple snatch-and-grab technique did not work, might they not slice off my hand to get at the gold? I promised to wear it tucked inside my sleeve whenever I was outside. My father insured it for a hefty sum. I screwed the cuff on dutifully. At any of our encounters, my father would examine it closely to see if I was taking proper care of his precious gift as if it were an investment.

Once I was out of sight in Australia, I took off what I thought of as a shackle—the symbolic irony of doing so in a land settled by convicts was not lost on me. I told my father I had placed it in a bank vault for security reasons as we had no safe at home.

As the price of gold soared, I wondered about selling it, thinking that I could buy something far more practical with its considerable worth. But guilt at ridding myself of his gilt made me hesitate, until one day I decided to take it to Cartier in Sydney to have it valued. The saleswoman greeted with me with deference. But the look on her face changed abruptly when I handed her the bracelet. Examining it with a magnifying glass held in her eye socket, she looked suddenly affronted, as if the gold band had emitted an unpleasant smell.

'Just one moment,' she said with abrupt rudeness before disappearing into a back room for a considerable length of time. She emerged with a look of contempt.

'Where did you buy this?' Her tone was bristling and brusque, not normally associated with luxury brand customer service.

'It was a gift—' I replied, summoning all the haughty dignity I could muster to add '—from my father,' as if the provenance would silence all doubt.

'We don't think it's ours. We'll have to send it away for verification,' she said, walking me to the door as if trying to evict a drunk and disorderly vagrant.

Out on the pavement, I felt disoriented by shock. My father never, but never, knowingly bought copies or knock-offs from markets; he was not interested in those kinds of bargains. He preferred the snob value of flagship stores, where his status was burnished with fawning and fussing, savouring the accoutrements and accessories that went with his purchases: the stiff cardboard boxes stamped with luxury brand logos, elaborate wrapping rituals and occasional little extras offered to regular patrons. There must be some mistake.

Six weeks later I received a peremptory letter from Cartier HQ in Paris. The bracelet was guilty as charged: a fake. In passing sentence, the company informed me that it had the legal right to impound and destroy it but had chosen not to, accepting that it had been given to me as a gift by a family member in good faith and had sentimental worth. I was to sign a contract guaranteeing that I would not offer it for sale as a Cartier Love Bracelet, or have it valued or insured as such. Doing so would result in prosecution.

Clearly, my status-symbol-conscious father had been royally scammed. But where? And how? He had bought me the bracelet on a trip to Rio and New York, where Cartier had two of their most prominent stores. Could this be an inside job, part of some elaborate criminal network? My father had been taken for a ride before. Shopping was one of his few hobbies and forms of relaxation. Protective of his dignity, I dared not ask him for details and risk humiliating him.

∼

While we were waiting for the verdict on my father's care, my mother collapsed in on herself. She slept all day to keep the world at bay, hardly touching food. The air in the apartment became at first stale with misery and then sour, like the smell of curdled milk. It was the stench of grief, oozing from my mother's pores like a sweat of sadness. Afraid to leave her alone, as she hinted at contemplating suicide, I stayed on, drifting between hospital visits. In an effort to create order, I cleaned and ironed: I needed visible results. On the rare occasions my mother got up for an hour or two in the afternoons, I distracted her with cupboard-sorting projects, but she was too lethargic to make decisions and too anxious to part with a single item, whether it was out-of-date spices or broken buttons. Overwhelmed by my parents' hoarding habits, I attempted to declutter. I wanted one task that would absorb and distract me, and make me feel that I was making tangible progress.

I went upstairs to my father's desk, the no-go sanctum he never allowed anyone to interfere with. I started to sort through his copious papers to see if there were outstanding bills to be paid, and to look for the instructions and guidelines he was always drafting about what to do 'in the event of my death'. As I sifted through files marked 'Insurance', 'Health Care', 'Car Records', other papers fell out covered in lurid graphics and noisy headlines.

Following the failure of the *rösti* venture, my father had signed up to several US-based gambling schemes and, despite pleading from my mother, was sending them money regularly. These proliferated, mushrooming out of control, so that he was receiving multiple appeals to win his life's fortune every day. Eventually recognising that he had got himself into a pickle, my father took himself off to a local meeting of Gamblers Anonymous. He found it so helpful that he attended for a further three nights in a row before declaring himself cured. That lasted six weeks. He had then relapsed, resorting to secrecy to hide his shameful habit, concealing the lottery correspondence.

The volume of it was staggering: I filled three large green garbage bags with it in a matter of hours. The quantity of paper was bad enough, the promises of imminent wealth patently ludicrous, but there was more. Among the pseudo cheques and the fake certificates of winnings there was a new twist: letters from clairvoyants with exotic names.

One was called Dame Antineas de Phénicée. Describing herself as *'Spiritualist, Numerologist, and Internationally Sworn Expert'*, she looked like a benign elderly maiden aunt in the black-and-white photograph on her letterhead. Dame Antineas congratulated my father on his discernment, *'and for your will to rid yourself of the burdens that have been weighing so heavily on you for such a long time'*. In that, she showed rare insight into his state of mind—at least he must have thought so. She promised to reveal to him the secrets of golden numbers of luck and fortune that would enable him to win really big sums in games of chance. Once he had done that, she vowed to send him more information on a *'fabulous gold piece'* to use to win scratch games, a coin charged with a power to fight bad luck and to protect against failure.

Another called herself Princess Zahia, a slave girl who apparently became a princess and lived in a non-specific Desert Emirate. Her photograph made her look like a middle-of-the-range escort, her dark hair cascading wildly, her feline eyes heavily kohled, her long neck emphasised by a broad choker of diamanté strands. Zahia's promises were couched in far more lavish and exotic terms. She introduced herself as a gorgeous bird living in a gilded cage: *'I am forbidden from going far from my*

Golden Palace where I have lived for several years. Consequently, I have many hours carefully chosen to bring you two gifts in my Princess hands which are among the most precious in the world: Love and Wealth.'

She continued somewhat breathlessly: 'My sumptuous magical residence has the incredible capacity of constantly reinforcing my supernatural powers of clairvoyance. I am writing to you in absolute secrecy, because during the last night of the Full Moon, three cards detached themselves from Nkonde's statuette [whatever that is]. They scattered your name in Golden Dust on my glass table and have shown three Directions of Life which are extremely precious for you.'

She became more intimate with each paragraph: 'I have to warn you, Harry, that from now on your first name and your surname are engraved in the pink granite wall in my bedroom. From now on I am living in total spirituality with you and with your mind.'

Then she reminded him of her own modest origins and the hardships she had endured: 'Often elements of my life as a little girl come back to me, when we lived with my very poor parents, on the banks of the Wadi Allaqi in Ethiopia . . . Like you, I have suffered. Like you, pain was imposed on me which was not mine. I did not have the choice to live the life that I wanted to. The overwhelming misfortune of which you are a victim, troubles of all kinds, are the source of intense frustration and a feeling of failure which emerges slyly in each of your thoughts. Yet I feel that you refuse to see yourself as a defeated person. I sense that deep down inside there is a rage to conquer, to elevate yourself above your current situation, to succeed.'

Zahia, is, at this point, truly telepathic.

Some of these letters came with gifts that purported to be talismans of magic and good fortune. There was a bingo pebble, meant to maximise winnings if you rubbed it before playing. Dame Antineas helpfully sent a bottle of oil, called Golden Fluid and containing glitter, which you were supposed to rub onto your hands. Its magic extract would, she wrote, attract luck and winning game numbers: *'It is a very special potion of grand occult powers having the ability to attract luck like a magnet. I suggest you reserve the Fluid for big jackpots.'* On the side of the bottle the contents were listed as liquid paraffin, triglyceride, perfume, polyethylene and prunus amygdalus dulcis (otherwise known as sweet almond oil). The label said the stuff was made by the Laboratoire Eliane, which listed its address as 140 Avenue des Champs-Elysées, no less.

Another self-styled clairvoyant and expert in divinatory sciences calling herself Maria Sarah had a more homely, almost rent-a-granny appearance, her smiling face appearing above a photograph of druids in a ceremony at a circle of monoliths next to the headline: *'Mr Baum, You have personally been granted a unique favour of prosperity and fortune so you are certain to receive in a very short time one hundred and eighty five thousand pounds.'*

Maria Sarah continued in finer print: *'My dear Harry, place your hand on your heart and prepare to jump for joy!'*

She went on to report that she was just recently back from a gathering in Brittany at a sacred circle for the ritual of 'Lunasad', which allowed three lucky people to benefit from a powerful magic gift of prosperity, at which my father's name was chosen and witnessed by hundreds of extra-talented mediums.

Over the next six pages she described the cult of the 'oracle of Ogham', illustrated with pictures of leaves from magic trees, before urging my father to spin a magic wheel of cardboard she had enclosed that would determine secret predictions for his future well-being, to be revealed in her next letter on receipt, naturally, of a cheque for thirty-two pounds (payable in two smaller monthly instalments if preferred, presumably to make it easier for pensioners on a limited budget).

To top it off, a fortune-teller named Julie Haley claimed to be able to marshal the precise number of clairvoyants required to help my father to win fabulous sums of money, saying: 'You need massive help . . . you need the total investment on not just one clairvoyant, 10 or 25 clairvoyants, but well and truly 57 clairvoyants, mediums and astrologists working in unison.'

Apparently the failure of an earlier attempt by a single medium had been blocked by my father's 'Nadis canal', which paralysed his 'Ener Chakral' when a detestable person cast a harmful influence over him creating a vast energy field filled with negative waves. Julie promised to do some Karmic work and in the meantime would send him a free 'Energital Captor' to ensure more financial wins when harmonised to his energies. All this in return for a modest donation, with options to tick a box for anything between thirty-five and twenty pounds. A bargain, wouldn't you say?

The small print at the bottom of all the payment forms is illuminating: 'The writer of this message may not be as per the photo and identity shown' and 'Due to the very nature of the proposal,

*where the user's conviction is essential, we are not bound by any*
*absolute obligation.'*

I find the bingo pebble and the magic oil at the back of a
desk drawer together with several strings of plastic fake pearls,
charms, shells, amulets and other dross my father had been
sent as free gifts. As if it were not bad enough that my father
had not automatically binned this garbage, most heart-rending
of all is a file of his handwritten draft replies to some of these
clairvoyants:

> *My dear Maria Sarah,*
> *I think that both my hand and my heart would function much*
> *better if I placed my hand on YOUR HEART.'*

He continues in a somewhat disturbing and threatening vein:

> *It is unlikely that you will escape from being put across my knee . . .*
> *there will come a time when it will be necessary and appropriate*
> *for you to ask (even BEG) for a ministration upon your derriere.*
> *Girls cannot be expected to administer one hundred and eighty five*
> *thousand pounds without.*

He then changes gear to complain about his recent frustration when attempting to bank two previous cheques issued
by Maria Sarah only to be declined by a bank clerk who told
my father they were *'a joke'*. One minute I am flooded with
revulsion at his pathetic threat of a playful beating, the next
I ache while visualising my father's confusion. I picture him

taking the bus along Wandsworth High Street, wearing the cap he has adopted to keep his bald head warm but that is so at odds with his former dandyish aesthetic. He has become just another old fella with a bus pass going up to the shops. I imagine him stooping to present his cheque to the teller, only to be dismissed, a pathetic elderly man who has been taken for a ride he does not understand.

Addressing an Australian lottery outfit, he fights back in a more familiar professional tone as an aggrieved consumer who recognises he has been exploited: *During the last few months I became the victim of your almost daily mailings and due to your promotional pressure came close to a nervous breakdown. Over the same period I allowed myself to be taken for a rather expensive ride by a total of approximately fifty Yanks . . . then you and your crew intensified your barrage to such an extent that I didn't and don't know whether I've won minus zero or not even that.*

He pleads to be removed from their mailing list. Of course they ignored his request, bombarding him with literature.

I am dumbfounded. To me, my father was still a rational man with a formidable analytical brain. But here, now, on the page, a stranger reveals himself to me: someone who was filled with doubts, seeking reassurance and certainty, asking for further details about the clairvoyants and their promises. How had they got his name? How did they know the troubles he had? When would the money come? Into which account? By when? He had sent several cheques already and had still not received anything: could there have been some mistake? His gullibility makes me feel ashamed and embarrassed on his behalf, but also amazed at how he had been able to hide his befuddled ramblings from us and maintain a façade of normality. It is disturbing to think that half the time when he was at his desk purportedly putting his affairs in order, he was clandestinely scrambling them into a further mess, as if a scrim of dementia had descended like a fine gauze over his consciousness.

He mentioned his upcoming cancer surgery in a lame appeal for sympathy that also betrayed his fear at facing the ordeal. I did not recognise my father. How long had he been like this? How much money had he actually sent to these people? The correspondence from them was ominously large, and my mother estimated that he was receiving forty or fifty envelopes a week from lotteries in various states. No wonder she was beside herself about it.

When she first became alarmed, she rang the British Consumers' Association, which told her there was nothing they could do to protect people against these sorts of scams; they were commonplace but did not fall within the jurisdiction of the European Union. The association pointed out that while many of the lotteries appeared to originate in the US, they were in fact based in other countries, including Australia, where the Australian Competition & Consumer Commission (ACCC) was aware of their existence but powerless to stop them. I make a mental note to find out more when I get home. In the meantime, I decide to Google Dame Antineas, just for the hell of it. Perhaps she has her own website where she offers more personalised predictions.

I find no such thing, but her name does come up on something called 'The Database of Scammers', which is where I read the following:

Posted by maxwellsteer:

*Jan 8 2007*

*My mother was addicted to scammery and probably gave away 40–50 thousand pounds in the preceding six years. She was certainly shelling out around 800 pounds a month when I and my siblings decided the situation was intolerable. There was no surface in her house on which anything could be put down. All were covered with foot-high piles of 'scamvelopes'. Way ahead was a conglomeration we think is called Black Tacos who either operate through 12 aliases or otherwise are a mailing house selling suckers' addresses to both lottery and psychic fraudsters such as 'the High Commission of International Games' or the preposterously named Dame Antineas de Phenicie. (sic)*

Now, like my father when he was robbed by Hamlett Isaacs, I too entertain murderous thoughts.

# CHAPTER 24

# Three women
# (Part one)

*'There were three of us in the marriage, so it was pretty crowded.'*

PRINCESS DIANA TO BBC *PANORAMA*

I am so anxious waiting for the news about whether my father has passed the requirements for admission to Nightingale House that I can find no useful way to make the minutes pass. I dare not leave the phone or my mother for more than a few moments. My neck and shoulders ache with a burning tension, I am so stiff I can barely turn my head. After days of unbearable suspense, the social worker calls and cannot conceal his pleasure in giving me the good news. At last, something positive.

Jubilant, I grab a bottle of champagne, jump on the bus and thrust it into his hands. He looks puzzled. 'I was just doing my job,' he says. 'But thank you, and good luck. Your father is one of the lucky ones.' It's hard to see it like that but I remind myself that I must.

At home, in a rare moment of respite from the gloom, my mother insists on opening more bubbles, a small celebration of a big victory. 'To you,' she says and I feel my heart ready to split. Mission accomplished, I book my return journey to Australia. I have no idea how my mother is going to cope on her own, but I simply have to leave. She gives my decision her blessing, but cannot conceal her dread. I promise to return in six weeks.

The day after I leave, my father is transferred by ambulance to his new home. He is calm but disoriented. The reception he gets could not be kinder or more thoughtful. My mother reports that staff lined up to greet him like a VIP. The carers made him a special cup of his favourite weak tea with lemon to help settle him. On the phone my mother sounds drained but relieved.

Papa is dosed with powerful antipsychotic medication but it is weeks before it takes effect. Meanwhile he wanders the corridors, intruding on other residents, sometimes attempting to get into bed with them as he did in hospital. Undeterred by the gate on the stairs, code on the lift and security at the front door, he persists in trying to escape. He steals clothing and chocolate and makes lewd comments to visitors.

When I visit a few weeks later, I often find him reading the papers. On closer inspection I notice they are upside down, but he seems to enjoy turning pages. He worries at the zipper of his document case obsessively and is endlessly searching for his car keys. I bring a bunch for him to play with and this appears to soothe him. Anything he holds is impossible to prise away, held by fingers like steel rods. He still has the power to hurt by crushing bones and biting. Mercifully, he appears undisturbed by a very distressed woman who sits nearby in the lounge screaming for hours on end 'I CAN'T SEE!' and whom no one can quiet. Although sighted, she is apparently reliving a traumatic memory of her childhood in the London Blitz.

At first, colleagues visit but they find the sight of my father so diminished too painful to endure and disappear, never to return. They are too ashamed to tell my mother how they feel and she is so angry with them that her resentment keeps them at bay, isolating her even further.

My father's old business brain has decided that he is staying in a poorly run hotel. One day he commandeers the nurses' station as his office and refuses to move. Repeating gestures hardwired into his deepest being, he finds a blank sheet of paper in a drawer, and scrawls a barely legible letter recommending a pay rise for all the staff. This endears him to his carers no end, earning him extra tea and biscuits. My mother, playing up to his general manager role, brings in his briefcase. While he is still mobile, he shuffles to and from his preferred chair, holding the case as if setting off for a meeting. Sometimes he cries in the middle of an incomplete sentence but it is like a spring shower and passes quickly. Maman feeds him with a spoon, as he fed me when I was a baby, pretending each was a different plane. 'Here comes a Caravelle, here comes a Boeing,' he used to say with each mouthful that landed. Now she does the same and he opens his mouth with mechanical obedience. The nurses claim he smiles if they mention my name.

He responds to an ever diminishing set of stimuli. Live music is performed regularly at Nightingale. One day a young soprano, part of a lunchtime concert trio, kneels at his feet to sing him an aria from *Carmen*, gently stroking his hand.

A year after our French reconciliation, my father turned eighty. To mark the occasion, he said he would like to hear Simon Rattle conduct Wagner's Ring Cycle at Aix-en-Provence. If I could secure the tickets, he would pay for the trip. We had a deal. What a long way we had come, he and I, since the first time he subjected me to Wagner at the preposterously precocious age of twelve, expecting me to sit through the tedium of a performance of *Das Rheingold* so I could have the privilege of seeing Herbert von Karajan conduct. As if I cared. The experience had exactly the opposite effect to the one my father intended: it put me off opera for the next decade. When I came round, I did so gradually, persuaded first by Mozart, then Bizet and Puccini. Wagner took another ten years.

Now those days glow in my memory like amber: long lunches on the terrace of the café where Cézanne had been a regular. Dusky pink suede peaches blushing in the market. And at night, we are transported to Valhalla: a monstrous family way more dysfunctional than ours playing out its warped destiny to the most sublime, transcendent anthems on earth. My father rises to his feet, part of a thunderous, tribal ovation. We hoot like the Valkyries, we bay like wolves, as only fanatics can. We are elated, freed of all our own ridiculous posturings by the absurd vanity of the gods.

I am so grateful for those precious halcyon days together, watching Papa now as the kind young singer takes his hands in hers and shows him how to clap. He repeats her gesture, fingers splayed like a child, tears rolling down his cheeks.

When he is taken on outings and stares out of the window of the Nightingale van, my mother, always by his side on these occasions, notices that he looks at the cars with more animation than usual. Once, seeing a Jaguar, he gives an almost imperceptible nod, as if saluting an old friend.

Several weeks after my father's move to the nursing home, I got an email out of the blue from a stranger in the UK. I'll call her Moira. She'd stumbled across an interview I'd given to BBC Radio Yorkshire on the seventieth anniversary of *Kindertransport*. Since my father was too ill to participate, I felt I should mark the occasion on his behalf, and had written a piece for a commemorative exhibition and anthology of memories by children and some of the families who took them in. The local BBC station asked me to elaborate on what I'd written and in the course of the conversation I explained that my father was now unable to recall this episode from his past.

Moira wrote that she was distressed to hear my father was unwell and wondered if I could tell her more. She had been a colleague and also his girlfriend before he married my mother and they had stayed in touch over the decades. She had married and been widowed for thirty years, had many grandchildren, and sounded active and independent. She had last seen my father in 2004, when he had taken her out to lunch.

I love the serendipity of such connections, the way strangers can find each other through the ether and how people with a tenuous link can choose whether or not to strengthen that bond. I wrote back and told her what I could, as gently as possible, suggesting that if she was thinking of visiting him, some times were better than others. I mentioned her to my mother. The two had never met, but my mother was aware of Moira's existence. 'Your father was still seeing a bit of her when he started seeing me,' she said. She was surprised but not upset to learn that my father had kept up his contact with her until so recently, even offering to accompany Moira to see my father to make it easier. It was a generous offer from someone normally wary and suspicious of strangers. My mother was changing and I could see it in the way she dealt with this moment. She absorbed the fact of this woman without hostility. Where once she might have shrugged the incident off as yet another minor annoyance, now she was acting with compassion. I admired her generosity. It took guts.

Showing equal pluck, Moira could not wait and drove herself all the way from Winchester to see my father unannounced. The visit was not a success and distressed her considerably. 'He did not open his eyes once while I was there,' she wrote in a subsequent email, 'and the only word he said over and over was "beast".' Undeterred, she returned a few days later, again alone. Afterwards, she spoke to my mother on the phone.

'I hear you had a special visitor,' my mother said the next day when she visited my father. No response. 'Moira?' she prompted, stroking his arm in encouragement. Waking from his near permanent stupor of dozing, he opened his watery eyes briefly and replied 'Yes' with a fleeting smile. So he remembered something, perhaps. Or maybe the sound of her name simply triggered a deeper memory.

Although her emails revealed strength of character, Moira was not ready to meet my mother. She wrote to me that when she had last seen my father, she had noticed tiny anomalies that perhaps family members would not pick up on, like the fact that he seemed unable to calculate the change to leave as a tip, which was extremely uncharacteristic given his talent for rapid mental arithmetic. She also said he had admitted that he and I were not on good terms. This was one year into our estrangement. I felt a stab of shame, imagining him telling her how disappointed he was in me.

By the time I was an adolescent, my father had gathered a strong and loyal team around him, including several women whom he promoted to senior positions, loyal deputies who proved they had his stamina for long hours and who seemed able to weather his tantrums, withering invective and irrational tyrannical edicts: he once pronounced in deadly seriousness that the wearing of culottes, which were fashionable at the time, was a sackable offence. Most of these female staff were single. Husbands or boyfriends would have resented my father's intrusions on weekends and evenings, and talked their partners into less demanding positions.

Increasingly, he was not home for dinner during the week. A husky voice became familiar on the phone—Helena, his trusted ally, his number two, ringing to say he was on his way. When I met her for the first time, I saw in her petite presence my mother in miniature: same olive skin, similarly strong nose, dark hair, dark eyes, definite foreign accent. But the similarity did not register as especially significant, given the stark difference: Helena was wedded to her career. She was all business, a professional woman who talked shop, went to conferences, attended meetings, talked about brochures, balance sheets, clients, destinations and hotel rates. She was always formal and polite to my mother and somewhat condescending to me. It was only many years later that my mother told me she had guessed that my father was having an affair with Helena.

No child wants to contemplate their parents' sex lives. I knew enough to tell me that my parents had long ceased to have any kind of intimate relationship. There were no Saturday afternoons when they closed the door of their bedroom on the sly pretext of a nap. My mother had dropped sufficient hints suggesting sex was never a source of pleasure and that it was only ever the means to an end: to have a child. Once that goal was achieved, she moved to another room where she slept in a single bed. The message was plain enough: from then on, conjugal rights were, I suspect, off the menu.

Little wonder that my father, for whom sex was probably a necessary recreational release, went looking elsewhere. Fair enough, I say, but by the same token I understand my mother's inability to satisfy his needs. Perhaps she was not an especially sexual creature, perhaps they were not compatible, or perhaps the secret trauma of rape never released her from its grasp. Despite this fundamental mismatch, in good times, my parents were affectionate towards each other. They walked down streets hand in hand or arm in arm. They hugged, and my father kissed my mother on the cheek when she cooked a favourite dish or looked especially smashing, to use one of his favourite compliments.

Eventually my father set Helena up in her own business, perhaps as a way of making up for not keeping more personal promises to her. He was extremely loyal and generous, if you looked at it one way, or controlling and paternalistic if you looked at it another. To him, Helena was family and he expected us to see it that way too; he had met her relatives overseas, stayed in their homes, and he relished the role of senior adviser and confidant over every move she made. He expected her to be present at major celebrations. When I arranged a small gathering at home to mark his seventy-fifth birthday, she was there to watch him blow out the candles, although my mother would much have preferred her not to be. The two maintained a civil façade though it was never more than cordial.

When Helena came to Sydney for a conference, my father wrote instructing me to take her out to dinner at the best restaurant in town and offering to pay. I settled for something a little less showy and we had a very pleasant adult evening together during which she told me that my father had promised to marry her. She was not bitter about the fact that it never came to pass. Perhaps she was even secretly a little relieved, as he was now frankly something of a nuisance, offering unsolicited advice on everything from where to take a holiday to where to buy property. She agreed that he had not prepared for retirement, that it did not suit him, that he was lost and bored and prone to stubborn prejudices and wild entrepreneurial schemes—all said in the slightly patronising but still lingeringly affectionate tone unique to former girlfriends and mistresses.

'He was so promiscuous,' she said of his careless way of buying gifts for her, later discovering that he had bulk-bought multiples to give to his wife and other female associates. I suddenly remembered an evening when I was ten or eleven and we were dining out overseas with business partners, including a tall, lean and stylish American woman with short cropped curls, long legs and throaty laugh I found thrilling. My mother admired a very modern, sculptural gold ring she was wearing.

'I have one just like that,' said my mother, genuinely amazed at the coincidence. Sure enough, my father had bought them both. My mother made a scene about it when we got back to the hotel.

When my father was diagnosed, Helena was loyal. Where other colleagues fell away spectacularly, Helena came to spend time with him regularly and always called my mother. The two became somewhat grudging and awkward allies. Though her manner was often frosty, my mother was grateful to Helena for not abandoning my father when he could no longer be of use to her.

I wish I could ask Helena what she saw in my father that made her cross the line from employee to lover. I don't want sordid details but I want to know whether the attraction was simply the headiness of doing deals together, winning business, wooing clients, pulling off bigger and bigger projects, seeing the cash flow and the stakes rise as the business's reputation grew and grew. Most probably it was that, together with the complicity that comes from being away, somewhere anonymous, in a good hotel. That's sexy enough when things are legitimate, but when they are not, it becomes truly intoxicating.

Am I promiscuous too? If not sexually, then socially: gathering people up with sudden enthusiasm and then being slightly cavalier about their feelings when their novelty fades? It is an accusation that has been levelled at me more than once.

I don't blame Helena for wanting my father to leave his family. At the time, there was nothing I wished for more. During one particularly nightmarish skiing holiday in my mid-teens, I sat my parents down and begged them to get divorced to stop the fighting. My mother would not countenance the idea.

Many years later, when my first marriage broke up, my father wrote to me that, in 1983, keenly aware of the historical symbolism of the location, he chose the forest of Compiègne where two armistices between the French and the Germans were signed in 1918 and in 1940 as the site for a solitary walk. Taking his cue from that anniversary, and defeated by my mother's sustained assault of tears, he privately negotiated his own peace treaty. Later he may have come to regret it, given that theirs was always an uneasy truce: they never seemed to achieve the autumnal harmony that other couples sometimes manage after spells of turbulence. There was no serenity between them, just milder or sharper tones of needling and wheedling.

But he did not give up his ways. Out of the blue he decided to quit smoking, having been a sixty-a-day man for decades. Recognising his habit was hardcore, he suddenly announced that he had booked himself in with a Russian hypnotist in Chicago for a weekend. When he came back, he never smoked again. Why did he resort to such extreme measures without notice? And why did he have to go to America to cure himself of the habit of a lifetime? Was it to please the wife and daughter who had been begging him to stop? I doubt it, as he had been ignoring our appeals for years. I suspect that it was to please someone with whom he was involved.

Several years later, another alarm bell rang when my father turned up with an uncharacteristic purchase: a pair of trainers. My father has never worn any kind of sports shoe. I have seen him walk through thick snow and on hot sand in leather loafers. Something was quite literally afoot.

Under sustained cross-examination from my mother, he confessed: he had planned to go walking with a younger acolyte from South Africa whom he had met at a conference many years earlier. I will call her Amber. He admitted they had been involved, but swore the relationship was over. Later, my mother, who was not normally a snoop, found the carelessly left receipts that so many wives seem destined to find when getting their husband's clothes ready for the drycleaner.

Scenes ensued. Amber was brazen enough to ring the house occasionally, and my mother would slam the phone down on her. My father played victim, claiming that he was being stalked and harassed. But my mother found out that my father was sending Amber money and managing her financial affairs, so the connection was not entirely broken. She worried he might change his will.

⁓

One day shortly after my father had become a Nightingale House resident, the postman making his rounds accosted my mother in the foyer of her building. 'Excuse me, Mrs Baum, your post-office box has overflowed and I haven't seen Mr Baum for some time so I thought I'd bring you your mail,' he said helpfully. My mother was not aware of having a post-office box. When she examined its contents, it turned out to be dozens of lottery notices, mixed in with letters postmarked from South Africa. My father had been devious enough to divert his mail to a secret address to hide the extent of two betrayals: one financial, the other emotional.

The lottery letters were easily disposed of. When I scrawled 'No Longer At This Address' on them, they stopped after a while. But the pile of correspondence from Johannesburg was harder to deal with. For days, then weeks, it sat on the hall table. Neither my mother nor I could decide what to do. Should we take my father his mail and risk upsetting him? Should we return the letters to their sender? Did Amber deserve an explanation for my father's total silence or could she simply interpret it as rejection? Were they still entangled in some way that meant she needed clarification that he would no longer be providing her with financial advice and support?

Eventually I got sick of their presence in our home and took them to him at the nursing home. He was by then too medicated with antipsychotics to register any interest. I am ashamed to confess that a few days later, when he was not in his room, I peeked inside his bedside table drawer, found the letters opened and took one to read at home. I wanted to know what Amber was like. I wondered how she wrote to my father, what the tone and pitch of her affection was, whether there would be any real intimacy on the page. I need not have worried: it was a long tedious description of having a new boiler fitted. At the very end she said she was praying for him and that she needed him strong. That reference to his physical being made me feel queasy.

I asked a colleague of my father's who knew Amber to tell her about his situation so that she would not write or call anymore. Months later, on another visit, I found an envelope taped to the back of a desk drawer I thought I had cleared. It was filled with large denominations of Euros and marked 'Amber'. I felt a flash of fury, thinking of him squirrelling away money for a mistress instead of offering to help me with airfares to come home. I grabbed the notes. Later, I spent them on a trip to Istanbul for Christmas with David and my mother. I didn't tell her how we could afford it.

I fantasised about Amber. I imagined myself going into her travel agency in Jo'Burg, pretending I was interested in some business and having meetings with her, and then suggesting dinner and getting to know her, seeing if I could get her to reveal herself to me without knowing my identity. Perhaps she had seen photographs of me, perhaps not. I wanted to know the story of the affair from her point of view and what she knew about his family . . . I asked myself whether at the end of such confidences I would reveal myself to her in a 'TA DAH!' moment and revel in her shock and shame.

There have been others but I don't know how serious any of them were. Occasional flings perhaps, or what today we would call fuck buddies. Did he use call girls? Easy enough to order one up with room service in hotels, or did he content himself with the porn channel?

Maybe he was more of an admirer than a seducer. As I sifted through files for essential documents, I came across caches of private correspondence to and from him—my father kept duplicate copies of all his missives. Some were to a woman in the US who had formerly been a nun. In one he mentioned her exquisitely beautiful hands and what a pleasure it had been to go shopping for fine calf-skin gloves for her in Florence. I remember him returning from that trip with multiple pairs for my mother and me, their supple, pointy-tipped fingers edged with tiny stitches and lined with silk for extra warmth. I felt sickened thinking of him writing to her with his own bleeding stumps, chewed nails and torn flesh.

# CHAPTER 25

# Grief

Back in Australia I am totally unprepared for the wash of anger that pushes me under like a rogue wave. It is so completely unexpected, unpredictable and violent that it frightens me. I did not love my father with this kind of ferocity, so why am I lashing out so fiercely and randomly?

I call a counsellor friend for advice. Grief is not her field, and she has limited time but offers to listen if I can meet her outside her workplace. A café is not private enough. 'Perhaps we could talk in the car?' she suggests. The very space that defined so much of how my father and I related: it feels right, familiar, safe. There is comfort, too, in sitting facing forward, not having to make eye contact, like in a confessional. I splutter out my confusion, clutching the wheel. Oncoming twilight conceals my distress from passers-by.

After an hour of listening, my friend hugs me across the handbrake. I drive home, exhausted by my outburst, but also calmer, like a volcano reverting to dormancy after an eruption. The muscle memory of each gesture, braking, accelerating, indicating, offers some consolation with its mechanical repetition and achievable mastery. Gestures I learned from my father, now encoded in me. I feel his presence when I disregard the speed limit or execute a particularly tight park.

I wonder if my father's muscles, atrophied as they now are, retain any patterns of the gestures of steering or changing gear now that everything else in his brain is bombed, blasted, smashed. I replay our last drive together in my mind, over and over, like picking at a scab: the utter banality of it, the lack of portent, of significance, in our mundane exchanges about the automatically retractable side mirrors, heated seats and silent Prius engine. If I had known we would never again be able to have a normal conversation, what would I have said instead?

Then comes the pain. Unfamiliar aches begin at my ankles, creeping up my legs to my buttocks and into my neck and shoulders, moving like a weather pattern from site to site, waking me at night like approaching thunder.

As a child, I used to love storms. If they came in the night, we would all get up and watch from the windows of my father's bedroom, energised by the spectacle. I think that at some primal, unconscious level, we were each reacting to the tempest within ourselves, charged by the electric violence raging in our psyches.

We whooped at the loudest crashes and lightning bolts as if we were at a fireworks display, and felt a new sense of peace when calm returned. But this storm is different: there is no climax. It does not pass.

The pain is corrosive, like rust eating into duco. It becomes more and more acute, combined with a deadening fatigue that leaves me breathless and bedridden for days. I feel as if I have battery acid in my veins and concrete in my limbs. Blood tests and X-rays show nothing out of the ordinary.

I give up exercising because it makes me feel worse. I lose three or four days of the week lying prostrate, dozing. I have occasional good days when my energy returns, but the aches always come back like a punishment, as if my body were saying, 'How dare you think you could cheat me?'

Eventually a doctor agrees with my internet diagnosis of chronic fatigue combined with chronic pain—something called fibromyalgia. 'It's a dustbin diagnosis,' he says, 'which means we just chuck all the symptoms into a bin that we can't explain and give it that name.'

The illness affects me for two years. Then one day, I realise I have had five, maybe six, days in a row symptom-free. I feel stronger, have more stamina, the soreness is less acute, less persistent, less frequent. I start making bolder plans, attempting half days and then full days in the city, reclaiming parts of my life.

Months earlier, I had agreed to do a public conversation with Helen Garner for the Sydney Writers' Festival about her then new book *The Spare Room*. A book about death, dying, and the testing of friendship. Subjects that were very close to the bone now, in front of nine hundred people. I had no idea how I would cope.

Usually there is so much adrenalin coursing through my body on these occasions that it acts as a protective barrier to an almost magical degree. When I psych myself up to get just nervous enough, I can feel it sharpening my synapses. Too relaxed, overconfident, I'm no good. But I also knew I was in totally uncharted territory and could not predict my own reactions to the emotional terrain of the book. I did not trust myself.

I wrote to Helen and told her of my fears. Unsentimental and yet completely sympathetic, having recently lost her mother and her sister, she reassured me and told me she would not let anything happen. But I knew it was my job and my responsibility to be in control. It was unfair to expect Helen to look after me. This was her moment in the sun.

Normally before one of these events, I prefer not to spend much time with the person I'm going to be interviewing. Otherwise all my energy is drained on small talk and we get stale with chitchat, trying to avoid the topics we'll discuss on stage. It's a trick I learned from Michael Parkinson. He made it a rule never to see his guests before they went on. At first I used to think it was slightly rude, but now I understand his thinking completely. Seeing them beforehand takes the edge off and dissipates the element of risk, an essential ingredient to give these exchanges some fizz, to make them sound vital and unrehearsed.

So it went against all my instincts to suggest to Helen that we have lunch before our event. We could do that and then spend the afternoon apart. I had a hunch it might make me feel safer.

We met at the Sydney Theatre bistro. She sat on the banquette facing into the room. We ordered the same salad as a main course, no wine. She wanted to know everything about what had happened in London. And of course, being Helen, she wanted forensic detail. She asked questions that were as sharp as scalpels, probing with the delicacy and precision of a surgeon. She told me about her own experiences of caring for her mother and sister. Within minutes, I was blubbering. So was she. Hunched over the crisp white linen tablecloth, we did not discreetly wipe away tears, we mopped up great floods, using our starched napkins the way you use bread to soak up sauce. Our waiter left us alone. Perhaps other diners wondered who was being so cruel to Helen as to upset her in public, but I didn't care. We cried about the things we had seen that we could not unsee, the suffering, the pain, the sorrow, the regret, the helplessness of daughters, the irrational rages that suddenly rushed at us from nowhere over the smallest thing. When we had finished, we hugged each other wordlessly and went our separate ways.

It was cleansing, cauterising. I had got it all out, shared it with her, and I knew she would not betray the trust we had established. Helen and I bonded through sorrow and letting our guard down that day over lunch. I draw on her for strength when I am feeling shaky and doubtful in purpose. Instead of summoning C.J. from *The West Wing*, I often ask myself, 'What would Helen do?' and push on.

Our Writers' Festival conversation was candid and well received, and proved to me that I could get back into the saddle, that normal life was there for me to go back to and that I had not completely lost my chops. It gave me confidence and courage. It emboldened me to ask braver, more direct and penetrating questions, and each time I was rewarded with reciprocal openness. It's as if the wisdom that comes with staring down sorrow and loss gains you entry to a new fellowship of humanity, where you are welcomed into a tender embrace and no one ever asks to see your wounds as proof of admittance. They just know you've earned your place among the survivors.

The day after our talk, I drive home from a meeting elated and relieved: I'm back in the professional saddle. I can sustain hours of equanimity without being ambushed by a sudden rush of tears or power surges of temper. My life is in gear. I can't wait to get home to tell David about how well things have gone.

I park at the top of our driveway. Those last few metres always give me a sense of satisfaction, as if I were scaling a small mountain, instead of just revving the engine to get up a very steep incline. The climb is symbolic of reaching our elevated sanctuary. Through the drawn curtains I can see David's silhouette on the sofa, about to watch the seven o'clock news, the unofficial cut-off point for our working day. I know the wine is already opened. I have a small window in which to debrief him before the headlines begin. I run inside.

As I begin my account of promising meetings, both of us become aware of an unfamiliar sound on the other side of the curtains. Something scraping, with the rhythm of a ricochet, like a tin can being kicked repeatedly along a wall. Metal tearing. Puzzled, we draw the curtains back.

Where we should see the bonnet of the car, there is a void.

A void.

Where the car should be.

A void.

Where the car—

David's eyes are suddenly stretched wide, round like those of a cartoon child. His mouth is a matching O of horror as he runs outside. Still not fully understanding what is happening, I follow in time to see our car sliding down the driveway, before coming to an abrupt halt at a peculiar angle, jack-knifed against a concrete retaining wall. The side mirrors have torn away fence posts on the descent. Then, the undercarriage falls out like the spilled guts of roadkill.

The enormity of what could have happened makes us both lightheaded with relief. The neighbours, brought out by the noise, look on in disbelief as we hug and punch the air, laughing. The car has not rolled down on to the main road or gathered speed and propelled itself across the street into another house. It could have been much, much worse.

When I tell friends of the incident, they nod wisely. Clearly, according to them, the episode demonstrates that I am still dealing with the aftermath of my father's decline. For months, I buy that interpretation. I am not myself, not ready to venture into the outside world, not self-possessed enough to regain control.

But today I am not so sure. Couldn't it just be that in an absent-minded moment of eagerness to share the news of my successful day, I had forgotten one small gesture of precaution and left the handbrake off? Just how symptomatic and symbolic was that one error? I wonder what my father would have made of the episode. As someone who tended to overreact with stinging criticism to the smallest misstep, sometimes he surprised me with uncharacteristic acceptance. I like to think he'd make light of the episode and say: 'It could have been worse, Baby. At least it was only a Holden, not a Mercedes 280 SL.'

# CHAPTER 26

# An unfinished daughter

When I started dating, I always gave boyfriends a brief précis of who my parents were. A skeleton story that was meant to intrigue them, suggesting there was more depth and mystery to me because I was such a mixture of cultures and there was so much drama in my parentage. Like the cynical writer of a soap opera teasing viewers into wanting to know what happened next, I worked the melodrama of loss.

I was using the same method of seduction as Scheherazade used to get herself out of a tight spot. Perhaps I, too, was fighting for survival by consciously constructing a narrative to give my existence a lustre that set me apart. Over the years it became a pat recitation I could deliver with such polish that I knew where to leave significant pauses for my listener to interject the odd exclamation of shock, horror or sympathy.

I did not attempt the same pattern of storytelling when I was getting to know the girls and women who would become my friends, and with whom the bond of intimacy was often stronger than with lovers. It was as if I knew that my female friends would hear my story differently and refuse to be taken in by it. If I was to earn their trust and their affection, they seemed to be saying, it would have to be not because of who my parents were, but because of who I was as a separate, distinct individual.

In Australia, that was easier. I was a blank canvas. If friends met my parents, they did so briefly, when I was already an adult. While I might have told them stories of my strict upbringing, face to face my parents appeared a little stiff and intimidating, but agreeable enough. Here I have no past, no roots or heritage on the map of this continent. It is liberating but also lonely, a sort of semi-orphaned state. And it will only get lonelier.

David was the first man to notice my strategy and call me on it in a way that was both sensitive and direct. 'I asked about you, not your parents,' he said the first time we had dinner. I was taken aback. My standard repertoire was not working. I had no idea what to say. The silence grew awkward. He waited patiently, his gentle dark eyes promising an attentive listener.

David is less like my father than any man I know. How many life lessons did I have to learn in order to avoid a repeating pattern of choosing men who dominated, bullied and abused me? Too many.

I chose men to work for who scared me, judged me, withheld approval and punished me. When I was at my most impression-able, in my early twenties, I dated and then lived with a damaged man who shared my father's values. After the relationship ended I was smart enough to realise how toxic it had been and to invest most of my salary in therapy. But though I identified the problem, I found it difficult to shake my tendency to be drawn to men who were charismatic but also critical.

When they first met, David and my father had nothing to say to each other. My father made a snap judgement. On the basis of scant evidence, he decided that David was a failure: a divorced man with no visible assets or means of support, and with the additional baggage of a child. He worried that David might depend on me financially, and that I might have to support us. He could not respect a man who would allow that to happen. His way of demonstrating his disapproval was simply to ignore David, quite literally. It was unnerving, rude and wearing. In restaurants he would ask me, 'What is David having?' instead of addressing him directly.

At first David made an effort to engage my father but one day I noticed a very polite but subtle shift. I asked David what was going on. 'Well, I can keep trying,' he said equably, 'but he's not going to change. And I think I will lose my self-respect if I keep trying, so I've decided to stop the tap dancing.' I admired his decision.

From then on, David met my father on his own terms and things very gradually started to improve. By the end of my parents' trip to France for our miraculous Christmas reconciliation, the transformation was complete. It hinged on the simplest thing: David's driving, and his ability to navigate Nice and its surroundings, to get us smoothly to Monte Carlo and Menton and back, find parking spots, remember one-way systems.

These navigational skills convinced my father that here was a man who could steer his daughter on the right path. He happily allowed himself to be a passenger and to be chauffeured, having previously always insisted on being at the wheel. It was a surrender made in deference to age, but also an acknowledgement of David's mastery. The car was literally the vehicle for a rapprochement. If my father had still owned a Jaguar, he would have let David drive it.

My mother, too, was not predisposed to David. I played it badly, announcing that we were going to marry before she'd met him and then informing her that he would be coming to London with me to visit. Never keen on houseguests, making an exception only for the Russians, she dreaded having a stranger under her roof who was also a *fait accompli* fiancé. Even worse, this meant it was highly unlikely that I would ever return to the UK to live.

When they met, she was thin-lipped and stern. But that lasted about twenty minutes. We were in the kitchen on our first evening, on our best behaviour, self-conscious and awkward in attempts to be falsely jolly. We were setting the table, which meant David was opening kitchen drawers looking for cutlery. What he found instead was my mother's remarkable, possibly definitive, collection of obscure, but globally comprehensive, cooking utensils. At first my mother looked faintly embarrassed, her guilty secret exposed, as if he'd been rootling through her underwear and found racy boudoir thongs mixed in with the sensible girdles.

Confident that he would rise to the occasion, I held up exhibit after exhibit, challenging David to guess their use. To my mother's astonishment and increasing delight, he identified them correctly. He got the cherry pitter, egg slice, decorative butter mould, zester, jar openers, grapefruit knife, even the nutmeg grater. As in any quiz show where the stakes are high, the questions got harder and harder. Some objects stumped us both completely. 'Oh, those are mussel holders,' said my mother, blithely demonstrating their steely castanet motion as if their function were self-evident. And this? 'A Dutch biscuit maker.' Of course. By now each implement prompted such mirth that within an hour, the table still unset, we were helplessly convulsed.

The bond between David and my mother grew and grew. When we took my mother to Istanbul for Christmas, we were alarmed at how uneven the cobbled streets were. In some cases, they were punctuated with large unmarked holes and vicious protruding spikes. David gallantly offered a slightly unsteady Maman his elbow to hang onto during our explorations. 'Elbow' has since become her permanent nickname for him.

One strange, strange thing: they look alike. David and I are often mistaken for siblings. Or, as I put it since we have both gone grey, a pair of schnauzers. The resemblance between us has grown stronger. He looks much more like my mother than like his own. Their skins are equally olive, their eyes equally deep set, brown and velvety, their foreheads high, their noses strong. I see Maman's features in David, especially in profile, and it gives me comfort to think that when she is no longer there an essence of her will linger in his face.

CHAPTER 27

# The unglazed heart

At Nightingale House my father dozes like *Alice in Wonderland*'s dormouse most of the day. His dementia is too severe for him to participate in any of the social activities. Sometimes they include him, wheeling him into a room for a drama workshop where he stares vacantly but cannot follow any directions to copy movements or gestures. Or they take him on a picnic where he does not notice his surroundings.

One determined volunteer comes in regularly to give a craft class. She brings bags of moist clay and terracotta for residents to shape and model, and wheels her trolley between each floor so that residents who cannot make it down to the well-equipped arts and craft centre are not left out. Some make lopsided plates and misshapen bowls, enjoying the slippery wet sensation of the material being shaped between their fingers, perhaps taking them back to the days of sandcastles and mud pies. The best works are displayed in the foyer.

Every time the craft volunteer invites my father to make something, he waves her away as if she were a buzzing insect. But she is not easily discouraged and always returns. My mother feels sorry for her, and tells her the situation is hopeless and not to waste her time. Papa had neither interest nor aptitude in his previous life for anything creative, so he will not develop them now.

When I was eight or nine, I caught a brief craft craze. It filled in solitary holiday *longueurs* and suited my non-sporty nature. At the time, making things was big for kids. On *Blue Peter*, the UK's most beloved children's program, born the same year as me, presenters were endlessly demonstrating things you could make with a loo-roll tube and a plastic bottle. The show was the first in the UK to use the phrase, 'Here's one I made earlier.' I was constantly asking Maman to save me empty bleach and detergent bottles to be recycled into something I'd seen on television, but my execution always let me down and left me feeling inadequate.

Inspiration came to me one day, however, after finishing a box of Cadbury's Dairy Chocolate Fingers. I decided to make something with it. Today we would call that recycling. I had noticed that my mother's evening clutch purse of crocodile skin was exactly the same shape as the biscuit pack: a shallow slim rectangle. I found an off-cut of felted dark-red material in her fabric box and wrapped the scrap around the box, tucking it into the inside lid and gluing it down around the sides. The effect was neat and pleasing. It opened and shut smoothly and I imagined her tucking a lipstick and powder compact in there for a night at the theatre. Thinking it looked perhaps a little bare as an evening accessory (the lizard bag had a gold and lapis clasp), I rummaged in her sewing kit and found a few sparkling beads that I stuck down on the centre of the lid in a circle, their facets catching the light like raindrops in sunshine. Perfect.

I presented the bag to my mother and she accepted it with just the right amount of surprise and delight. A few evenings later, proud of my handiwork, I watched her leave for the opera in her appropriately chocolate-coloured mink stole, clutching my bag in her jewelled hand. So I was devastated when I later found it shoved at the back of the glove compartment, understanding in a flash that she had never used it.

My mother's manual accomplishments were discouraging. She had endless patience and skill, excelling at needlework, tapestry, knitting and all crafts. I tried to copy her, but anything that required counting and a regular repeated gesture following a pattern defeated me. My mother blamed it on my being left-handed, saying it made everything awkward, being done back to front. Still, she encouraged me to find me practical hobbies, buying me a book that became my constant companion. A paperback published by Penguin called *Something To Do* became a substitute friend. Divided into twelve chapters, one for each month, it suggested various projects, half of them indoors and half outdoors. Many were quite tricky and required a level of manual coordination and precision I could not manage. I rarely did the outdoor ones unless they involved collecting shells, leaves or feathers.

Next came a kit that supplied moulds, with different-coloured clear and opaque resins to pour into and set, like buttons or shells. I made pendants with it and sold them at school. A year later I was given a miniature kiln and some cut-out copper jewellery bases, together with a set of enamels that came in little shakers like salt. You created stencilled patterns and made your own designs and then fired them. They came out molten, glazed shiny and hard like glossy jam tarts. I made rings and pendants and again sold them at school. They were so popular I even took orders, showing precocious entrepreneurial flair. There was high demand for one design: a disc pendant on a white background with a scarlet heart at its centre. It was bold and graphic, and I managed to perfect the enamelling technique so that it didn't bubble or craze.

The weeks at the nursing home pass without incident. Except that one day, my mother is stopped by the craft volunteer.

'Your husband has made something,' she says with evident satisfaction.

My mother does not believe her. There must have been some mistake.

'Oh no, most definitely Harry Baum, he made something last week.'

My mother asks what it is.

'A terracotta heart. Unglazed. When it's been fired I will give it to you. I'm sure he means it to be a gift to you.'

An unglazed heart. Which is what mine feels like these days. Exposed. Fragile. Breakable.

I think of my father's stumpy spatula fingers shaping the mineral mud. It's hard to imagine. I remember my little glazed heart from the kiln-firing days, a small red pumping organ, stylised into a shape we recognise globally as symbolising love, now devalued as a graphic used in countless commercial promotions and transactions and even turned into a verb, deforming the language in a way my father would call an abomination: 'I heart NY.'

As a child who suffered from a lack of dexterity, I strained for mastery of a skill that comes with practice. Awkward and clumsy, my first attempts had been thrown in the bin, lopsided, off-centre, imperfect. I try to imagine my father making something wonky and unfinished, something in which, as his former self, he would have taken no pride or pleasure. He hated to get his hands dirty. But in the end, conscious or not, the heart is all that matters. Even though he was lost to us, wrapped in a thick blanket of fog, however briefly, some part of him knew that. And now I know it too.

# CHAPTER 28

# The memory box

Six years after his diagnosis, my father is a husk. He can no longer speak intelligibly. He barely opens his eyes to sip from a cup or be fed. He is incontinent and wears pads. He drools from his medication. His utterances are gobbledegook, mostly noises, sometimes rising in volume and resembling the revving of a car engine. When he sees me, sometimes these incoherent sounds become more urgent and deliberate, as if he is straining to say something important. He grips my hand, crushing my knuckles. From the cadence of these unformed utterances I recognise that he is asking me about money, the urgency of his tone exactly the same as it would have been when he could articulate concern about my use of credit cards and levels of debt.

Once I left home, the opening gambit of our conversations was never 'How are you?' but 'How's your bank balance?' or

'How's the mortgage?' or 'Have you paid off your credit card?' Instead of praise for anything I had published he would say, 'I hope they paid you well.'

When I was a student and first began managing the monthly allowance my father gave me, he required me to undertake an audit whenever I came back to London. I was expected to show evidence that I could balance my chequebook, presenting the stubs for scrutiny just as I had once had to present my bitten nails. If I overspent he would quote Polonius from *Hamlet*—'Neither a borrower nor a lender be'—and chastise me. Then, once I promised to do better, he would top up my account. There were annual lessons in budgeting that I tuned out of with showy yawns, resenting these demonstrations of control. Later, he signed me up to investment policies I did not request, committing me to long-terms saving plans without consulting me. I protested his interference by pretending to be cavalier about earning and spending.

My mother was totally financially dependent on him. Until my father became demented she had never used her credit card to pay for a meal. Now in her eighties, she was suddenly forced to disentangle his complicated arrangements and multiple squirrelling of gold coins here, bonds there. My father's savings were byzantine in their complexity and scattered through dozens of different portfolios. Partly due to bad luck, they yielded disappointingly little for all his efforts, his dream of wealth and of passing on a large sum never realised. He knew this before his health failed him, and it was the cause of gnawing bitterness and corrosive regret. If one word were to sum up the second half of my father's life, it would be 'disappointment'.

My mother's unflagging devotion to the shell of her husband earns the admiration of the carers at Nightingale House. She visits every second day without fail, greeting my father with a cheery 'Hello, HB' though he fails to acknowledge her in any way. She combs my father's few remaining strands of hair, kissing his forehead, holding and stroking his hand, feeding him, making a fuss when he has not been shaved or dressed by lunchtime or is wearing someone else's clothes. She is ferociously vigilant of his dignity, and vocal about any aspects of his care that are neglected or substandard. Always searching for a way to unlock my father, she reads all the literature on the latest research into dementia and buys him a soft toy to cuddle, hoping it might give him pleasure. It soon falls from his lap, but she tucks it back into the crook of his elbow, over and over again, lifting his hand to stroke its synthetic coat.

It is soul-destroying to watch and is taking its toll on her. She is increasingly frail, fearful, frugal and yet still capable of moments of ferocity on my father's behalf, like a tigress suddenly roused to snarling anger in defence of her cubs. Her world has shrunk to the scale of necessity, reduced to bare basics. In moments of devastating candour, she admits that she is lonely and has no confidence socially. She joins a carers' support group in the hope of meeting people in similar circumstances. I admire her bravery and praise her for venturing out on this late quest. A few months later she is jubilant on Skype, announcing with great pride that she has made a friend and cannot wait for me to meet her. The implied need for approval in her voice echoes my own, many years before.

I think back to her petty jealousy of my friends when they got too close and threatened to steal me from her. Her dislikes were sudden, irrational and ferocious. One minute she was enthusiastic about Sabine, a sparky, outgoing girl I met at university, because she was French: she enjoyed hearing her language being well spoken by a compatriot from a cultured Parisian family; it soothed her homesickness to compare notes with Sabine about Britain's failings and strange customs; they bonded over shared frustrations, such as the lack of minced veal at British butchers. But then, one holiday, when Sabine came to stay and her large, boisterous personality filled the house (and for once, charmed my father), my mother announced without warning that Sabine would have to leave, immediately. She could not stand to have her in the house one second longer. Going upstairs to tell Sabine, whose family had extended open-ended hospitality to me in Paris on several occasions, that she was no longer welcome and must pack her bags was one of the most awkward moments of my life. Now I ask myself why I didn't refuse point-blank to do my mother's bidding or tell her to do it herself. Why I didn't march out of the house with my friend and not come back? I was too compliant, like a Stockholm syndrome hostage.

My friendship with Sabine survived, strengthened by her forgiving nature and persistent efforts to win my mother over. Ten years later, in tears, my mother apologised for her juvenile jealousy. Her pride had been wounded when Sabine teased her about her French being out of date, and she had lashed out in revenge.

I am determined to like any friend my mother makes. I watch with almost parental delight as this fellow carer becomes her confidante. At the age of eighty-three, she is discovering that it can be more fun to go to the cinema with someone than on your own and that going out for a pizza can be the highlight of your week.

As a long-term resident of the nursing home, my father is one of the first to be moved to a new wing and given a brighter, more spacious room with a view of the gardens to which he never looks out. It is the equivalent of an upgrade to a suite in a posh hotel.

'He won't notice,' says my mother with a shrug.

From the very beginning of my father's institutional life, she has refused to bring anything personal from home to decorate his walls and shelves in case it gets stolen by other wandering residents. As a result, his bedroom is bare and spartan by comparison with those of others, whose families have brought in cushions, furniture, photographs and tchotchkes to add homey cheer and personality to counter the nursing-home decor. She tracks his few possessions with the fervour of a drug sniffer dog, retrieving them triumphantly from other rooms and constantly sewing name tags into new clothes, as if sending him off to boarding school, fearful lest one sock go missing.

Now, there is to be a memory box outside each room, to give a sense of each resident's identity and interests. A small lockable perspex container with a single shelf and a light so that its contents can be clearly seen even at night. My mother struggles to find things to put in it, worrying that they will be misplaced.

'I'm not sure it's secure,' she says, as if a safe or strongbox were preferable for his few modest possessions.

I come up with a list of objects of little or no value, to illustrate my father's few tangible enthusiasms.

'What about a Toblerone, the giant ones he liked to buy in bulk?' I suggest via our daily Skype call, remembering the way he could eat a whole block in one sitting.

'He has no teeth anymore.'

'No, I mean just the packaging.'

'Maybe . . .' she says, resistant to any purchase.

'And a CD of one of his favourites, Bach or Beethoven?'

'He never played them, he didn't know how to turn on the machine. And besides, someone will pinch the disc.'

'Well, just the box then,' I say encouragingly.

'Or a photograph of us at Buckingham Palace when he got his MBE?'

I wonder if that was his proudest day. At lunch afterwards in a restaurant on Park Lane in his pale-grey morning suit, his top hat tucked under his chair, he could not stop beaming. 'Not bad for a refugee,' he said softly, almost to himself, as we raised our glasses of champagne in a toast.

'Perhaps . . .'

'What about a couple of maps and a *Michelin Guide?*'

She does not argue with this. Instead it prompts a suggestion of her own: his passport. A poignant document, proof of an identity remade and now lost. No visas necessary for where he is now or will eventually be going.

What would I put in my box? A pair of earrings, seashells, a poem and an artwork by David, a luggage tag, my wedding ring, a phial of saffron threads to remind me of sunny flavours. The condolence-card reply from Jackie Kennedy. Photographs of my parents, images of friends. This book.

Possessions say so little, in the end. We cherish them, invest them with meaning, but their eloquence becomes muted with time. At a certain point, the things you want are not things. They are people and sensations. The sound of rolling thunder approaching, the folding ripple of a small wave in a sheltered bay, the feeling of large warm drops of rain on your forearm, the smell of basil, coffee, garlic, baking bread. Laughter. Love. Friendship. Beauty. Kindness. Music. The creative spark and flair of making a bouquet of flowers, or a meal eaten in fellowship, or finding the right words to put on the page.

While we haggle over the contents of the memory box, I notice that my mother is more graciously resigned to my father holding her hostage than I expected. Ever hopeful that he will respond with some small sign of appreciation, she makes sure he is taken on outings with other residents, hoping to stimulate any part of his brain that remains undamaged. She pushes his wheelchair through parks and gardens and points things out to him from the window of the Nightingale bus, returning exhausted but often uplifted by the tiniest sign.' I think he really enjoyed himself,' she says later, and I am amazed at her new capacity to find the positive in even the slightest flicker of his eye.

'He seems to like the hand massages,' she says of a program of new treatments being trialled, though he still chews his fingers raw in unchecked compulsion. Therapists confirm her observations, saying they have glimpsed fleeting smiles. He is less agitated, more peaceful. There are still flashes of anger, rare outbursts that appear out of nowhere. Being pushed along an unfamiliar corridor to the terrace, he cries suddenly for no apparent reason, as if suddenly afraid. While he is visibly declining, my mother is ageing more imperceptibly. No one notices because her skin remains unlined and her child-like manner deceives strangers into believing she is a decade younger.

And that's not all. At Nightingale House, she receives unexpected compliments. When a carer describes her as 'good with people', she repeats the phrase to me frequently. She has also learned to see comedy in her visits and its absurdities. One day she see my father holding hands with a woman. When my mother bends to kiss him on the forehead, the woman asks tartly, 'And who are you?'

To which my mother replies, 'I'm Harry's wife.'

The woman, who is rather well groomed and nicely dressed, becomes rattled: 'No, you're not. I'm his wife.'

Instead of arguing, my mother laughs. 'If you say so.'

On her next visit, she discovers she has an admirer of her own. A resident in the same wing greets her with a polite salutation, and then, moving along rather faster than propriety would suggest, touches her on the breast and announces himself as her husband. Instead of getting flustered and offended, my

ONLY

mother recounts the episode with a flirtatious smile in her voice. 'So now I have two, too,' she says.

I could not do what she does. I'm ashamed to admit that on some visits to my father, I found the experience such an ordeal that I just sat in the car rather than face what waited for me on the second floor.

Forty per cent of the nursing home's residents have no visitors whatsoever, and are entirely dependent on the goodwill of volunteers who do not reach everyone on their rounds. When my mother sees a new face, she has the confidence to approach in greeting, setting aside her natural timidity and reserve. She is stronger and steelier than either of us knew.

Which comes in handy. In an attempt to reduce costs due to severe budget cuts, within days of my father's move to the new wing the NHS threatens to withdraw the funding for his care.

Just as I fought the system to get him admitted, my mother decides she will take up the struggle to keep him there. Energised by defiance rather than cowed by officialdom, she swings into action with method: she studies all the official literature to understand the assessment criteria and launches a carefully considered counterattack in a comprehensive report stating her case, rebutting the arguments with calm reasoning and judicious observations from staff.

The wait for a decision stretches over two agonising months, during which she eats less and sleeps little. On Skype I notice that her cheeks are hollow. Her world shrinks to one and only one concern. She is under siege. Every decision, however small, is put on hold. 'I can't think about that now,' is her stock answer

336

to any question. Finally, an official letter arrives. To everyone's amazement, she's won.

The triumph in her voice via Skype is almost palpable. The confidence boost acts like a power surge, prompting her to quit the antidepressants she has been taking since my father was admitted. Bursting with pride, she cannot wait to tell me that other carer visitors at the facility have asked if she would be an advocate on their behalf.

As a tentative mature-age student who never completed a basic education, my mother dreaded writing essays when she took high-school level Russian exams in her fifties. It put her off studying for a degree, despite her natural aptitude and her passion for the literature. Now here she is, in her mid-eighties, able to mount a cogent argument and defeat a powerful authority. It is never too late for victory.

# CHAPTER 29

# Long-distance death

In the end, the call I had dreaded since moving to Australia was not a call at all. It was an email from my mother's friend in London telling me my father had suddenly been taken to hospital with acute pneumonia and was not responding to treatment. My mother was with him and had been told to expect the worst.

Taking a break from her vigil by his side, Maman had later left an uncharacteristically garbled message on my mobile. She sounded marooned, disoriented with shock. Alone in the middle of the night, words deserted her: 'He's got . . . oh . . . what is it . . . what do you call it . . . ? Anyway, it's not looking good . . . so there you are . . .' She abandoned the sentence in mid-air, leaving meaning to drift like smoke.

I reached her at the hospital, where they had no bed to offer but had volunteered a sofa for her to rest on. She sounded dazed, like someone wounded wandering around the scene of an accident who has not yet been attended to by emergency services.

'Shall I come now?' I asked, trying to sound upbeat and helpful.

'I don't know,' she replied, sincerely forlorn and bewildered. 'I can't make a decision.'

Six hours later, my father was dead.

My mother had been by his side, watching and above all hearing him struggle for every breath.

'It was terrible. The nurse said he was in pain,' she told me, sparing me nothing. 'He made noises like a hot water bottle.' I thought about the slooshing sound the water makes when it is moving around in its rubber sheath. Until then I had found it vaguely comforting. Was that what she meant? Then I thought of the sound the hot water bottle makes when you expel the air before turning the stopper tight. A breath.

Why did he die in pain? I had a sanitised view of death, imagining morphine would be given in any situation. But it turns out that pneumonia is an exception, because the opiate narrows the airways, making it even harder to breathe. Surely, if someone was dying anyway, that wouldn't matter, and morphine could make their decline gentler, easier? Apparently not. Perhaps my mother was not sure what to ask for or wasn't aware how medical staff use euphemisms like 'We can give him something to make him more comfortable'. Every time the nurse asked her if she would like to be alone with her husband for his final moments, Maman begged her to stay.

Listening to my mother talk about my father's death, I wondered how much of her helplessness as a child by her grandfather's bedside haunted her in my father's final hours. Except that now she was an adult and, to my mind at least, waiting to be released from years of being hostage to a man who had long since vanished. When I Skyped her, she did not turn the camera on, preferring to remain invisible in her distress.

'Did you hold his hand? Did you tell him it was alright to go?' I asked, lamely resorting to movie clichés.

'Oh, he wasn't listening,' she snapped. 'His eyes were open but not focusing on anything. He had no idea I was there.' She sounded accusing. But really the right word is aggrieved.

'Still, perhaps he could hear you,' I insisted. Who was I trying to comfort? My mother or myself?

'I don't think so,' she said. In her pain and trauma, I think she wanted me to suffer a little of what she had endured, rather than make it easier in my imagination. Perhaps so she would not have to feel so alone with it all. I wanted to hear her sound relieved that it was over. But there was no relief.

'I'm on my way,' I said. 'I'll be there as soon as I can.'

You say you'll jump on a plane, but it's not that simple. Flights from Australia do not depart hourly like European shuttles. They are full at short notice. It takes a day to disengage from life, cancel work, think about what to pack, organise technology. I had no idea how long I would be gone for or what the weather would do. It was technically autumn, but the temperatures I read online suggested an Indian summer. How long would that last?

I felt calm. Detached. It had happened. At last, at last. And at least I was not in the air, racing to get there, uncertain. At least I knew the outcome. That made it easier, didn't it? Within minutes, it was as if I was enclosed under a bell jar, sealed into a vacuum by a special kind of loneliness that stole up on me like a predator. Intellectually, I knew I was not alone. David was beside me, literally as well as figuratively. He would follow me to London within a matter of days. But meanwhile it was as if a vapour had seeped into the air, making me feel apart, disconnected, as if the molecular structure of the atmosphere had changed.

Seeking to escape that toxicity, I went for a walk on the beach and experienced another strange sensation: while I was stepping over the soft sand I felt myself ageing, as though I could detect it at a cellular level, as if my skin were leathering and becoming a reptilian carapace I would never shed. *So this is how it is, from now on,* I heard deep, deep inside in a voice I did not recognise. My older self had taken possession, an unwelcome squatter who had moved into the basement and was not going to budge anytime soon.

I went into efficiency mode. I would organise the funeral on the plane and start on the eulogy. I would make a list of people to contact. I would not waste the flight time. I launched myself into Competent Caroline mode, a state I knew brought out the best in me. Efficient, practical, calm, in control. In a crisis, I was my father's daughter. But when I got to the airport I was not quite so assured. Waves of tears crashed over me at the check-in counter—enough to earn me access to the business club lounge. No upgrade on compassionate grounds, but still, something.

'We're full, I'm sorry,' said the ground staff supervisor. Every crumb of kindness made me feel so grateful I only wept more.

Even at an airport, always a place of heightened emotions, there are prescribed zones for crying. You are supposed to do it all before you go through to Departures and have pulled yourself together by the time you get to Immigration. No one cries at Passport Control, Security and beyond. You shop, you eat, you buy a magazine and some nuts, you people-watch, but you do not sob. If you do, you feel you are letting the side down, failing the team. You are spreading unnecessary alarm like germs. In these times of heightened vigilance, someone might report your distress and complain.

On the plane, I kept to myself. Normally chatty to help time pass in a more bearable way, I'd make basic conversation with a neighbour when meals were served. But not this time. I had no desire to impose my feelings on anyone or take an interest in their reasons for travelling. No film or book could hold my attention.

David had arranged for a driver to meet me at Heathrow. We chatted a little. I called my mother to say I was minutes away. I told the driver the reason for my visit. He nodded to me in the rear-vision mirror.

'I lost my daughter last year,' he said, jolting me as abruptly as if we'd hit another car. He said it so calmly. 'She was thirteen.'

I asked how it happened. 'An accident,' he replied, matter-of-factly. 'She was on a ski lift and she fell off it and died of internal injuries.'

By now we were at the gates to my mother's home.

'I'm so sorry,' I stammered as he unloaded my suitcase. He shook my hand and smiled the smile of the permanently wounded.

'She was my favourite.' That confession pierced my heart. Perhaps only a stranger could be told such a painfully intimate admission.

My mother opened the door to me in a cobalt-blue waffle-weave dressing gown that I would see her wear for the next three weeks, its yoke uncharacteristically grubby. Catching my focus immediately and anticipating criticism, she lobbed a pre-emptive explanation: 'It's toothpaste, it doesn't come out.'

Beneath her defiant ferocity I sensed fear and alarm, panic and dread. She had obtained a death certificate, but now, with that one formality processed, she had no idea what to do next. She had the name of a funeral director, but wanted me to take charge.

'I don't care what you do, it means nothing to me,' she said with the Gallic shrug that punctuates so many of her statements. One day, I would like to investigate how the French have turned that sudden movement of raising and dropping the shoulders into a gesture of national eloquence, expressing everything from contempt to acceptance.

Wandsworth is as unlovely and unloved a part of south London today as it was in my childhood. It has resisted gentrification or perhaps not been offered the option, unlike Clapham and Battersea. As a child, I remember passing these rows of identical narrow red-brick *Coronation Street*–style terraces on the way to school and seeing small children with sooty faces playing barefoot like Dickensian urchins around the back of Young's brewery, the area's main employer. Its headquarters on the Wandle, a waterway feeding into the Thames, looked like a Victorian poorhouse. The company delivered its cargo of barrels to pubs around the city on carts pulled by heavy-limbed dray horses. The industrial revolution did not appear to have lifted the prosperity or working conditions of the borough in two centuries, despite the proliferation of high-street chains and shopping centres with branches of Uniqlo and Wagamama. Why would anyone want to linger here? Gillman Funeral Directors defied the drab streetscape with its dazzling white façade and interiors, blindingly bright in their denial of decay, like a row of perfect teeth in an otherwise ravaged face.

The first shock was how long it takes to get a date at a London crematorium. The city is busy dying and you enter a queue, just as you do everywhere else. We could not find a venue any earlier than ten days hence. How would we fill all that time, I wondered. With so little family and such a small social circle, arrangements would only take up so many hours.

'What do you like about your job?' I asked Kelly, our funeral organiser, slipping into journalist mode to cope and for the benefit of my mother, who could not even bear to look at the list of services available. I noticed Kelly's tattoos as well as her long spatula-like acrylic nails, which prevented her from holding her pen normally, forcing her hand into a peculiarly awkward, almost simian clench.

'Customer satisfaction,' replied Kelly with cheery conviction.

Not this customer. I had imagined we could choose a cardboard coffin (known in the trade as a Barbara Cartland, which I am sure she would have loathed, given that she was not one for plain packaging of any kind) as a budget option. But the eco options (water hyacinth, bamboo, cardboard) cost exactly double the more traditional timber options. So we settled on a coffin called Rippon (but which would have been more aptly called Rip-off). No trimmings. No flowers. We would choose the music and I would conduct the service.

'You are very brave,' said Kelly admiringly.

Overconfident, I missed the warning in her comment. I thought back to hosting my father-in-law's funeral at which the role of MC had fallen to me by default. I had, if I am totally honest, enjoyed the role—being emotionally detached I had revelled in using the skills of my working life to welcome the congregation at that modest family gathering and settle them into a mood that was not too sombre, for the benefit of the young children present. I did not want their first experience of this rite to be frightening. The only thing that shocked us all was my mother-in-law's sobbing the moment she saw the coffin. It was like her laughter, completely uninhibited and full-throated. Impolite in volume. There was no stopping it, no matter how much her son and daughter squeezed her from both sides as if applied pressure could contain her grief, like a tourniquet on a bleeding wound.

At home I wrote a list of my father's colleagues to call and email. Back in her dressing gown, my mother sighed, becoming more and more agitated.

'I don't want to see these people. Where have they been for the past six years?' she said, her voice catching with resentment. If she had a shopfront, she could advertise: 'Long-term grudges a speciality'. Once again, as it had six years before and more mildly ever since, the apartment smelled of sour milk. She was curdled with sorrow and anger, interspersed with flashes of unsparing self-awareness. 'I know I'm only feeling sorry for myself,' she would say hotly, as if someone was arguing with her.

Sometimes her behaviour embarrassed me. When she met a fellow resident of her building in the elevator or foyer, she would barrel up to them, ignoring the proprieties of personal space and say, 'Do you know my husband died?', waiting for a reaction that was never up to the standard she expected. If she savoured their discomfiture, it was short-lived. Ultimately, everyone disappointed her. 'I don't know how to be,' she said, flinging her arms from her sides in a gesture of helplessness.

The next day, we went to Nightingale House to empty my father's room. But within thirty seconds of crossing the threshold, my mother bolted like a spooked horse.

'I'll wait for you downstairs,' she said, making her escape to avoid the sympathy of carers she was not ready to face. They, too, were grieving: some had gone on rostered leave and returned to find Mr Baum gone forever and were dealing with their own shock after six years of his dominant presence. Each came and hugged me as I emptied out the flimsy drawers and cupboards.

Someone went to find the key to the memory box. I took his car keys, passport, Michelin guide and photographs from the perspex shelves. His presence was wiped from the place. All that remained as proof of his existence was a pencil portrait in a hallway as part of a series commissioned by the home. Mournful, haggard, his eyes baleful and vacant, his cheeks sagging. It was not a likeness I wanted to own.

Downstairs, my mother was sitting on the terrace, having a cup of tea and watching a group of residents, most of them in wheelchairs, being led through a class in flower arranging.

'It's so nice here,' she said with a wistful little smile. 'I wish I were Jewish.'

I took that to mean: I wish I belonged here. Or somewhere. The implied question, too frightening to utter—*What will happen to me if I need care?*—remained unasked, hovering over us like small puffs of cloud above an active volcano.

Perhaps, she ventured, if we had to have some kind of reception or wake after the funeral, we could have it here? We were shown to a function room, round, bright, chintzily intimate and overlooking the garden. More importantly, it was offered free of charge.

I worried that the setting might be too grim and put some people off.

'Fine,' retorted my mother.

We were introduced to a young black woman from catering whose name tag announced her as Efficiency. She lived up to it, making notes about smoked salmon sandwiches and suggesting chocolate brownies. Perfect. My father adored them.

Exhausted by decision-making and negotiation, we were in bed by eight o'clock. Jet lag and anxiety make terrible bedfellows.

The morning brought mail, which my mother opened but did not read: she checked the condolences cards to see who they were from but ignored the messages.

'Ha!' she would say when she received one from someone she despised.

As more and more former colleagues made it clear they would like to attend the funeral, she grew increasingly hostile to the whole occasion.

There was a brief reprieve when I chose music for the service. Part of me wanted to give my father the rousing flamboyant send-off he would have relished with the 'Ride of the Valkyries' in all its spirited grandeur. To my surprise, my mother, who detests Wagner, agreed that it was a suitable choice and did not leave the room as she usually did when I played the opening of Act III of *Die Walküre* to check the time cues.

But then, scanning his CD collection I had an inspired and irreverent idea to close proceedings with something unexpected and humorous that would cause a ripple of initial shock but send everyone out with a smile. My father adored the satirical brilliance of Tom Lehrer. His lyrics made my father's shoulders shake with laughter, even when he knew them by heart. On a compilation album that included family favourites like 'New Math' and 'The Vatican Rag' we found a darkly apocalyptic ditty called 'We Will All Go Together When We Go'. Some might consider it tasteless, but that only pleased my mother more. Asked to choose between Lehrer and Wagner, she opted for Lehrer as a way of provoking the congregation.

But her satisfaction proved short-lived. With every hour that passed I watched my mother decline into taciturn numbness. She did *The Times* crossword with a cup of black coffee and then retreated to bed for the rest of the day. She was not sure she would come to the funeral at all, and no amount of cajoling, or suggesting that it might be cathartic, would sway her. I would not force her, could not, but with each hour that passed my confusion grew: who was she to defy a tradition that had endured for centuries? What was this really about? What was she grieving for at this point? A man she had lost six years ago? A sense of purpose wrenched from her and now casting her adrift? Why did this have to manifest in such an extreme form?

By the middle of the week I was at breaking point. Exhausted from sleepless strain I decided to defuse the situation and take some of the pressure off. I had to admit to myself that this funeral was not like my father-in-law's and was not the same as hosting an engagement, however stressful, at the Sydney Opera House. I understood in my core than I could not get through the ambitious production I had choreographed and be a caring daughter to my surviving parent while honouring the one who had just died. My mother needed my support more than any fine words or carefully curated images and sounds. Against my nature, I did a total U-turn and decided the funeral should be a private, family-only affair. I could not put her through the ordeal of having to greet people she loathed in such a charged and painful setting.

This was no small change of heart. By now people had booked airfares to come from overseas and word had gone out via industry websites. I had to send around urgent emails notifying as many as possible of changed circumstances without going into too much detail as to the reasons. There would be a wake, to which friends and associates were welcome, but the cremation would be behind closed doors. The blowback was immediate and fierce. Some expressed open hostility, others protested in stony silence.

My mother's immediate relief and gratitude were countered by my searing awareness of having displeased and disappointed others. After twenty-four hours, remorse had built up tension in my body like a poison. I remembered this sensation of toxins flooding my veins from when the fibromyalgia first appeared six years earlier. I did not want to encourage a recurrence. Taking a long walk in the nearby park to give myself courage, I rang those I knew would be most upset by my decision and allowed them to vent. It was unpleasant and deeply uncomfortable. Did people honestly feel they had a greater claim to pain than my mother? And if they did, how had they demonstrated that in my father's final years?

Caught between two factions, I felt I could do nothing right and had failed everyone. The hours dragged on with not enough to do. Now there was no order of service for which to select passages. The photo montage would be screened at afternoon tea instead of at the crematorium. The music choices would be reduced to just one simple short piece without a farewell fanfare of pomp or subversion. Day after day was a limbo of misery.

'Can you get rid of his clothes?' my mother asked suddenly one morning. When I had offered to do this six years before and every year since, she had refused. Now she wanted all trace of him gone. Relieved to be given a task to pass the time, David and I began the process of emptying my father's extensive wardrobe. We bagged up more than forty suits (some of them almost gangsterish in their cut and swagger: what was my father thinking when he ordered an off-white silk suit with wide lapels fit only for Bugsy Malone?) together with tuxedos, dinner and sports jackets, a handful of casual brushed-cotton shirts, gaudily printed silk summer shirts brought back from Indonesian conferences that only Nelson Mandela could get away with and V-neck cashmere sweaters. Alongside his handstitched, monogrammed pure cotton business shirts I found a collection of dozens of spare collars and cuffs, as stiff and pristine as index cards in a stationery cupboard. Everything wearable went to a Jewish charity for the homeless. There must be some pretty nattily dressed people sleeping rough on the streets of London.

Drawers spilled with cashmere-lined scarves, soft leather gloves, belts with Gucci buckles, opera glasses in snakeskin cases, gold shirt studs, boxes of collar stiffeners. A tooled leather case container a silver shoe horn and bootlace hook, precious mementos from his Viennese childhood. The trappings and accessories of external finery and display, of vanity and status. And the Hermès ties, of course, ribbons of colour like medieval pennants. I chose one for David to wear at the funeral: the only time I have ever seen him in one. And set another aside as a gift to the director of my father's care home.

Finally, the day that could not be put off arrived. I had rehearsed my eulogy, trying to take the sting out of the most emotionally risky passages and marking the pages up with stage directions: Breathe and Slow Down . . . I had delegated the job of finishing its delivery to David if I broke down too badly to recover. I resolved to bring no expectation and pressure to how my mother chose to play it. By mid-morning she came out to consult me about which black dress to wear given the unpredictable weather, and asked me to show her how to tie a scarf in the current fashion. When it was time to go, I took a Valium and half-filled a water bottle with vodka tonic, nestling it in my bag.

We got to the crematorium early, as we do everywhere we go. I turned on the radio. It was playing one of my father's favourite pieces of music, Beethoven's 'Eroica' Symphony, the stirring fourth movement he liked to conduct, brandishing one of my mother's fine flexible metal knitting needles. The memory too fresh, I turned it off. Moments later, the hearse arrived, drawing up level with us so that we were looking straight at the coffin.

'Is that it?' my mother whispered. When I nodded she rolled her eyes. 'Quelle comédie,' she muttered, using one of her favourite expressions of dismay.

I turned the car to face the other way, parking under a willow tree looking onto a bed of wilting roses, and got out to greet the funeral director and give him the CD of Vladimir Horowitz playing Liszt's Consolation No. 3.

I took a swig of vodka to steel myself. Mum pretended to be shocked. Each taking an elbow, David and I led her forward, bearing her weight as though she were an invalid, her face to the ground, never looking up. When the coffin was brought in and placed on the dais, she bent further forward, like someone about to vomit. A moment that would normally be solemn and silent was punctuated by her constant murmurings of 'Jesus Christ, can we go now, is it over?' while we each stroked an arm trying to reassure and calm her. After an agonising minute attempting to find enough stillness to listen to the shimmering music while saying a final goodbye, I gave up.

I nodded to the director to close the curtains. Before they completed their automated beige glide, we rose to leave the way we came in from a space all of us agreed was perfectly vile. Where was the usual side exit into a prettier tended garden suggesting life's continuity and nature's eternal renewal? Certainly not at the Lambeth Crematorium in Tooting, where I defy anyone to find any solace or grace. Instead of bodies, they should burn the place down.

# CHAPTER 30

# Three women
# (Part two)

There is a famous photograph, taken in 1953 at the state funeral of King George VI, of three present and future queens of England in mourning: Queen Mary, wearing a severe wimple that frames her stern face and grey curls and in an old-fashioned floor-length dress, looking as if she has stepped out of a portrait by Rembrandt; Elizabeth, the Queen Mother in profile, her eyes closed mid-blink; and her shy young daughter Elizabeth: all veiled and huddled together. The two younger women wear dresses that are more modern, exposing pale calves and high heels. They are glamorously austere in their solemnity, potent icons of power and mystery: majesty in grief, three inscrutable women embodying the past, present and future, facing their destiny through the fine gauze of their veils.

After my father's funeral we drove from the crematorium to the nursing home in a heightened state, a potent adrenalin of indignation coursing through our veins at the ugliness of it all. The green plastic cushions, the nasty pleats in the synthetic curtains, the absurdly high plinth on which the coffin rested, all provoked a uniting scorn and dismay.

At Nightingale House I fortified myself in the car park with another nip of vodka to meet many people I did not know at all, and others I had not seen for more than thirty-five years, including one who had been the subject of a teenage crush.

Mixed in with the men in suits, most of whom wore Hermès ties in tribute to my father, were the three equivalents of those queenly royal personages, like figures in a triptych.

My mother, firmly in David's vigilant but tender grasp, enthroned in a high-backed front row chair from which she did not move, receiving condolences as guests leaned forward to acknowledge her status as mourner-in-chief and first lady of sorrow, as if paying homage to their sovereign.

Slipping in discreetly, my father's earlier love, Moira, arrived from the country, smart in black velvet, her blue eyes finding me instantly and putting me at immediate ease. We had a kind of familiarity that bypassed all formal introductions and small talk. She walked towards my mother with no-nonsense British backbone.

Red-eyed and a little late, Helena, his colleague-turned-mistress, came in disarray from a gathering of colleagues at the pub. Denied access to the funeral, they had mounted an alternative protest/tribute down the road (which my father, who loathed pubs, would have hated). She was wearing a colour she thought of as my father's signature blue, which he used in his company logo and promotional material—a cool clear electric cobalt. To my eyes, her palette was a little off-key. The anger of her phone conversation with me just days earlier, full of bitterness, had abated into more considered and accepting sorrow. Too distracted, I did not introduce her to Moira. Later, she revealed that my father had told her about Moira and I regretted not facilitating their encounter. But I was not the hostess at a cocktail party, I was the daughter at my father's funeral, and had other concerns and priorities.

After the eulogy, Helena came to me, slightly tipsy, tearful and unexpectedly needy. 'Give me something of his, won't you?' she begged, causing me to lose my composure. I assured her that I had already selected one of his favourite silk scarves for her, with its luxuriously tasselled fringing. Moira asked for nothing, prompting me to make a note to send her a keepsake.

Hours later, sorting through my father's seemingly endless files and papers, in an attempt to make space physically and emotionally, I found notes he made under the heading 'If I survive', with a list of people to notify following his operation. Half of them were now dead. On the back was a second heading: 'If I had two hundred and fifty thousand pounds (plus)'. Itemised with costings were objects of desire and demonstrations of largesse. They included spending almost half that amount on the newest Jaguar. And a generous gift to Amber, his secret lover in South

Africa, proving that he had not truly severed the relationship. All of this presumably was to be funded by lottery wins. In the stationery drawer where he kept labels already printed out for regular correspondence, I found her address. *Cheating bastard*, I thought. I winced as if physically wounded. Should I tell her it was all over? Did I owe her anything? She had not heard from my father now for several years and would perhaps assume he was already dead. What do to?

Night and day the question gnawed and gnawed at me. What was my duty to him? What was decent? Considerate? Why was I even thinking of letting her know? I worried away at this as though trying to untie a frayed piece of rope with ragged fingernails. I fantasised about using my best stationery, stiff card embossed with a small gold pineapple just like the one on the charm bracelet my father had assembled for me, to write her just one line: '*My father Harry Baum died on September 16, 2014. No further correspondence will be entered into.*'

Formal, official, officious, forbidding. Final. And that's when I understood my motive. It was not pure or honourable, it was dark and dirty and filled with righteousness and rage. I wanted to hurt her as she had hurt us. I wanted revenge, I wanted to exact agony, I wanted to send her a letter that would blow up in her face like a grenade. That little golden pineapple looked almost exactly like an exploding missile. Once I recognised the impulse, I felt ashamed. But with time came a kind of freedom. The note remained unwritten.

# CHAPTER 31

# Trio

In the weeks after the funeral, my mother found no solace, closure or strength. She retreated from the world into the cave of her bed, lying there for up to twenty-three hours out of twenty-four, dozing on Valium, then medicated with antidepressants and sleeping tablets. She did not answer the phone and could only occasionally be coaxed out for half an hour to have a cup of coffee, or visit the library or, on the day before my departure, go to the cinema—our favourite form of escapism.

She wanted my father's ashes hidden somewhere she would not find them, outside the apartment. Surprised by the weight of his remains, I stashed him in a basement locker until I could take him to Paris and sprinkle him as close to his hero Napoleon as possible. On this we agreed.

Ever practical, Maman said, 'You'll have to do it at night, into the Seine.' But she was adamant that she did not want to be part of it. He would want us to go and have a good meal somewhere, I said. But the tyranny of the *Michelin Guide* was over and my mother shook her head in emphatic refusal. There would be no final pilgrimage and no sentimental *adieux*.

Marooned on a sea of sadness and loneliness, my mother was unsure where she belonged or wanted to be. With us in Australia, or by herself in England, where her modest rituals and routes are embedded and ingrained? The short straight drive to Sainsbury's, the direct bus to the Victoria and Albert Museum, the library and its half-hearted book club, the monthly French conversation group. And who knows, perhaps when her equilibrium is restored, a return to Nightingale House one day, as a volunteer, as they suggested. It was too soon for decisions. All questions, choices and options were deferred until signs of recovery appeared like spring buds on bare branches.

It was not safe to leave her so David stayed on while I came back to Australia to fulfil work commitments. He made a list of all the handyman jobs that needed doing around the place and took my father's extensive library to a second-hand dealer. My mother found David's practical skill and quiet presence soothing. When he devised an elaborate truss system of pulleys to take a heavy recliner over the handrail of the apartment's mezzanine, she watched with eyes like saucers, muttering, 'It's like having a circus act at home . . . *Incroyable . . .*' clearly enjoying this demonstration of his strength and ingenuity.

Back in Australia, people were kind and sympathetic, but there is a use-by date for everything, a statute of limitations on grief. I wish the custom of wearing a black armband could be reinstated to signal fragility and a need for gentle treatment. We are all in too much of a hurry now to move on, to demonstrate a resilience we may not feel. I long for the unspoken subtleties of the Victorian mourning code with its spectrum of colours from ebony to crimson, indicating various stages of recovery. I find solace on the beach, in rockpools blooming with spring algae and the freckling of baby mollusc shells forming from tiny dots. Huge tides and big storms have shifted sand, reconfiguring the topography: a perfect mirror of my own inner landscape, equally altered.

David's special rapport with my mother is confirmed once again. I marvel at his infinite patience, his ability to appreciate tiny signs of progress ('She got up', 'She ran a bath', 'She had a second helping at dinner'). He is neither prescriptive nor judgemental of setbacks. He is not offended by her self-absorption and stubborn resistance to advice. One day she surprises him by trying out a walking stick that she has previously refused to use, cajoled into it by his seemingly casual mention of how helpful his mother finds her cane. He has the knack.

He devotes himself to her without fuss or complaint and without any expectation of gratitude. When she is in bed, he undertakes little tasks she will not notice: he bleaches all the teacups, removing the accretion of tannin that has stained them an unsightly brown. He even wrests that goddamn blue dressing gown from her and manages to remove the toothpaste stains, returning it before she's noticed it has gone. But it feels different when she wraps herself in it, no longer stale with that ingrained odour of bereavement: 'This feels nice,' she says.

As they talk to me on the screen I notice small signs of progress: she pretends to flirt with David, coquettishly boasting of the delicious dinner he cooked her or their plans to see a film. For now, they are there and I am here. Connected, separated, but together. In a few months we will all be reunited for Christmas on my side of the world. She is using the deadline of that trip to complete a fiendishly difficult Guernsey sweater for David, having been unable to pick up her knitting since my father's death. The wool is dark, making the task harder, but she is determined to finish it.

We are three. A trio rather than a triangle. For now, at least, our three sides make a harmonious shape.

# EPILOGUE

# Only

For better or worse, as an only child, and as a woman without children, the defining relationship for the first part of my life has been with my parents. They are the sole custodians of my childhood, without any qualification or alternative version that could be supplied by siblings. I listen to arguments at other people's dinner tables—those 'that's not how it happened' stories, supplemented and contradicted with anecdotes that amplify the official version of family holidays, accidents, disasters, triumphs. They sound like stereo, while my life is mono.

I am the end of the line. After me, our family perishes, leaving no genetic trail to be mapped by future generations. I often think of all the effort my parents put into surviving and overcoming huge obstacles. Both were keen for a fresh start, for new beginnings, for birth as rebirth. I am the result of that striving, carrying all their hopes, dreams and expectations. It has been a constant pressure, making me cautious where others might have been more reckless. I have never felt entirely free of that awareness unique to singletons of being priceless, an artefact without a copy or slightly different draft. From an early age I understood the responsibility that came with there being no spare if they lost me. I was always sensible, always careful. Precious cargo. I played safe, always protecting the investment my parents had made.

Like anyone, I had goals, dreams and ambitions. I pursued some with single-minded application. Some called it selfish, unfeeling, ungrateful, when I moved to the other side of the world. Looking back, I see that I did it unthinkingly and insensitively. I could have been more understanding, gentler, kinder.

It was not entirely conscious, but I resolved not to have children early, around the age of twelve. And I never wavered. Motherhood held no appeal for me, and I never felt the hormonal or genetic pull to reproduce, as strong in others as the force of gravity. Career and friends would compensate, and maybe, if I was lucky, love for and from someone else who might perhaps see past my status as an only child. Funny how, in writing that expression just now, I realise that it never allows you to grow up: even in your fifties, the description keeps you stuck in infancy, a version of those foetuses one sees preserved in formaldehyde in museums, curled up on themselves and floating like pale pickles in jars. Whether you are the youngest or the eldest among siblings, you nevertheless mature. But when you're an only child, you never seem to ripen. The word 'child' sticks to you like chewing gum on a shoe.

Statistically, when only children have families, they are more likely to have only children themselves. That fact surprises me, as I had imagined they'd be keen for exactly the opposite, for expansive, boisterous broods and tribes. But apparently not. Perhaps, by the time they become parents themselves, they realise with gratitude what focus and attention can do to nurture an individual to their fullest potential. Or perhaps they don't have faith in their ability to spread their resources, love and attention further and would rather concentrate on maximising opportunities for one. Being an only child still carries a stigma. Recently a woman, still fertile enough to contemplate a second child, asked me with earnest intensity whether she thought being an only had ruined my life and left me somehow disabled or a social misfit. She saw nothing tactless or offensive about the question or the implication that only children are handicapped.

When I was a little girl I could feel my parents' pride in me like heat from the sun. My good manners earned me approval at home and admiration beyond. I basked in approbation and affection.

As I grew older and did well at school, my good grades were praised and boasted of. If there had been medals for achievement, they would have been prominently displayed rather than hidden in a drawer. No one ever teased me for being brainy or bookish. Promise and achievement were everything, and I was eager to please, thriving on encouragement, like a plant that produces showy blooms when fed extra nutrients.

Much later I learned that love comes in two varieties: conditional and unconditional.

As children, my parents never had the security that comes from love without extenuating clauses, so it was hardly surprising that they could not pass that on. Especially when it came to my father, the approval and independence I craved were always qualified, subject to negotiations that began with the words 'only if' and 'only when' so that my status as an only child became fused in my mind with 'only' used as an adverb of condition.

As an adult, seeing love consistently offered without expectation gutted me. My first reaction was ugly: piercing, poisonous jealousy followed by waves of shame. Who would I have been, if I'd been allowed that freedom to disappoint?

When I botched admission to Oxford, moved to Australia, ended my first marriage, when my career did not go to plan, these episodes summoned up the spectre of failure and earned judgement or condemnation—sometimes silent, but no less eloquent.

Between the watershed moments there were many other minor opportunities to stumble: a forgotten anniversary, a lack of sufficient gratitude for a loan, a careless disregard for precious possessions borrowed. Such was the accuracy of my radar that I could interpret the subtlest nuances in my parents' voices—on the phone, in a letter or in person—communicating a wide spectrum of dismay.

'I only want you to be happy,' my mother insisted, unable to provide me with a template of how to go about such a thing. When I seemed to manage it with David, she told us how much pleasure it gave her, before suddenly bursting into tears, leaving me heartsick on her behalf.

Over time the cumulative evidence persuaded me that I was a bad daughter. Estrangement cemented that conviction; reconciliation pulled us back from the edge of the precipice just in time. But beyond that chasm, there was always the potential for another in a seemingly endless canyon of disapproval.

So it came as a surprise to me when, on the birthday following my father's illness, my mother sent me a card with the words 'To the Best Daughter in the World' printed on its cover. Years on, I have been unable to throw that card away. At some later date, I may need proof that I did something right and that when push came to shove, however falteringly, I was a good daughter after all.

# Acknowledgements

This memoir is the culmination of five years of stitching together fragments written over a considerably longer time. If Susan Wyndham had not asked me to contribute to *My Mother, My Father*, an anthology on losing a parent, I would not have had the incentive and validation required to tell the rest of this story.

Thank you to Kris Olsson for a generously constructive reading of a very incomplete first draft at a crucial stage. Your comments steered me off a dangerous reef.

The raw material of this manuscript was developed at two week-long intensive writers' retreats run by Charlotte Wood. I arrived at the first one in bad shape from my father's funeral. I would like to thank fellow writers Carolyn Swindell, James Tierney and Cath Hickie for their tact, kindness, patience and encouragement, which got me over the line; on the second retreat Kris Olsson, Susan Wyndham, Julie Bail, Ashley Hay and Sandra Hogan provided words of support to push the project forward. Charlotte's low-key but ever-present guidance, combined with the bountiful nourishment she provided each evening at dinner, made the experience of writing more focused and even occasionally joyful. Her friendship has been a continued source of strength, pleasure, solace and mirth. But I still don't get camping.

I owe Ailsa Piper a huge debt for two meticulously close reads of the first and last drafts and so much more.

To my publisher Jane Palfreyman: I will never forget the moment I read your email response to the manuscript. I was sitting under a canopy in Jaipur listening to golden paragraphs tumbling effortlessly from Colm Toibin's lips when I felt my phone vibrate in my pocket and sneaked a look. Your connection with the story and fierce desire to take it on were so overwhelming I cried for joy most of the rest of the day.

Ali Lavau showed me how to lick the manuscript into a more coherent shape; thank you also to editors Christa Munns and Susin Chow, to Nicola Young for her forensic proofreading, to Andy Palmer and the marketing team at Allen & Unwin.

I would also like to express my thanks, in no particular order to: *Good Weekend* magazine editors Fenella Souter and Ben Naparstek, who commissioned early sketches of what later became chapters; Aviva Tuffield, Hannie Rayson, Meredith Jaffe, Lee Kofman, Maria Katsonis, Agnès Varda, Antonia Case, Sabine Amoore Pinon, Christine Jordan, Peta Landman, Marie-France

Casalis, Laura Kroetsch, Rosemary Neill, Ariane Allard for research into my grandparents' death, Patti Miller for the writing exercise that prompted the Kennedy story, David Hughes, Mary Minzly, Valerie Redgrove, the most gifted teacher who believed and was gone much too soon, Alison Manning for coaching wisdom, Bundanon Artist-in-Residence program for allowing me to share my husband's stay to undertake uninterrupted rewrites with wombats, Helen Garner, Magda Szubanski, Geraldine Brooks, Richard Glover, Elizabeth Gilbert—and anyone who ever said, after hearing one of my family anecdotes, 'You should write a book,' making me believe there might be a readership for these stories.

I accept full responsibility for liberties I have taken with time: close observers of the events of 22 November 1963 have pointed out that mothers waiting at my school would not yet have heard the news. But that is the way I remember it.

During the course of writing, I read many memoirs, of which *Boy, Lost* by Kris Olsson, *H is for Hawk* by Helen Macdonald, *Fierce Attachments* by Vivian Gornick, *Flesh Wounds* by Richard Glover and *Reckoning* by Magda Szubanski all provided me with much-needed injections of determination and truth serum. Mary Karr's *The Liars' Club* gave me a pure shot of adrenalin, reminding me to be fearless and get down the physical details.

Finally, I wish to thank the two people to whom this book is dedicated: my mother Jacqueline, who was brave enough to let me share her story and took the cover photograph; I am sorry for any pain the telling of it has caused her. And my husband David, who read many drafts, laughed, cried and read again, always with invaluable suggestions and much-needed tech support. Your grace in the world humbles me daily and your love shows me what is possible.